HELPING AMERICA VOTE

A repeat of the Florida debacle in the 2000 presidential election is the fear of every election administrator. Despite the relatively complication-free 2008 and 2010 elections, we are working with fairly new federal legislation designed to ease election administration problems. The implementation of the Help America Vote Act of 2002 (HAVA) raises the question, how effective have reforms been? Could another Florida happen?

Helping America Vote is focused on the conflict between values of access and integrity in U.S. election administration. Kropf and Kimball examine both what was included in HAVA and what was not. Widespread agreement that voting equipment was a problem made technology the centerpiece of the legislation, and it has remedied a number of pressing concerns. But there is still reason to be concerned about key aspects of electronic voting, ballot design, and the politics of partisan administrators. It takes a legitimacy crisis for serious election reforms to happen at the federal level, and seemingly, the crisis has passed. However, the risk is still very much present for the electoral process to fail. What are the implications for democracy when we attempt reform?

Martha Kropf is Associate Professor of Political Science at the University of North Carolina-Charlotte.

David C. Kimball is Associate Professor of Political Science at the University of Missouri-St. Louis.

Controversies in Electoral Democracy and Representation

Matthew J. Streb, Series Editor

The Routledge series *Controversies in Electoral Democracy and Representation* presents cutting- edge scholarship and innovative thinking on a broad range of issues relating to democratic practice and theory. An electoral democracy, to be effective, must show a strong relationship between representation and a fair, open election process. Designed to foster debate and challenge assumptions about how elections and democratic representation *should* work, titles in the series present a strong but fair argument on topics related to elections, voting behavior, party and media involvement, representation, and democratic theory.

Titles in the series:

Rethinking American Electoral Democracy
Matthew J. Streb

Redistricting and Representation: Why Competitive Elections Are Bad for America
Thomas L. Brunell

Fault Lines: Why the Republicans Lost Congress
Edited by Jeffery J. Mondak and Dona-Gene Mitchell

In Defense of Judicial Elections
Chris W. Bonneau and Melinda Gann Hall

Congressional Representation and Constituents: The Case for Increasing the U.S. House of Representatives
Brian Frederick

The Imperfect Primary: Oddities, Biases, and Strengths of U.S. Presidential Nomination Politics
Barbara Norrander

Rethinking American Electoral Democracy, 2nd Edition
Matthew J. Streb

Helping America Vote: The Limits of Election Reform
Martha Kropf and David C. Kimball

Third Party Blues: The Truth and Consequences of Two-Party Dominance
Scot Schraufnagel

Forthcoming:
In Defense of Politicians
Stephen K. Medvic

HELPING AMERICA VOTE

The Limits of Election Reform

Martha Kropf
University of North Carolina-Charlotte

David C. Kimball
University of Missouri-St. Louis

Routledge
Taylor & Francis Group

NEW YORK AND LONDON

First published 2012
by Routledge
711 Third Avenue, New York, NY 10017

Simultaneously published in the UK
by Routledge
2 Park Square, Milton Park, Abingdon, Oxon OX14 4RN

Routledge is an imprint of the Taylor & Francis Group, an informa business

Library of Congress Cataloging in Publication Data
Kropf, Martha E.
    Helping America vote : the limits of election reform / Martha Kropf,
David C. Kimball.
      p. cm.
    Includes index.
    1. Elections–United States. 2. Elections–United States–Management.
    3. Election law–United States. 4. United States. Help America Vote
    Act of 2002. I. Kimball, David C., 1966- II. Title.
    JK1976.K76   2011
    324.6'30973—dc23   2011026284

ISBN13: 978-0-415-80407-3 (hbk)
ISBN 13: 978-0-415-80408-0 (pbk)
ISBN13: 978-0-203-87031-0 (ebk)

Typeset in Bembo
by Cenveo publisher services

To John Szmer, Gwendolyn and Zachary Szmer
Dr. Donald and Gwendolyn Kropf
Martha Kropf

To Laura Arnold, Carol Kimball, Andy, Will and Mary Kimball
David C. Kimball

CONTENTS

List of Figures and Tables   *viii*

Acknowledgements   *x*

1   Introduction: The Context of Election Reform   1

2   How Does Definition of the Problem Affect the Solution?   15

3   Did the Reforms Increase Accuracy?   34

4   At What Cost? The Unintended Consequences of Reform   55

5   We Mostly Eliminated the Butterfly Ballot…Isn't
     That Enough?   71

6   Defining the Problem in Human Terms: Who
     Implements Reform?   96

7   Conclusion: What Have Reforms Accomplished?   112

Notes on the text   *119*

References   *139*

Index   *151*

LIST OF FIGURES AND TABLES

Figures

2.1 Use of Punch Cards, Lever Machines, and Paper Ballots,
2000–2010   30
2.2 Use of Central-Count and Precinct-Count Optical Scan
Systems, 2000–2010   31
2.3 Use of Full-Face and Scrolling Touch-Screen Systems,
2000–2010   32
3.1 Changes in Residual Votes by Changes in Voting
Technology, 2000–2004   39
3.2 Changes in Residual Votes by Changes in Voting
Technology, 2000–2008   39
3.3 Residual Votes by Racial Composition of
Counties, 2000–2008   48
3.4 Residual Votes by Median Household Income of
Counties, 2000–2008   48
3.5 Residual Votes on New Jersey Ballot Measures by Voting
Equipment, 2006–2010   51
3.6 Residual Votes on Louisiana Ballot Measures by Voting
Equipment, 2008–2010   52
5.1 Residual Votes in Florida in 2000 Election by
Voting Technology   72
5.2 Palm Beach County "Butterfly" Ballot Used in the 2000
Presidential Election   73
5.3 Residual Votes in Florida in 2000 Election by Ballot Design   74
6.1 Methods of Selecting Local Election Officials in 2004   99

6.2 Party Affiliation of Local Election Officials in 2004   100
6.3 Expected Number of Accepted Provisional Ballots in the 2004
     General Election by Partisanship of Local Official and
     Jurisdiction's Voters   106

Tables

2.1 Voting Equipment Used in the United States Since 2000   29
3.1 Residual Vote Rates in Recent Presidential Elections   37
3.2 The Impact of Voting Equipment Changes on Residual
     Vote Rate, 2000 and 2004 Presidential Elections
     (Fixed Effects Regression)   42
3.3 The Impact of Voting Equipment Changes on Residual
     Vote Rate, 2000 and 2008 Presidential Elections
     (Fixed Effects Regression)   44
3.4 Racial and Economic Disparity in Residual Votes by
     Voting Technology, 2000 Presidential Election   47
4.1 Polling Place Consolidation, 2000–2008   66
4.2 The Impact of Polling Place Consolidation on Voter Turnout
     2000 and 2008 Presidential Elections (Fixed Effects Regression)   68
5.1 Frequency of Desirable Ballot Features in Sample Counties,
     2000 and 2004   81
5.2 Impact of Institutional Factors on Residual Votes: 2002 and 2004
     General Elections   85
5.3 Impact of Institutional Factors on Overvotes and Undervotes:
     2002 and 2004 General Elections   87
5.4 Ballot Initiatives and Referendums Examined in 2004   90
5.5 Predictors of Residual Votes on Ballot Measures
     in the 2004 Election   92

ACKNOWLEDGEMENTS

Since this is a book about election administration, we are especially grateful to the many election officials who have spoken to us or helped us gather more data about elections. We are also grateful to Lindsay Battles, Jessica Curtis, Cassie Gross, Jeremiah Olson, and Matthew Owings for research assistance. We would also like to thank Dr. John Szmer for his ideas and encouragement.

Thanks to the Election Assistance Commission for its Election Day Survey, a welcome source of information about elections in the United States.

We thank the University of Missouri Research Board and the National Science Foundation for supporting some of the research that appears in these pages. We alone are responsible for the interpretations in this book.

Finally, we would like to thank the people at Routledge for encouraging us to complete this book, and for their patience with us. Matt Streb, Michael Kerns, and Mary Altman bore the bulk of this work. We are grateful to Mike Alvarez for reviewing the proposal. His comments led to several changes.

M. K.
D.C.K.

1

INTRODUCTION

The Context of Election Reform

Minnesota's 2008 senate race between incumbent Republican Senator Norm Coleman and Democratic candidate Al Franken was anything but a *Saturday Night Live* skit. The vote count was so close that the margin triggered an automatic recount and several months of wrangling. And, of course, in Alaska in 2008, we didn't know that Republican incumbent Ted Stevens had lost his seat in the U.S. Senate until two weeks after Election Day. Georgia's Senate race triggered a run-off election on December 2, 2008 between the top two candidates because no one won a majority of the votes. Such issues from the 2008 general election don't seem like a big deal—the Democrats got the majority in the Senate and probably were a bit ambivalent about the prospect of a filibuster-proof majority. The bottom line is that delays, recounts, run-offs, and even unlikely events (such as a candidate who never campaigned winning a primary in South Carolina in 2010) happen on almost every Election Day somewhere in this country.

Eventually, if close elections don't affect a lot of people, we tend to forget them. In 2006, there were several elections which went unsettled for weeks, including one marred by voting equipment errors in Florida. Moreover, in 2004, it took two recounts (one by machine, one by hand) to settle the race for governor in the state of Washington.[1] Individual events such as these do not cause the collective breath holding that took place in the aftermath of the 2000 election. There is nothing quite like *not* having a president-elect for 36 days, particularly in a society used to knowing who would be president before they go to bed on election night. And, if there is a scapegoat—like poor voting equipment—it makes it easy for policymakers to quickly propose solutions for such a crisis and claim credit for having done so. Of course, in the world of lawmaking, no law is ever passed easily, particularly when the legislation concerns a policy over which the U.S. federal government has traditionally had limited influence.

When the United States Congress passed the Help America Vote Act of 2002 (HAVA), everyone knew it was not perfect, but policymakers argued that events—especially in Florida—from the 2000 election seemed to demand a change in election procedure. The equipment used to cast ballots was at the center of criticism. Modernizing voting equipment became an important part of the federal legislation. Further, several states—such as Florida—embraced new electronic voting equipment well before the U.S. Congress could act.

Interestingly, despite what some called "historic" changes in Florida, just a few short years after the fateful election, Florida was at the center of another disputed election. In 2007, Florida's state legislature decided to rid the state of the electronic voting equipment it so quickly embraced following the 2000 election. By 2012, the state even planned to get rid of equipment required by federal law for voters with disabilities.[2] The Help America Vote Act had required such accessible equipment. However, then-Governor Charlie Crist cited commonly discussed problems with electronic equipment such as potential vulnerability to computer hackers, potential unreliability, and voters' lack of confidence in the machines.[3]

However, arguably the most important triggering event for the state change was the election for the state's 13th congressional district under the nation's spotlight in 2006. In that race, there were an estimated 13,000 ballots that contained no vote in the 13th district race, whose outcome was decided by fewer than 500 votes. Some scholars blamed ballot usability, but the larger problem looming—at least to policymakers—seemed the lack of accountability of the equipment.[4] Voters could not check a ballot to ensure their intended vote was properly recorded by the equipment. The focus had shifted from worrying about whether the old voting equipment had properly recorded the intended votes to whether the new equipment did. Integrity of the elections emerged as a problem in both 2000 and 2007, but what motivated the switchback?

In the case of the equipment switch in Florida in 2007, and in other states, policymakers were responding to fears about the legitimacy of the electoral system. Simply put, Florida officials did not want "another Florida." In the 2000 election, Florida became the scapegoat for a variety of election problems. We saw one of the closest, most controversial elections in our history play out in Florida. Given the advanced state of broadcast media and the Internet, citizens had the opportunity to follow each grimy detail of the election dispute. The public clearly saw that, especially in such a close election, the way in which an election is administered matters. If even one part of a complex system of measuring citizen preferences for government fails, the public can question the legitimacy of the system. Florida was the center of attention because the outcome of the election came down to Florida, where 537 votes separated two candidates. In that fateful election, multiple problems came to light including problems with voting equipment, ballot usability, lists of registered voters, and recount procedures. These multiple system failures caused federal and state policymakers to reconsider the election system. Ultimately, President George W. Bush signed the Help America Vote Act into law in October 2002.

The signing and subsequent implementation of HAVA, along with a variety of state reforms, raises the question: Have we fixed the glitches? Could another Florida happen? Florida's reaction to electronic equipment in 2007 raises a related question: What are the unintended consequences of changes we set into motion with HAVA? Finally, is it possible for the federal government to fix the nuts and bolts of election administration in a relatively complete manner? Although it is just one example, that Florida banned electronic equipment in 2007 is an indication that there are doubts about whether we actually fixed the election system. What motivated the switchback in Florida is actually part of the answer about whether we have fixed the system. In our haste to address the election problem, our policymakers focused heavily on fixing the problem of voting equipment quickly. This book explores the positive, negative, and neutral consequences of being hellbent on changing our voting equipment. Using the data we have gathered in more than ten years of studying election reform, this book explores these important questions. Exploring the questions ten years after the passage of HAVA gives us analytic leverage to determine whether there is the potential for "another Florida," even though many people are starting to take elections for granted again.

Why Should We Care? It's Legitimacy, Stupid...

It is important to note that the election system seemed to work in 2000, even with the complex system failures in the mechanics of the election. The fact is we inaugurated a new president in January 2001, who was even re-elected four years later. However, policymakers (especially Democrats) worried that the winning candidate did not "legitimately" win the election. Perhaps upon hearing the word "legitimacy" citizens may not understand it as political theorists might. For the typical citizen, legitimacy may have a lot to do with perceived authority of the government, as well as the confidence and trust citizens have in the government. In theorizing about elections, legitimacy is a key reason to hold democratic elections—the citizens decide who makes policy for them, but also accept the results in the case that their preferred candidates lose. Citizens of a democratic government accept the results because the process for political change is outlined in law in advance and is systematic.

Results of a Pew Center public opinion poll taken after the 2000 election indicated that the public did not initially accept the Bush win as legitimate. However, the analysis included with the poll conceded that as time passed, a majority of people believed that Bush legitimately won the election. But that also meant that about half did not accept the results.

No matter who wins the presidency, George W. Bush or Al Gore, many Americans think that the victor will come to office because of the way the voting was conducted or counted rather than because he legitimately won the election in Florida.[5]

It would be going much too far to say that as a result of the 2000 election citizens were ready to revolt and place Al Gore in power (though there might have been a liberal Democrat or two who threatened to move to Canada). On a more micro level, political scientists emphasize legitimacy, trust in government and confidence in government because these concepts affect our willingness to participate in government and to accept its authority. In some ways, such concepts may even have more importance than voting decisions. In fact, in the past decade, confidence that one's ballot has been counted accurately has become a central measure of how well elections are managed.[6]

In considering what makes for a legitimate election, over time, our courts and policy now emphasize that every citizen should have a vote, but only one vote (hence, "one man, one vote").[7] Every person should have a say, and citizens expect that when they cast a vote, the vote will count in a final tabulation deciding who holds a particular office. This access problem with elections has resulted in discussions of increasing the franchise and increasing voter turnout by making it easier to register or to vote.[8] Over time, increasing the franchise has meant reforms such as allowing those without property to vote, allowing women to vote or most recently, instituting federal policies (the Voting Rights Act) to stop efforts to block African Americans from voting, and allowing those aged 18–21 to vote.[9] From the perspective of easing registration burdens and making voting easier, election reforms have focused on solutions such as Election Day registration, pre-election day voting, and mail-only voting. Furthermore, a fundamental question of access has dealt with the question of how easy or hard it should be to register and to vote. Finally, when a voter attempts to vote, the ballot should be usable—that is, it should be clear where the voter registers his preference. Once the voter has cast a vote, the equipment should count it as the voter intended. Ironically, many of the preceding "access" reforms tend to exacerbate the existing socio-economic bias in the electorate,[10] though the value of access is often touted as a Democratic value.

On the other hand, citizens also perceive a legitimate election as one in which the winning candidate did not cheat or maliciously alter the results. Furthermore, those that vote should be qualified to vote. That is to say, this country should have integrity in our elections. Every *citizen* gets to vote once and only once. Even if a citizen has economic interests in one jurisdiction, but lives in another, that citizen typically votes where he or she lives.[11] An important corollary is that dead people do not have the right to vote. Furthermore, vote tabulating equipment should correctly register the vote count. Moreover, when we recount the votes, as many states and jurisdictions do in the case of very close elections, we should be able to replicate the results. In other words, in a recount, the results returned the first time around should be the same as the results received the second time around. Solutions for such problems have focused on implementing voter registration regimes, which were adopted in many states between the late 1800s and the First World War,[12] and requiring voters to show identification, which has become a popular call following Republican takeovers of several state legislatures following the 2010 election. Often, "integrity" reforms are touted as Republican ones.

Our country had been dealing with election problems framed in terms of access and integrity since the founding of the country, especially since the framers failed to give the federal government significantly more power than they did over elections and left to the states most decisions about voting rights.[13] However, over time and especially recently, the debate of access and integrity has taken on a partisan and rather polemic cast, as if the two are opposites. In considering the access versus integrity debate, the accepted wisdom is that Democrats prefer to expand the electorate while Republicans do not. In strategic terms, this is because the demographic profile of non-voters is more similar to the Democratic Party's constituency.[14] Thus, conservatives and Republicans tend to be more interested in measures to prevent fraud,[15] which may reduce voter turnout, while liberals and Democrats tend to be more concerned about removing barriers to voting and increasing turnout.[16] The motives of either party may not be pure. Both want to win elections, but the polarized debate limits the type of election reforms that could realistically pass congressional muster. The high degree of partisan polemics in our country also affects the implementation—that is, the day-to-day operation—of election reforms, as noted in later chapters.

In this political environment, the close and contentious election of 2000 took place. There was significant question about who might become president all during the campaign—Democrat Al Gore had served as vice-president for eight years. Republican George W. Bush had served as governor of Texas; his father had served as president for four years. Public opinion polls were too close to call as Election Day approached and the candidates were fighting multiple battles in so-called "battleground states." The election was not decided for 36 days, due in large part to multiple election system failures. The failures exposed weaknesses in our election system. Thus, the United States Congress felt compelled to act.

What Was the Triggering Event?

As we approach the 2012 election, and in the wake of electing our first African American president, students of elections start to forget the chaos of the 2000 election. Voting equipment selection was not uniform across the country, or even within states. Much voting equipment was selected by local election officials. Voter registration databases had various weaknesses, especially where it concerned official purges of (usually) ineligible voters. Among other election problems, the 2000 election revealed to the general public that they could not take vote tabulating equipment for granted. Before 2000, there were certainly cases of questionable ballot counting, but most citizens took the administration elections for granted. The public simply did not know the magnitude of the problem. Not only that, but in Florida, there were charges that African Americans had been purged from registration lists for political reasons (due to a questionable felon purge) and many people worked desperately to establish that they were in fact eligible to vote. Combine that with charges of fraud and dead people voting, and the election was—well—a mess.

Political junkies watching the election returns in 2000 initially heard that Al Gore won the state of Florida, but it was not long before the television networks changed their call. As the night wore on, journalists and viewers realized that the results of the election hinged on Florida, even though the election was close in other battleground states as well. Due to the closeness of the election in Florida, there was an automatic recount, which when completed gave Bush a lead of only a bit more than 300 votes out of more than 6 million. But soon the question was: What ballots actually counted? More specifically, what counted as a vote on a punch card ballot? What about ballots with pregnant chads? Dimpled chads? Hanging chads? Party lawyers, interest group representatives, experts and journalists soon began highlighting the potential problems with punch card ballots.

A back-and-forth contest began in the courts and Bush lawyers and Gore lawyers argued about which counties to recount, how to count ballots and what deadlines should be met.[17] By the end of November, Florida Secretary of State Katherine Harris (R) certified the election results, giving Bush a 537-vote lead. By December 9, the U.S. Supreme Court decided to halt all manual recounts and soon made a decision in *Bush v. Gore* that made Bush the election winner. On December 13, 2000, Al Gore conceded the election "for the sake of our unity of the people and the strength of our democracy...."[18] Florida highlighted major administrative breakdowns in the election system: ballot counting issues and database issues.

It should be noted that there were multiple system failures in the 2000 election; Florida was simply the most high-profile case. Other states, such as Missouri, allegedly had fraud with dogs and dead people being registered to vote (there were other states and other problems after all). Georgia had high error with voting equipment just like Florida. But it was Florida's punch card ballots that became the center of attention, because Florida's results held up the country.

Punch Card Ballots

The most noticeable breakdown in the system seemed to be with vote tabulating equipment, especially in Florida. Indeed, the punch card ballots and visions of recounts with election officials closely examining ballots was an enduring vision that dominated the rhetoric following the election. As election night 2000 wore on, it become clear that not only was the race as close as a few thousand votes, there were also some peculiar election results in some counties in Florida. In Palm Beach County, conversation turned to butterfly ballots—in which the ten presidential candidates were presented in two columns.[19] Some argued the ballot caused a large number of votes for third-party candidates such as Pat Buchanan. Right after the election, *Miami Herald* reporter Peter Whoriskey noted that:

> [i]f the Palm Beach County election results can be believed, the Lakes of Delray is a hotbed of support for Patrick Buchanan. More people there cast votes for Buchanan than any other precinct in the county. Trouble is, no one in the predominantly liberal, predominantly Jewish retirement condo community seems to believe that's possible.[20]

Also, in Palm Beach, as well as other counties, large numbers of "spoiled" ballots or ballots for which no vote was registered were highlighted. What was very disturbing about the situation was that the results of the election depended on the assumptions made about types of counting rules adopted as well as which counties were actually recounted.[21]

The conversation soon turned less on ballot usability and more on voting equipment, which had a certain irony to those in the election reform community before all this took place. Roy Saltman had studied voting technology for years as a computer scientist in the Institute for Computer Sciences and Technology in the National Bureau of Standards (now NIST). For 30 years, he noted that punch card voting was inferior equipment, "destined to show its defects in public"—something that Saltman argued most election officials recognized:

> Some election officials, inured to the mistakes made by voters as an expected human condition, thought the system adequate. Others hesitated to speak out because they feared to propose significant expenditures to the local political leadership, and the remainder quietly prayed that the elections that they personally administered would not be close. There was no chorus of election officials demanding change.[22]

There may have been other motivations for the lack of change in equipment, used by about one-third of Americans in the 1998 election.[23] Indeed, until the 2000 election, punch cards for the most part provided quick results the media and the public demanded. Furthermore, most vote tabulating equipment is not perfect. There are trade-offs among the different types of technology.[24]

However, at that point, failing to recognize the punch card problems (both in computerized tabulation and the inherent weaknesses of having to punch out chads) meant that the defects in the vote tabulating equipment might cause unpredictable problems. Even the Supreme Court in its *Bush v. Gore* opinion seemed to agree that policymakers would have to address punch cards. The *per curiam* opinion of the Court read:

> This case has shown that punch card balloting machines can produce an unfortunate number of ballots which are not punched in a clean, complete

way by the voter. After the current counting, it is likely legislative bodies nationwide will examine ways to improve the mechanisms and machinery for voting.[25]

A close election could (and did) cause a triggering event to change public policy.

The Florida election rhetoric was framed in terms of voting equipment, but voting equipment was framed in the more traditional sense of access to the franchise. Access to the franchise demanded that we modernize voting equipment; and many charged that poor and minority voters were most likely to use such voting equipment,[26] even though it was not clear that was the case nationwide.[27]

However, there did appear to be scholarly agreement that in election jurisdictions with more minorities—particularly African Americans—there were higher levels of what some called "error" or "lost votes."[28] Scholars started calling the "lost votes" by another name: residual ballots—simply the difference between the number of ballots cast in a given location and the number of votes cast for the presidency. Scholars had recognized that just because a vote was not recorded for an office did not mean that the voter intended it that way.[29] Scholars began to talk more in terms of overvotes and undervotes, rather than simply residual ballots even though much research—including our own—analyzes residual votes. However one analyzes the accuracy of the equipment, the close and controversial nature of the 2000 election and the real struggle for power it represented touched a sore point that had to do with remaining inequities in the system for selecting government. Given the inequities, the public seemed to demand that something be done. Thus, many policymakers defined the problem of elections as one of voting equipment, but also in equal protection terms as access to proper vote counting technology.

Database Errors

Election Day 2000 revealed another set of problems—this set of problems was with the voter registration databases, on which each precinct relied to determine who could vote and who could not. As the day wore on, large numbers of voters noted they were turned away from the polls, especially in Florida. But it was not just Florida. The United States Commission on Civil Rights contended that this happened nationwide, that potentially two to three million people had lost their right to vote due to "clerical and administrative errors."[30] This type of problem could always happen due to human error (potential voters and election administrators), but the problem was exacerbated in Florida because of a purge of voters prior to Election Day. The U.S. Commission on Civil Rights released a report in June 2001 called, "Voting Irregularities in Florida During the 2000 Presidential Election." They noted that as a result of a fraudulent mayor's election in 1997 where apparently dead people voted, Florida's legislature decided to contract with a private company to conduct voter registration list purges.[31] The list, especially of felons[32]—included people who were not felons.[33] While officials pared the list somewhat, the U.S. Commission on Civil Rights reported that most of the reportedly ineligible voters were African American. This too, was an important image from the 2000 election, raising questions about access to the franchise.

The Other Florida? A Platform for Integrity

While punch cards provided some of the most enduring images guiding election reform, a different aspect of the integrity problem definition was more clearly highlighted in other states, such as Missouri, particularly in St. Louis City. "In 2000, Missouri came in second only to Florida in the number of allegations made about both voter fraud and vote suppression," noted Tova Wang from the Century Foundation.[34] Republicans believed that many people improperly voted and continued to push the point for several months after the election. In June 2001, Republican Senator Christopher ("Kit") Bond from Missouri—who became an important spokesperson for the integrity side of the election problem definition—wrote an editorial in the *Washington Post*:

> Though dead for 10 years, St. Louis Alderman Albert "Red" Villa actually registered to vote this spring in the city's mayoral primary. Ritzy Mekler, a mixed breed dog, was also registered to vote in St. Louis. And a recent canvass found that hundreds of city voters apparently are mailing in absentee ballots from abandoned buildings and vacant lots.[35]

Then Secretary of State Matt Blunt issued a report alleging that at least 1,200 people were allowed to vote improperly.[36] Democrats went to court on Election Day because they charged that up to 33,000 voters had been "improperly thrown off the rolls, causing hours of delays to prove they were eligible to vote."[37] Senator Bond called for a federal investigation of the irregularities occurring on Election Day. Through all this, the *St. Louis Post-Dispatch* reported that about 400 people had been allowed to vote anyway, despite being ineligible. Ultimately, a federal lawsuit compelled the St. Louis City Election Board to clean up the voting rolls, but the question still remained as to what to do in such situations. Had Missouri's election been as close as Florida's, then the rhetoric resulting from these lawsuits might have taken center stage and we would be talking about fraud far more than we are today.[38] As it was, concerns about voter fraud formed the basis of an integrity frame in terms of ensuring that only those who are eligible to vote do vote.

The Result: Some State Legislation, Federal Legislation

Consequently, Florida "moved quickly after the 2000 election to enact comprehensive reforms, including funding to replace voting equipment."[39] Florida also made punch card ballots illegal. A couple of other states quickly took the initiative to pass election reforms. Less than a year after the 2000 election, Georgia passed legislation that would remove all the state's lever, punch card and even optical scan ballots, in favor of electronic voting systems.[40] In 2001, Maryland also passed legislation to replace its voting equipment.[41] Ultimately Congress passed the Help America Vote Act of 2002 (HAVA), which observers noted was a difficult-to-achieve compromise:

> HAVA was very much a compromise between contending forces in Congress, a compromise that was barely achieved before the 2002 elections because of the difficulty of obtaining bipartisan agreement on various aspects of election administration. Broadly speaking, one side of the pre-HAVA debate tended to emphasize the importance of promoting access to the electoral process through measures that facilitate voter registration and the like. By contrast, the other side tended to emphasize the need for protective measures to prevent voting fraud.[42]

Seemingly, the piece of the legislation that caused the most controversy was a requirement for voter identification, not voting equipment.[43] The requirement that first-time voters who registered by mail show some identification angered Hispanic civil rights advocates and caused Hillary Clinton and Charles Schumer (both Democrats from New York) to be the lone senators to vote against the compromise version of HAVA.[44] However, even amidst the partisan debate about the values of access and integrity, there was agreement. Some voting equipment was not working as intended. A centerpiece of the legislation was the authorization of funds to replace antiquated voting equipment, the biggest federal investment in election administration ever. Because of the decentralized nature of election administration, the reforms enacted since 2000 represented the most widespread changes in American election procedures in decades.

HAVA gave state and local jurisdictions a deadline of 2006 to implement the required reforms. Since a few general elections have occurred since that deadline, this is an ideal time to evaluate the impact of the Act, especially in terms of its ability to safeguard the legitimacy of American presidential elections. In this book, we analyze our data from several years of election-related research on a variety of aspects of election reform—as well as media coverage—in order to conduct this evaluation. Here is a preview of what we find. Because of the way many policymakers defined the problem of election administration (as voting equipment), the federal legislation designed to solve the problem is not as holistic as it could be. Our data indicate that the Act led to positive outcomes in terms of the accuracy of vote counting—at the top of the ballot. However, our protections against a ballot design meltdown are minimal and there are real potential problems with ballot usability that have not been addressed.

Provisional votes provide some measure of protection for voters against clerical and administrative errors, yet the rules used and even the people applying the rules are in question. Electronic voting machines seem to have increased worries about legitimacy and have already been discarded in many jurisdictions. All in all, we argue our country has reduced our risk of another national-level legitimacy crisis resulting from election administration. In some ways, however, there are still glitches in the system, the most important of which is pretty much unavoidable; people administer elections. However, state policymakers could make changes in the way local election administrators are selected, particularly to limit the role of partisanship in election administration. If states and localities were willing to yield more control to the federal government, that might help address inequities that cause legitimacy issues. We may not see another episode like the 2000 election for quite some time, but we argue the risk is still there. Despite HAVA, local-level legitimacy problems and recount battles are likely to continue. It is not fair to ask any legislation to be perfect, but some risks are predictable and to a certain extent, preventable.

The Framework for Analysis

We are most interested in evaluating how the conflict between access and integrity resulted in the Help America Vote Act. Such an analysis requires both what was included in the Act, and what was not. However, we think that such consequences emanate from the ways in which policymakers and advocacy groups frame and address the policy problems. Such consequences are not random, as some might argue,[45] but are predictable based on the way we define the issue. This is similar to the idea that Bryan Jones and Frank Baumgartner emphasize about information processing in their book, *The Politics of Attention*:

> Once a signal is detected and interpreted, a debate about the proper solution may occur. Solving public problems is neither simple nor straightforward. Each solution may have multiple implications for the problem and various 'side consequences' going beyond the first problem.[46]

They continue by noting that this is important "because the aspect of the policy that is emphasized in the debate…often determines the outcome."[47] Thus, we argue one must understand the agenda setting stage in order to evaluate the policy. Further, we show that in general, there are specific issues that HAVA de-emphasizes which our data and analysis of the situation in the past ten years indicate are important. All in all, in the process of policymaking, how policymakers conceptualize and define a policy problem is central to determine how to address the problem.[48] We note that such an approach demands an understanding that academics, such as ourselves, also play a role in problem definition.

Overview of the Book

Each of the chapters in this book highlights original research indicating that while some of the changes due to HAVA were positive, overall election reform was somewhat limited in its ability to improve problems. Chapter 2 discusses the various definitions of the election administration problem as outlined by academics, advocacy groups and policymakers, as well as the posited solution resulting from each definition. However, Chapter 2 also shows the most important output of the federal legislation: older versions of voting equipment were replaced by newer and usually better technology.

After the 2000 election, it became clear that voting equipment was defined as the most obvious source of election administration problems. Furthermore, the problem was defined in terms of lost votes for president and other contests at the top of the ballot. Thus, the centerpiece of HAVA was the replacement of outdated voting equipment. The largest part of the more than $3 billion Congress appropriated was intended to provide electronic and optical scan voting equipment.

The research presented in Chapter 3 indicates that most new voting equipment now includes an error prevention mechanism, the critical factor in reducing voting errors for contests at the top of the ballot, such as the presidency. However, while some scholars have examined residual votes (undervoting and overvoting) on races such as that for Senate, House of Representatives and gubernatorial races,[49] very few have examined races toward the bottom of the ballot, such as ballot measures. Surprisingly, our evidence shows that some electronic machines perform worse than punch card machines when it comes to residual votes at the bottom of the ballot.

We are aware of very little work that has explored the unintended consequences of election reforms. Chapter 4 does just that, in examining the legitimacy issues risking the maximal performance of HAVA. HAVA strongly encouraged states to replace older voting equipment but did not provide funding to cover the entire cost of new equipment. Furthermore, many citizens are concerned about electronic voting equipment, particularly its integrity. Some states had buyer's remorse and spent more money to replace voting technology purchased quickly after the 2000 election. As a result, state and local election authorities have been exploring ways to minimize the cost of new voting equipment. One option that several jurisdictions have chosen or are considering is to consolidate polling places or reduce the number of voting booths. However, evidence suggests that consolidating polling places reduces voter turnout.

Chapter 5 indicates that voting equipment problems encompass mechanical issues such as whether one can punch out a chad completely. But the usability of ballots and other election materials is an issue that extends beyond technology. We think the strong focus on equipment itself drowned out other usability aspects of voting. Thus, those implementing election reform may not do enough to ensure that voting equipment transparently communicates the will of the electorate. HAVA provides that the Election Assistance Commission (EAC), along with the National Institute of Standards and Technology and a Technical Guidelines Committee will communicate voluntary standards for the design of election materials. But, voluntary standards may not be widely implemented.[50] Thus, by changing to optical scan ballots but failing to factor in ballot formatting and usability issues, election administrators may not prevent certain voting errors. We outline the results of two studies of ballots used in the 2002 and the 2004 elections. We show that several ballot design features influence voting errors at the top and bottom of the ballot. Several simple graphic design changes can improve the voting experience. Yet ballot design was not a salient agenda item for policymakers during and after HAVA.

It is also important to consider that any and all election reform changes will be implemented by local election officials in counties and townships all over the country. Chapter 6 examines the background, policy preferences, and behavior of the people who manage elections in the United States. We find that roughly half of election officials are members of a major political party, and that Republican and Democratic election officials tend to have different policy preferences on some critical areas of election management. Most importantly, we provide some evidence that election officials may manipulate election procedures to aid their political party. Our evidence here comes from provisional voting, something required by HAVA and implemented for the first time in most states after the 2000 election. Over 1.92 million provisional ballots were cast, and over 1.24 million of them were counted as valid ballots in the 2004 election, the first general election held under HAVA's requirements. We find that the casting and counting of provisional ballots was related to the partisanship of local election officials. Thus, we caution that we cannot just interpret election problems in terms of the mechanics of ballots and equipment (a simple solution). We should also consider the politics of the officials who are interpreting and applying the laws. HAVA did not address the political activities of election officials or the ways in which election officials are selected.

Conclusion

Roy Saltman predicted that as long as the public received quick results of elections, and that if there was no real question about who won, then confidence in the election administration system (especially voting equipment relying on computers for tabulation) would be maintained.[51] Certainly, in various localities, there were situations where results were delayed and questions asked about vote tabulation,[52] but such events were rather localized and did not involve a significant portion of the United States population, which one might consider key in order for a problem to be considered by Congress. Indeed, the 2000 presidential election, with its 36-day crisis combined with endless media discussions of counts and recounts of ballots and questionable results, shook public confidence in the legitimacy of the presidential election.

Any time we attempt reforms in elections, we are making a statement about democracy and how best to accomplish democratic and legitimate elections. Should democracy be about increasing access to those denied it? In ensuring a voter is able to vote and that his or her vote counts, we are ensuring access. Of course, our democratic principles have determined that "one man one vote" takes center stage as well; for many that means protecting the integrity of the election by working to prevent fraud. Of course, the problems highlighted in the 2000 election were complex, and politics in the United States often attempt to simplify problems in order to produce solutions. In some ways, it is actually sort of ironic that the Carter Baker Commission said, "in a world of problems that often defy any solution, the weaknesses in election administration are, to a very great degree, problems that government actually can solve."[53] When policymakers deal with a crisis situation however, the way we deal with the problem is mostly due to the way we perceive the problem and who is able to dominate the symbolic rhetoric surrounding the problem. Voting equipment took center stage in the passage of HAVA.

Avoiding "another Florida" is not all it is cracked up to be. In the pages that follow, we show that election reform can be helpful, but what we have done so far may not prevent the legitimacy problems that our country has tried so hard to avoid. We show that the headlong rush into changes may have created unintended consequences. We hope to raise questions about issues that will both increase the access to voting and improve the integrity and therefore legitimacy of elections. We hope that two relatively smooth elections in 2008 and 2010 did not lull us into a false sense of security about our democracy.

2

HOW DOES DEFINITION OF THE PROBLEM AFFECT THE SOLUTION?

The only modern technology on display in many precincts Tuesday were the laptops, cellphones and Palm Pilots in the hands of the hapless voters trapped in lines of three hours or more. (The cellphones came in particularly handy for the voters who emerged from poll purgatory to discover their cars had been towed for exceeding time limits on parking.)[1]

(Editorial, *Atlanta Journal and Constitution*, November 13, 2000)

Within the surreal tableau of election 2000, there is this: the dramatic incongruities of technology. It is as if American society now has one foot in the slick world of high-tech advertisements, and another stuck somewhere back around carbon copies and adding machines.[2]

(Peter S. Goodman, *Washington Post*, November 10, 2000)

As the dust from the 2000 election settled, it began to dawn on Americans that perhaps the types of technology we were using to cast and tabulate votes was not keeping pace with the technological development to which so many of us have become inured. In 2000, many citizens had Internet connections and mobile phones, satellite television and broadband cable television. We had long entered the days of the 24-hour news cycle. We were in the digital age, but apparently, many Americans were still voting on old-fashioned voting machines, and not touch-screen computers. Punch card voting technology—used by approximately one-third of the population—was first used in the 1890 Census.[3] Approximately 18 percent of the population (including all of the state of New York), used mechanical lever machines—the so-called "900-pound behemoths." These machines were first introduced in New York in 1892, and had not been manufactured for more than 15 years.[4] Still other jurisdictions used paper ballots, which election officials counted by hand.

With just a bit of study, it was clear that the 2000 election in Florida was not a single problem but a set of problems. Indeed, election administration is very complex, particularly since elections are managed by state and local officials. Chapter 1 discussed three aspects of Election Day 2000 that informed debate among most political actors until and after the U.S. Congress passed HAVA in 2002. The punch card problems in Florida (and elsewhere, as it turned out), the voter registration database problems in Florida (and elsewhere) and the potential fraud allegations in Missouri (and elsewhere) provided the information used to shape the political rhetoric. But as with most triggering events, political actors could characterize the 2000 election in different ways, most likely because of partisan politics, but also because of interest group pressures, academic research shaping the topics and of course, the actions of political entrepreneurs looking to score political points. Examining the evidence gathered before and after the 2000 election, one certainly cannot conclude that voting equipment alone was the source of all the election problems. However, observers soon realized that the political debate seemed to surround the democratic values partisans said they wanted to maximize in administering elections: Republicans wanted to maximize integrity; Democrats wanted to maximize access. Modernizing voting equipment seemed to maximize both sets of partisans' values and new voting equipment became a leading solution. Yet, other aspects of election policy often polarized the parties, delaying federal legislation and funding that states needed for modernizing elections.

Aspects of the Problem of the 2000 Crisis

How did the quickly emerging consensus about voting equipment affect the solutions we adopted, and what intended or unintended policy outputs ensued? Many scholars have detailed the various aspects of HAVA, but how in particular did the Act address the election problems defined and highlighted by the 2000 crisis in Florida? Understanding this question will help us analyze the potential problems neither defined nor addressed in the Act. However, the goal of this chapter is to illustrate some of the rhetoric and actions on the part of policymakers that led us to this conclusion. This chapter indicates that policymakers with varying political agendas and ideas focused on differing aspects of what happened in the 2000 election; yet one way of solving the election problem—more modern voting equipment—was agreed upon by most partisan politicians on both sides. It seemed an obvious fix.

The Values of Access and Integrity

In analyzing problems, policymakers typically consider political concerns as well as core values. In the debate leading to the passage of HAVA the values of access and integrity were often discussed and presented as if they were at odds. As we note in Chapter 1, in debates about election reforms Democrats often take the side of increased access to voting while Republicans take the side of protecting the integrity of elections. This is because it is assumed that if non-voters participate in future elections, they are more likely to vote for Democratic candidates. Both parties want to win elections. The growing degree of partisan polarization in other areas of politics found its way into election reform discussions. These partisan tensions were evident in the debate over HAVA. Democrats wanted to replace error-prone voting equipment and allow provisional ballots for voters wrongly left off voter lists, while Republicans wanted more rigorous voter identification requirements and statewide registration databases that would provide more accurate voter lists. New voting equipment also appealed to Republicans as a way to ensure the integrity of the vote count. However, a Republican-led provision requiring first-time mail registrants to show photo identification in order to vote nearly derailed the legislation. Our country continued to witness the partisan debate over election laws well after HAVA passed, on issues such as Election Day registration and voting rights for felons. Partisan bickering was also observed with respect to poll watchers and voter registration in several battleground states shortly before the 2004 presidential election.

Voting Equipment and Punch Card Ballots

At its most basic level, policymakers, media reports, researchers, think tanks and interest groups alike defined a portion of the Election Day problem as a matter of vote tabulating technology simply not being modern enough. More accurately, scholars found that certain types of equipment were more accurate than other types in terms of registering the intent of the voter. Defining problematic voting technology was one of the most accepted issues in election reform from 2000 to 2003. However, where the ultimate blame lay for such a problem was in question. Was it inadequately educated voters who simply did not possess the requisite skills to cast their vote (and if they couldn't, then perhaps they shouldn't), or was it that the equipment itself was inherently flawed?[5] As it happened, the blame for mistakes in registering any particular voter's intent did not matter. Policymakers would not soon forget members of Florida canvassing boards squinting over every dimpled chad, an image which questioned the integrity and accuracy of the final vote count. Academics began work evaluating voting equipment accuracy and the prevalence of different types of equipment.[6] This academic work helped define the problem of voting equipment.

Voting technology itself became a civil rights issue not only for minority voters but also for disabled voters. The media and many political entrepreneurs charged that the people most likely to use inferior equipment were those who were poor and minorities. The problem has been framed as a civil rights issue, analyzing the relationship between residual votes and race. Evidence had existed to that effect, but the research community provided further evidence. The work showed that residual votes were more common in precincts and counties with large populations of racial and ethnic minorities. Furthermore, scholars noted there appeared to be an interaction between demographic variables and some voting methods and ballot features. The association between socioeconomic measures and voting mistakes was weaker in places using equipment (such as error correction mechanisms) or ballot features (such as a straight-party option) that made it easier for voters to complete a valid ballot.[7] By the same token, the elevated rate of residual votes associated with confusing ballots and voting technology tends to fall disproportionately in precincts and counties with high concentrations of poor, elderly or minority voters.

Federalism: What Is the Responsibility of the National Government?

The Supreme Court seemed to have spoken in *Bush v. Gore*, the decision of the Supreme Court to stop the ballot recount in Florida. The decision suggested that the federal government did have some role in tabulating votes because the process by which ballots were recounted violated the equal protection and due process. But in a way, the Court tried to limit the precedent set by the ruling.

> The recount process, in its features here described, is inconsistent with the minimum procedures necessary to protect the fundamental right of each voter in the special instance of a statewide recount under the authority of a single state judicial officer. Our consideration is limited to the present circumstances, for the problem of equal protection in election processes generally presents many complexities.[8]

While punch card ballots and old-fashioned equipment more generally were a relatively simple way to define the problem of elections, more complicated was the issue of whether equipment should be uniform across states or within states. Central to the entire crisis was the problem revealed by the lack of uniformity in voting equipment, ballot design, vote counting rules and in database management issues. The system of elections in the United States was (and is) variously called "hyper-federal," "hyper-decentralized," and "hyper-local." Voting equipment was, for the most part, selected by local election officials. Thus, there was debate about whether the federal government should impose some sort of uniformity in voting equipment to insure equal protection of voters.

Decrying the lack of federal minimum standards for voting equipment, Representative John Conyers (D-MI) wrote in an editorial in the *New York Times*, "America has tried leaving election decisions to each state. We have no minimum federal voting rights standards for voting machines. The result: In the 2000 presidential election, 1.5 million ballots were discarded due to defective voting equipment." He went on to comment "that states have been slow in outlawing discrimination"[9] and suggested that states would be slow in changing equipment as well without federal involvement. Other policymakers responded that having the federal government determine things such as voting equipment for localities was unprecedented federal involvement in elections. However, some who made such arguments seemed somewhat willing to compromise, providing there were many more fraud-fighting techniques employed in elections.

Thus, part of the struggle to define the problem of elections was over what actions the United States government should take and which level of government should establish election laws. The issue arose in many different contexts, both state and federal, within legislative and judicial branches.[10] Was the federal government the appropriate actor to address the issues of voting equipment, standards for ballot design and faulty voter databases?[11] Certainly, the federal government had stepped in before. Most recently, Congress had passed the National Voter Registration Act of 1993, which governed the purging of registration rolls and mandated that citizens could register to vote at a state Division of Motor Vehicles (DMV) office or at a public assistance office. Such regulation was designed to increase voting access. Not only that, but the Voting Rights Act (and amendments) had provided specific guidelines to local jurisdictions, going so far as to make some jurisdictions obtain clearance before making even the smallest election-related change. However, for the most part, elections had been under the jurisdiction of states and localities.[12]

While policymakers seemed to agree in general that election jurisdictions were using inadequate voting equipment, the way in which the federal government might go about implementing a change in technology was under question. The prominent report "To Assure Pride and Confidence in the Electoral Process," prepared by the National Commission on Federal Election Reform, made a variety of recommendations about federal involvement, yet its suggestions were rather conservative, as they suggested a "carrot" approach to voting equipment changes and reforms in administration. In response, Senator Christopher Dodd (D-CT) and the House co-sponsor of his bill, Rep. John Conyers Jr. (D-Mich.) held a news conference. The two "were joined at a news conference by members of the Congressional Black Caucus and the Congressional Hispanic Caucus in contending that anything short of uniform federal rules for fair elections would leave the door open to more Florida-type abuses."[13]

Not Just Old Equipment, But...

Old-fashioned voting equipment became the most pressing and recognized aspect of the election problem, but the problems sparked the investigation of other aspects of election administration, which became important in federal and state debates about what could be done to reform elections in our country. The battle of election reform following 2000 allowed policymakers long interested in various aspects of reform to raise other related issues. Another enduring image of the election was voters either standing in line or denied access to the vote due to registration problems. For example, the purge of voter lists on the part of Florida officials was controversial.[14] In addition, as many as three million votes were "lost" due to registration problems.[15] While some states allowed potential voters to vote an "affidavit ballot" if they thought they should be on the registration list, many did not. Such affidavit ballots would allow the voter's ballot to count if in fact there was a mix-up or administrative error, and indeed, the voter should have been allowed to vote.

The rhetoric after the 2000 election seemed to indicate that these lost votes were particularly a problem. However, the registration problem noted here also had other sides. The problems with registration databases were also framed in terms of the level of the management. In particular, some argued that allowing local election officials to maintain the registration database was an inherently flawed idea. Since many local jurisdictions all over the country had separate and sometimes not even computerized voter registration databases, this could allow some individuals to vote twice. However, another prominent way of framing the problem was the idea that the purges that had been conducted were inadequate, leaving vast numbers of dead people and illegal voters on lists. As noted in the previous chapter, Missouri Senator Christopher ("Kit") Bond charged that the database problems enabled fraud. Purging voter rolls was complicated by the federal law governing purges, the National Voter Registration Act of 1993 (more commonly known as Motor Voter). Six months after the 2000 election, Bond wrote an editorial in the *Washington Post* where he charged that there were many dead people on the voter rolls, facilitating "organized vote fraud."[16] In that same editorial, Bond argued that a main solution to the problem as he defined it would be to require "some sort of notarization or authorization" on mail-in voter registration cards. Conservatives charged that another way to reduce fraud would be to require that first-time voters who registered by mail must show some sort of identification when they presented themselves at the polls on Election Day. However, that provision proved very controversial. Ultimately some of this language appeared in HAVA, yet these reforms were eclipsed by the amount of money spent on voting equipment.

(Some) States Took Quick Action on Voting Equipment

In the meantime, while the representatives in the U.S. House and Senate were wrangling over the particulars of election reform, many state policymakers across the country took the matter into their own hands. State lawmakers and election study commissions also defined the problem of elections as one of voting equipment, though many state commission reports identified a number of other problems in the system. Much of the state-level discussion also centered around a lack of uniformity; prior to 2000, localities made their own decisions about what vote tabulating equipment to purchase. Perhaps state lawmakers should determine the equipment, and provide at least part of the funding for its purchase. Secretaries of state and other election administrators sometimes comforted those worried about the expense by saying that the federal government would come through with funding. Just a few examples show that it was not just punch card voting machines at the center of attention. Rather, the debate focused on older technology more generally.

Indeed, by mid-2001, when some states were seen as not taking action soon enough, the American Civil Liberties Union and other groups filed several federal discrimination lawsuits. Defendants included California, where the lawsuit charged that "punch-card ballots such as those that led to problems in Florida violate the civil rights of minority voters."[17]

Some states quickly took initiative to pass election reforms, especially where reforms concerned voting equipment: Florida was the first to adopt new voting equipment. Less than a year after the 2000 election, Georgia did the same, but adopted all DRE equipment.[18] In 2001, Maryland also passed legislation to replace its voting equipment, though actual changes were somewhat slower there. Even some states that never had punch cards adopted changes (the example here is Iowa). Certainly, not all states moved forward with changes to equipment, partially because there was not always a perceived need to do so, or there was worry that the federal government would not pass legislation (and the related budget bills) to fund changes in very expensive equipment. States such as New York were caught up in partisan bickering and also had difficulties reconciling new equipment with old election laws.

Florida

Florida "moved quickly after the 2000 election to enact comprehensive reforms, including funding to replace voting equipment."[19] Republican Governor Jeb Bush started early 2001 by establishing a task force to make election recommendations on the best way to rid the state of punch card ballots. However, the task force's recommendation that all counties use optical scan ballots met with opposition, since some county officials wanted to use direct recording electronic (DRE) machines. When he proposed his budget for the next fiscal year, Governor Jeb Bush (R) announced that he was setting aside $30.5 million for election initiatives, and that voting equipment was his "top priority."[20] And, after a couple of short months of negotiating, the Florida House and Senate announced the parties had compromised. Similar to a later compromise announced by the U.S. Congress, there was agreement on voting equipment, according to the *Miami Herald*. "Both the Senate and House have agreed to ban punch-card ballots, and both insist on electronic equipment counting ballots in each voting precinct starting next year."[21] On May 4, 2001, the House voted 120–0 and the Senate voted 39–1 in favor of the new legislation, which would ban punch card ballots. The bill would also require manual review of ballots when there was a close election.[22] Later that year, newspapers announced that then-Palm Beach County Supervisor of Elections Theresa LePore—also known as Madame Butterfly after the ballots she designed—planned on selling their punch card machines on eBay. Ironically, Florida was also one of the first states to abandon DREs following a Sarasota County incident amid national concerns about the integrity of DREs.

Georgia

The 2000 election crisis in Florida highlighted the lack of uniformity and use of antiquated voting equipment in states all over the country, including Georgia. But fairly quickly, analyses revealed that Georgia had a high level of residual votes, with close to 100,000 citizens either failing to vote for president or some problem with vote casting or tabulation, and the media reports indicated there was a large racial disparity in undervotes, that is, the ballots where no vote for president was registered.[23] And, reports indicated that the residual vote rate in Georgia was actually higher than her more infamous sister Florida.[24] Secretary of State Cathy Cox used this information and the triggering event in Florida to advance a legislative agenda that included new electronic voting machines throughout the state, to be piloted in municipal elections in specified locations. The new equipment would likely be paid for over three to five years. As with other states' election officials, she hoped the federal government would fund some of the machines.

> Cox said she hopes the state will not have to foot the bill for the entire system. Vote-counting problems occurred nationwide, and Florida's highly publicized travails have prompted legislation in Congress. Bills introduced by both Democrats and Republicans would provide block grants to states that choose to modernize their voting machinery.[25]

The 2001 legislative session ended with the lawmakers approving Cox's voting equipment plan, but not dedicating funds for new equipment purchases. However, the state was on track for the new voting equipment purchases by 2004. As a result, the state would have uniform, modern equipment throughout.

Maryland

Relative to Florida, Maryland did not make its decision quickly. Much of the analysis of what was the correct decision to make did not appear to take place until after the state made the decision to purchase electronic voting machines. Interestingly, through examining the state over time, one can see that officials quickly identified a need for modernized voting equipment, yet took their time in purchasing it because of later concerns about security of the machines. A 2003 report noting several severe security concerns was released the day before the state announced the purchase of Diebold voting machines (Accuvote TSx machines) for a total of $55.6 million.[26] Fairly quickly, the state delayed the 11,000 touch-screen purchase, asking for a review of the system's security.[27] Maryland eventually released the hold and bought the DREs, with the Republican Governor Robert L. Ehrlich noting that Diebold had promised to fix the problems noted in the review.[28] Maryland moved ahead with the purchase and use of the Diebold machines, and even published a brochure attempting to combat what they said were "myths" about electronic voting.[29] While there has been a debate in the legislature, Maryland continues to use its touch-screen voting machines.

Iowa

While punch card voting equipment was the center of attention in the early 2000s, the definition of the problem was not just about the usability of punch card ballots, but rather about older voting technology more generally. A case in point is the state of Iowa. The *Sioux City Journal* bragged, "Iowans never will have to worry about hanging chads, the little pieces of paper knocked out in punch-card ballots...that type of voting method was outlawed in Iowa 20 years ago by lawmakers who foresaw the potential problems."[30] Iowa may have stopped using punch cards 20 years before the 2000 election, but then-Secretary of State Chet Culver (Democrat) noted that many counties still used lever machines and hand-counted paper ballots. Thus, one of the state's first priorities was modernizing, even though by mid-2001, the state's task force studying the issue decided that local election officials should decide what kind of equipment to use in each county.[31] While Iowa's lead election administrator, Culver, jumped into modern technology, the state legislature was somewhat slower.

At first, the state legislature struggled to pass the funding necessary to help modernize voting equipment. But, by 2002, with the passage of HAVA, Culver announced that "[h]elp is on the way" to the counties that used either hand-counted paper ballots or "old-fashioned lever machines, often held together with rubber bands and paper clips."[32] However, noted a task force studying the issue, counties should have the choice about the best kind of voting equipment for them, and Culver assured them that the federal government would assist the states. By 2006, most counties in the state had modernized their voting equipment. Later during the decade, the state legislature, gripped by concerns about the security of paperless voting, reversed course and required all counties to purchase optical scanning technology.

The Help America Vote Act of 2002

After the U.S. House and Senate initially passed election reform legislation, there were difficulties in getting any legislation through a conference committee to resolve differences between the bills. Democrats believed that Republicans were reducing access to elections for African Americans and Latinos by requiring identification to vote. The Republicans believed that by not endorsing some identification, the Democrats were endorsing election fraud. The debate on Capitol Hill took on a polarized partisan characteristic. However, there was some agreement, according to one partisan observer. Warren Christopher wrote in the *New York Times*,

> [d]espite the charged environment, the parties remain agreed on the core of the bill—critically needed federal money to buy new voting equipment and minimum standards on the conduct of federal elections like accessibility for disabled voters, multilingual voting materials and provisions for voters to correct errors in their voting.[33]

All in all, voting equipment changes increased access to the franchise and the integrity of the process. Provisional voting and statewide voter registration databases were, for the most part, agreed upon as well.

Certainly, observers have characterized the provisions of HAVA as a balancing act between the values of access and integrity.[34] However, both Republicans and Democrats noted the importance of new voting equipment as well as minimum standards for it in praising the eventual compromise. In the conference committee report, Missouri Senator Christopher Bond spent most of the time discussing how the bill would prevent fraud, but also lauded the part on which the Congress members agreed.

> This final compromise bill—and it is a compromise in the truest sense of the word—tries to address each of the fundamental problems we have discovered. For starters, this bill provides $3.9 billion in funding over the next 5 years to help States and localities improve and update their voting systems. In addition to providing this financial help, we also provide specific minimum requirements for the voting systems so that we can be assured that the machinery meets minimum error rates and that voters are given the opportunity to correct any errors that they have made prior to their vote being cast.[35]

Senator Edward Kennedy (D-MA) supported the bill but said new identification requirements were problematic.

> It requires the invalidation of a registration when a voter inadvertently forgets to check off a duplicative "citizenship box." It requires that, when registering to vote, voters must either provide their driver's license number, or, if they lack one, the last four digits of their Social Security number. We all have a strong interest in preventing voter fraud, but these requirements may not be an effective way to verify voter identify and, at the same time, they are very likely to create unnecessary barriers for voters.[36]

What was seemingly the easiest to agree to? Some voting equipment was not working as intended. A centerpiece of the legislation was the authorization of funds to replace antiquated voting equipment.

All in all, what did HAVA do? First, HAVA provided for the replacement of voting equipment, and jurisdictions should adopt equipment which would allow a voter to check her ballot for errors. Second, HAVA provided for independent and private access to voting for disabled voters. Third, HAVA provided for provisional ballots. In terms of integrity, HAVA required statewide voter registration databases. HAVA also provided that first-time voters who registered by mail must show identification. Not only that, but HAVA would work to provide equal protection within states, rather than among states.[37] The bill authorized close to $4 billion in funds to induce states to meet the requirements of the federal law. First and foremost, the law offered grant funds for states to use to update voting equipment. But, the law also allowed grant funds to be used for such activities as recruiting and training election officials and poll workers; educating voters; and assuring access for voters with physical disabilities. The federal legislation also required states to establish an administrative grievance process to handle voters' complaints. In order to take advantage of the grants, states were required to appropriate a 5 percent match and submit a state plan detailing how the funds would be spent and how the state would meet the new federal requirements.

The Solution to the Most Visible Problem Defined: New Equipment

HAVA provided inducements to states and localities to change voting equipment. In particular, the Act encouraged changing from lever and punch card machines to optical scanning (precinct counters) and electronic equipment. Title III of the Act specified that voting systems used in federal elections should meet several standards. First, the voter should be able to verify independently and privately that his vote was cast as intended. Furthermore, the voter should be able to change the ballot if he desires. If the person casts too many votes for a contest, the system should provide notification and allow the opportunity to correct any mistake.

Members of Congress who did not want to force the purchase of new equipment noted that such standards could also be met by "establishing a voter education program specific to that voting system that notifies each voter of the effect of casting multiple votes for an office" and provide the voter with instructions on how to correct the ballot. Furthermore, the Act also specified that each precinct must "be accessible for individuals with disabilities, including nonvisual accessibility for the blind and visually impaired, in a manner that provides the same opportunity for access and participation (including privacy and independence) as for other voters." The Act specifically mentioned that the requirement for accessibility could be satisfied by the use of an electronic voting system. Finally, the error rates of the equipment could not exceed federal guidelines set out by the Federal Election Commission. Unless they received a waiver, in order to receive funds to replace voting equipment, states had to replace them by January 1, 2006.

Consequently, roughly 70 percent of counties have switched to new voting equipment since the 2000 election. A significant number of counties adopted new voting equipment before each of the last three general elections. However, the largest amount of change occurred before the 2006 election. This is likely due to the 2006 HAVA deadline for localities to adopt new voting machinery in order to receive federal funds to help pay for them.

HAVA Was Not Just About Voting Equipment

In addition to the federal funding for new voting equipment, HAVA included some other provisions. To avoid turning people away from the polls on Election Day, Section 302 of HAVA required states to allow people to vote in a provisional ballot when they believe they are registered but their names do not appear on the voter list at their polling place. The justification for provisional voting was that sometimes people are wrongly removed from the voting registry because of database errors or because the would-be voter recently moved.[38] Data entry errors and general administrative mistakes are also possible. Since HAVA also requires that first-time voters who registered by mail show some sort of identification and some states have various voter identification laws, some states also use provisional voting in a case where a person lacks the proper identification. Finally, if the courts specified that polls stay open late for whatever reason, the individuals who vote late must vote in a provisional ballot, according to HAVA. At the time of passage, seven states were exempt from the provisions, due to the fact that they had either Election Day Registration (Idaho, Maine, Minnesota, New Hampshire, Wisconsin and Wyoming) or no voter registration (North Dakota). The provisional ballots voted were to be segregated from the rest of the ballots until the eligibility of the voter could be determined. Election officials would determine whether or not the voter was eligible to vote and then the voter was to be notified in writing whether his vote counted or not. HAVA required that provisional voting standards be in place by January 1, 2004—well in advance of the 2004 election.

However, HAVA left some discretion to the states as to the implementation of provisional voting standards. First, the legislation did not specify that a voter must be in the proper polling place in order to cast a vote. However, HAVA only stated that the person must state he is an "eligible voter within the jurisdiction" but did not specify what "jurisdiction" means, whether it be election authority or precinct. Different states have applied that standard differently since the implementation of provisional voting. In the 2004 election, 17 states chose to count provisional ballots cast outside the correct precinct; 27 did not count those cast at the wrong precinct.

Another aspect of discretion is that states were allowed to specify the "time frame in which election officials must verify whether a provisional ballot should be counted before certifying the results of an election."[39] Finally, HAVA did not stop states from expanding provisional ballots to other categories of voters.[40] Thus, there is variation in the way in which provisional ballots are implemented.

HAVA and Statewide Voter Registration Database

Access and integrity came together in the debate over voter registration. Sarah Liebschutz and Daniel Palazzolo argued that it was "a good example of how the two sides advanced their separate goals through a compromise."[41] HAVA established that states develop a "single, uniform, official, centralized, interactive computerized statewide voter registration list defined, maintained, and administered at the State level that contains the name and registration information of every legally registered voter in the State and assigns a unique identifier to each legally registered voter in the State."[42] According to the legislation, the database should contain the name of every legally registered voter and be connected with other state agency databases. Not only that, but all local and state election officials should have access to it. Despite the seemingly firm wording of the statute, the legislation and subsequent guidelines seemed to leave at least some discretion to state and local authorities about the division of authority in this matter. In particular, there is some discretion in terms of who exactly would construct and maintain the lists (state or local officials). Other unresolved questions include whether the construction of the registration database should be outsourced or whether it should be conducted by in-house specialists.[43]

HAVA and the Creation of the Election Assistance Commission

HAVA established a new board to oversee this activity known as the Election Assistance Commission (EAC). Due to the partisan nature of the battle that created the legislation, the board received no rulemaking authority and only could hand down voluntary guidelines in consultation with the National Institute for Standards and Technology. The president appointed the bipartisan commission, with the advice and consent of the Senate. The commission was to serve as a national clearinghouse of election information and provide voluntary guidelines on election administration to states and localities.

Another part of HAVA requires the EAC to commission periodic studies of election administration. "The purpose of these studies is to promote methods for voting and administering elections, including provisional voting, that are convenient, accessible and easy to use; that yield accurate, secure and expeditious voting systems; that afford each registered and eligible voter an equal opportunity to vote and to have that vote counted; and that are efficient."[44] The EAC faced controversy over the reports it commissioned concerning voter identification and election fraud. In 2007, Congress held hearings to investigate and the EAC also asked its inspector general to investigate the obligations of the commission in terms of these studies.[45] Another problem: delay in the nomination and confirmation of commission members. The Commission was to be in place in February of 2003, but was not operating until nearly a year later.[46] Since the body was charged with distributing the grant funding portion of HAVA appropriation (states had to meet various requirements such as publishing state plans for reform in order to obtain the funds), no grant funds could be distributed until the commission was in place.[47]

The Main Policy Output: Changes in Voting Equipment

Whatever problems the EAC had and however slow the federal efforts might have been, the major thrust of the legislation was to enable the replacement of old equipment, and that has happened. We collected information on the voting technology used in each state and county in each general election from 2000 to 2010.[48] Generally, voters used five different methods of voting in the United States during this period: hand-counted paper ballots, lever machines, punch card ballots, optical scan systems, and DRE machines. Table 2.1 describes these systems in more detail and indicates the percentage of counties using each system in the last six general elections. With punch card ballots, voters use a tool to punch out holes in the ballot card next to their chosen candidates. Votes are then counted by a card reader machine. Punch card methods can be divided between Votomatic varieties (in which the punch card is separate from the booklet listing the offices and issues up for election) and the Datavote system (in which offices and candidates are printed directly on the punch card). On lever machines, all contests are listed on the face of the machine and voters pull down a lever next to their chosen candidate. Votes are counted mechanically inside the lever machine. In optical scan systems, voters mark a paper ballot with a pen or pencil and votes are counted by a scanning machine. With DREs (sometimes called "touch screen" systems), candidates are listed on a computer screen and voters push a button or touch the screen next to their chosen candidate. The DRE machine records and counts the votes.

Paper ballots, punch cards and lever machines are older voting systems that have been used for decades in the United States. Optical scan balloting and DRE machines are newer types of voting equipment. Optical scan systems vary depending on where ballots are counted: at a central location (like the county courthouse) or at the voting precinct. One advantage of the precinct-count optical scan systems is that they give voters a chance to discover and correct potential mistakes.[49] The central-count systems do not have such an error-correction feature.[50]

DRE machines can be divided into two different varieties. Older DREs (such as the Shouptronic 1242) and some new models were designed to mimic

TABLE 2.1 Voting Equipment Used in the United States Since 2000

Technology	Description	Percent of Counties Using System						
		2000	2002	2004	2006	2008	2010
Punch Card–Votomatic	Punch card is inserted behind booklet with ballot choices—voter uses stylus to punch out holes in card. Ballots counted by card reader machine.	16.4	14.0	10.2	0.4	0.3	0.2
Punch Card–Datavote	Ballot choices are printed on punch card—voter punches out hole next to chosen candidate. Ballots counted by card reader.	1.4	0.8	0.5	0.0	0.0	0.0
Lever Machine	Candidates listed by levers on a machine—voter pulls down the lever next to chosen candidate. Machine records and counts votes.	12.8	9.4	7.7	2.2	2.0	0.0
Paper Ballot	Candidates are listed on a sheet of paper—voter marks box next to chosen candidate. Ballots counted by hand.	10.6	9.5	9.2	2.5	1.9	1.9
Full-face DRE	Candidates listed on a full-face computerized screen—voter pushes button next to chosen candidate. Machine records and counts votes.	9.7	10.2	9.9	7.7	6.6	4.3
Scrolling DRE	Candidates listed on a scrolling computer screen—voter touches screen next to chosen candidate. Machine records and counts votes.	1.0	7.3	11.5	31.3	28.9	29.2
Optical Scan–Central Count	Voter darkens an oval or arrow next to chosen candidate on paper ballot. Ballots counted by computer scanner at a central location.	30.0	27.7	26.0	12.5	12.1	12.3
Optical Scan–Precinct Count	Voter darkens an oval or arrow next to chosen candidate on paper ballot. Ballots scanned at the precinct, allowing voter to find and fix errors.	15.3	18.0	22.4	42.0	42.4	46.2
Mixed	More than one voting method used.	2.7	3.2	2.7	1.4	5.9	5.9

N = 3,123 counties

lever machines. These DREs present the entire full-faced ballot at once and typically use a push-button interface. Most of the newer generation of DREs (such as the iVotronic and Accuvote-TS machines) typically use a touch-screen interface in which voters scroll through the offices and issues on the ballot, with only one or two contests appearing on the screen at one time.

Some states began replacing older voting equipment quickly, anticipating federal funding. Table 2.1 indicates that there were a number of changes in equipment before the federal government took action in 2002. Almost 100 counties junked the punch card voting machines between 2000 and 2002. A little more than 100 counties dropped the use of lever machines. About 200 counties began using touch screen DREs prior to 2002. Overall, voting technology changed dramatically over the last decade. By 2010, roughly 75 percent of local jurisdictions had switched to a different type of voting equipment than they had used in 2000. Most of the changes were made by the end of 2006, due to the deadline imposed by HAVA to qualify for the federal voting equipment funds.

Since the number of voters varies dramatically from one county to the next, we also estimated the number of ballots cast on each type of voting equipment in each general election since 2000. We gathered data on the number of ballots cast in each county for the last six general elections in the United States. Figure 2.1 shows the percentage of ballots cast on old voting technology (paper ballots, punch cards, and lever machines) each year in the United States. As the graph shows, old voting equipment is now almost extinct in the United States. Punch card ballots only remain in use in five Idaho counties. Hand-counted paper ballots are still used, but only in a dwindling number of small, rural counties.

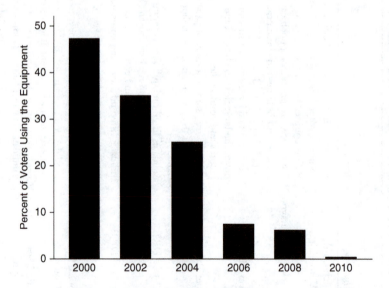

FIGURE 2.1 Use of Punch Cards, Lever Machines, and Paper Ballots, 2000–2010

Finally, after New York switched to an optical scan system in 2010, lever machines are no longer used in general elections in the United States.[51]

However, to focus only on the shift from old technology to optical scan or touch screen voting machines is to miss two other important changes in voting equipment in the United States. Within optical scan and DRE systems, there has been a shift toward more voter-friendly versions of the equipment. Among optical scan systems, ballots are counted at a central location or at the precinct. One reason why the distinction is important is that the precinct-count version offers an error detection feature to voters, while the central-count system does not. Figure 2.2 shows the share of ballots cast on each type of optical scan system. In 2000, precinct-count and central-count systems were used in roughly equal amounts. Since 2000, the percentage of ballots cast on precinct-count optical scan systems has increased sharply, while the percentage of ballots cast on central-count systems has declined. There has been a slight increase in voting on central count systems in 2008 and 2010 as some counties in Western states (primarily in Washington) have recently switched to vote-by-mail systems.[52] In vote-by-mail systems, an optical scan ballot is mailed to voters. After completed ballots are returned to the county election office, all ballots are counted at that central location. Despite the increase in voting by mail, in 2010 over 60 percent of ballots were cast on optical scan systems and roughly 80 percent of optical scan ballots were cast on precinct-count systems.

The final change in voting equipment involves the type of electronic voting machines used in the United States. Recall that some DRE machines have a

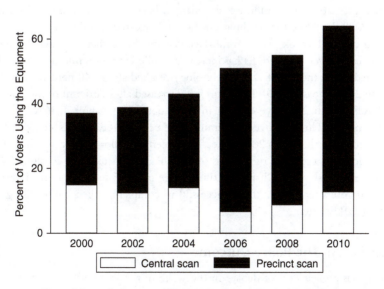

FIGURE 2.2 Use of Central-Count and Precinct-Count Optical Scan Systems, 2000–2010

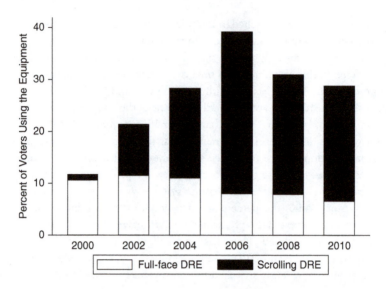

FIGURE 2.3 Use of Full-Face and Scrolling Touch-Screen Systems, 2000–2010

full-face layout in which the entire ballot appears at once on a very large screen or device, usually mimicking the layout of lever machines. Other DREs have a scrolling layout, where just one or two contests appear on the screen at one time. After making a vote in a contest, the voter then scrolls to the next screen and the next contest. Figure 2.3 indicates the share of ballots cast on both DRE systems since 2000. In 2000, the scrolling DREs barely existed and the vast majority of voting on DREs took place on full-face systems. Since then, the percentage of ballots cast on scrolling DREs has increased, while voting on full-face DREs has declined. After the use of DRE technology reached almost 40 percent of ballots cast in 2006, the use of DRE systems has decreased after criticism of the security of DRE machines. As we explain in more detail in Chapter 4, states such as California and Florida moved to eliminate the use of DRE systems after the 2006 election. Nevertheless, in 2010 almost 30 percent of ballots were cast using DRE technology, and roughly two-thirds of the DRE voters used the scrolling ballot layout. As we show in Chapter 3, this change in DRE technology is important because voters tend to be more successful in completing their ballots using the *scrolling* DRE system.

Conclusion: The Policy Outcome

There was a great deal of debate in the wake of the 2000 election; with many competing definitions of what the main problems were holding up the outcome of the election. Ultimately, the problem definition that legislators seemed to agree on most was that our country needed modern voting equipment; it became the centerpiece of HAVA—the part on which we spent the most money. With the vision of modern technology in mind, our country has made vast strides over the past decade: roughly 70 percent of counties have switched to new voting equipment since the 2000 election, with the largest amount immediately preceding federal 2006 deadline. However, the main problem definition had a few consequences, both intended and unintended. In the next chapter, we turn to one intended consequence: more accurate elections. However, the remainder of the book will explore unintended consequences and a few "what if" questions.

3

DID THE REFORMS INCREASE ACCURACY?

> Criticize Floridians, if you must, for their voting skills during the presidential election of 2000, but at least give them points for style and creativity. In spoiling their ballots, many demonstrated considerable ingenuity.[1]
>
> (Martin Merzer, *Miami Herald*, April 4, 2001)

As the previous chapter indicates, in the wake of the controversy surrounding the 2000 presidential election, reformers and policymakers initially viewed the problem of election administration as one defined by the lack of modern voting equipment. The recount of ballots in Florida revealed to the world difficulties with casting and counting punch card ballots. Thus, the federal government and some states first examined ways to modernize voting equipment in the United States. In 2002, Congress passed the Help America Vote Act (HAVA). The main thrust of HAVA was to encourage states and localities to change their voting equipment in order to promote greater accuracy in the casting and counting of votes. The large majority of federal funding to states authorized by HAVA was intended to purchase new voting equipment.

In addition, Section 301 of HAVA includes voting standards that encourage states to use technology that will detect and prevent "error." DREs prevent voters from selecting more than one candidate in a contest and thus prevent any overvotes. In addition, some DRE systems remind voters about contests they may have skipped in a ballot review screen, and thus may reduce undervotes. Similarly, in precinct-count optical scan systems, the scanner is programmed to notify voters if the ballot contains overvotes. Precinct-count optical scan systems and DREs tend to reduce residual votes because of the error-prevention features in these systems. In contrast, punch card ballots and optical scan ballots counted at a central location do not offer such an error prevention feature and tend to produce higher rates of voting mistakes.[2]

When it comes to voting equipment, HAVA largely achieved its intended effect. As we noted in the previous chapter, between 2000 and 2010, roughly three of every four local jurisdictions in the United States adopted new voting equipment. A small number of localities motivated by some of the problems in the election of 2000 purchased new voting technology before passage of HAVA. However, the vast majority of states and counties switched to new voting equipment after 2002 with the assistance of HAVA funding. In this chapter we examine whether the changes in voting equipment affected the accuracy of casting votes in the United States. We show that elections are more "accurate" but that some contests are less accurate than others. Indeed, not all technology is created equal.

How We Know Elections Are More Accurate: Measuring Accuracy

One measure of the accuracy of the election system focuses on "residual" votes, the difference between the total number of ballots cast in an election and the number of valid votes cast in a particular contest.[3] We use this measure to evaluate accuracy because we cannot look over a voter's shoulder when they are voting. We do have a secret ballot after all. We don't typically examine the ballots or ballot images cast by individual voters, but if we did, we could not connect a particular voter's attributes to that ballot. Thus, we examine residual votes cast in an election jurisdiction, usually a county—we can obtain information about the jurisdiction in the aggregate (e.g., a certain percentage of the county residents has a college degree). For the election reform community, the main goal of adopting new voting equipment was to reduce the number of residual votes, particularly in high-profile contests like presidential elections. When there are a large number of residual votes in an election, there are concerns that many voters were unable to cast their votes as intended. Furthermore, as seen in Florida, the disposition of ballots with residual votes is a source of controversy in the event of a recount or an extremely close election.

We show that the shift to new voting equipment has succeeded in reducing the number of residual votes in presidential elections. Most particularly, systems such as optical scan systems, which notify the voter in the case of an "error" (HAVA language) before the voter casts the vote have been effective. We should note that some previous analyses examining voting equipment over time have not separated these so-called precinct-count optical scan systems from central count machines when analyzing residual vote. Interestingly, some state policymakers, worried about security, have chosen central count systems over precinct-count systems. However, this chapter's analysis, which distinguishes between the two systems, shows that precinct-count machines—where a voter is alerted to an error—have a comparative advantage over central count machines.

Furthermore, this chapter's analysis shows why it is important to distinguish between full-face and scrolling DREs. In particular, voting systems that display the entire ballot at once (lever machines and full-face electronic voting machines) tend to produce substantially higher rates of residual votes on ballot measures because voters are more likely to miss down-ballot contests on full-face ballots. The good news is that due to changes in voting equipment, today fewer voters cast their ballots on full-face systems than did so in 2000. While voters no longer use punch card equipment, voters are often using optical scan ballots that are counted centrally, though full-face machines are not as common.

Voting Equipment and Residual Votes in Presidential Elections

A number of studies note that the residual vote rate (the percentage of ballots cast with residual votes for a particular contest) varies by type of voting equipment.[4] Residual votes occur as a result of undervotes (where voters record no selection) or overvotes (where voters select too many candidates, thus spoiling the ballot). Most observers agree that overvotes are due to voter mistakes, a result of confusion with the voting equipment or ballot design. In contrast, undervotes may be intentional or unintentional. Intentional reasons for undervoting include voter fatigue, a lack of desirable choices, or little information about a contest. Unintentional examples of undervoting include cases where voters miss some contests on the ballot or try but fail to record their choice.

Since most jurisdictions do not or have not always compiled separate counts of undervotes and overvotes in elections, there is some ambiguity about the sources of residual votes. We know from several surveys that less than 1 percent of voters in presidential elections report that they intentionally skipped the presidential contest.[5] Thus, if the voting equipment or ballot design has no impact on voters, we should observe residual vote rates no higher than around one percent in presidential elections. More generally, if all residual votes are intended by the voters, then we should not observe substantially different rates of residual votes on different types of voting equipment or ballot designs.

Gathering Data to Analyze Accuracy

We gathered data on turnout and election returns to compute residual vote rates for every county in the 2000, 2004 and 2008 presidential elections. Elections are administered at the county level in all but nine states. In the nine states where elections are administered by municipalities or townships, we still collected or aggregated the data to the county level. In four states (Illinois, Missouri, Maryland, and Virginia), some cities have separate election administration authorities. These cities are treated as separate jurisdictions in our data. We treat Alaska as one observation, since elections are administered by the Alaska state government. Adding the District of Columbia as another observation produces a total of 3,123 geographic units that cover the entire country for which we have voting equipment and election data. We gathered much of the data from state election offices. However, at least ten states do not collect or report reliable data on the total number of ballots cast in elections by county, which is crucial to calculate the number of residual votes.[6] For those states, we contacted individual counties to request the needed data. In other states we also contacted county election officials to correct errors in data reported by states.[7] While the data we gathered reflect the vast majority of counties in the United States, we are missing data on residual votes for a small number of counties. Nevertheless, we have managed to gather residual vote data for a larger portion of the country than previous studies.[8] As we show below, states and localities have improved at compiling residual vote data, so the number of missing observations has declined since 2000.

Table 3.1 provides a summary of the data, including the residual vote rate for each type of voting equipment in the last three elections. Overall, the residual vote rate dropped from 1.8 percent in 2000 to 1.1 percent in 2004 and 2008. This may seem like a small change, but in a nation with more than 130 million voters in the most recent presidential election that translates to almost 1 million fewer residual votes. In addition, recall that previous studies indicate that a bit less than 1 percent of voters report intentionally skipping the presidential contest. Thus, a residual vote rate only slightly above 1 percent in the two most recent presidential elections is not much more than one would expect if there were no problems with the voting equipment and ballot design. The numbers in Table 3.1 indicate that while newer voting methods such as optical scan systems and DREs produce fewer residual votes than punch card ballots, systems with an error prevention feature (as in precinct-count optical scan systems and DREs) tend to have a lower rate of residual votes than systems without an error prevention feature (such as punch cards, paper ballots, and central-count optical scan systems). This suggests

TABLE 3.1 Residual Vote Rates in Recent Presidential Elections

Technology	Percent of Residual Votes in:		
	2000	2004	2008
Punch Card–Votomatic	2.8	1.8	—
Punch Card–DataVote	1.2	—	—
Lever Machine	1.7	1.0	1.1
Paper Ballot	1.8	1.7	1.8
Full-face DRE	1.6	1.2	1.3
Scrolling DRE	—	1.0	1.3
Optical Scan–Central Count	1.8	1.7	1.3
Optical Scan–Precinct Count	0.9	0.7	0.9
Mixed Systems	1.1	1.0	1.0
National Residual Vote Rate	1.8 (N=2,873)	1.1 (N=3,037)	1.1 (N=3,018)

Note: Cells left blank indicate technology that was used in very few jurisdictions.

that changing to new voting equipment helped lower the number of residual votes in presidential elections.

Other Explanations for Residual Votes?

However, there are some other potential explanations for the higher rates of residual votes observed in some counties, and for the reduction in residual votes since 2000. For example, studies indicate that unrecorded votes are more common in communities with large concentrations of people who are non-white, elderly, poor, or lacking a high school degree.[9] It is possible that counties using punch cards or central-count optical scan systems are above the national average in these demographic characteristics. In addition, residual votes may be higher in some counties than in others because of other election administration practices or different local political cultures. For example, some counties may do more than other counties to educate voters how to properly use the voting equipment. Finally, in the wake of the 2000 election and the passage of HAVA there was more scrutiny of voting equipment from public officials and the news media.[10] The increased attention to voting technology may have induced voters and election officials to be more careful in using and operating voting equipment. Thus, further analysis is needed to sort out competing explanations for the variation in residual votes that we observe.

One way to control for alternative explanations is to examine the change in residual vote rates from one election to another within the same counties.[11] Roughly one-fourth of the counties switched to new voting equipment by 2004, and approximately two-thirds of the counties adopted new voting equipment by 2008. Demographic characteristics of counties tend to remain fairly stable over a four-year or eight-year period. Thus, we can compare the change in residual vote rates in counties that switched to new voting equipment with counties that made no change after the 2000 election, knowing that demographic factors account for few of those changes.

Figure 3.1 shows the results of such a comparison for the 2000 and 2004 elections. As expected, the residual vote rate declined more in the counties that switched to new voting equipment. In counties that adopted new voting equipment after 2000, the residual vote rate dropped from 2.2 percent in 2000 to 0.9 percent in 2004, a decline of 1.3 percentage points. For counties that made no change in voting technology, the residual vote rate declined from 1.6 percent in 2000 to 1.2 percent in 2004, a decline of just 0.4 percentage points. Many of the counties that did not change their voting technology had already adopted newer equipment (optical scan or DRE systems) before the 2000 election. The counties that adopted new voting equipment started with a higher residual vote rate in 2000, when they were still using older voting methods.

Figure 3.2 presents a similar comparison for the 2000 and 2008 elections. The same patterns hold. In counties that adopted new voting equipment after 2000

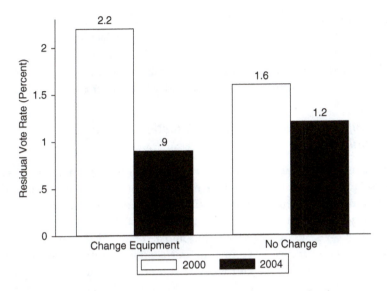

FIGURE 3.1 Changes in Residual Votes by Changes in Voting Technology, 2000–2004

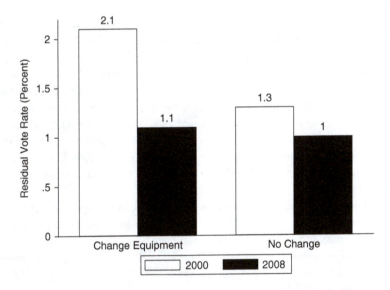

FIGURE 3.2 Changes in Residual Votes by Changes in Voting Technology, 2000–2008

the residual vote rate was cut in half, dropping from 2.1 percent in 2000 to 1.1 percent in 2008. For counties that made no change in voting technology, the residual vote rate declined from 1.3 percent in 2000 to 1.0 percent in 2004, a decline of just 0.3 percentage points. This provides stronger evidence that replacing old voting equipment helped reduce residual votes in presidential elections.

Did Equipment or Increased Voter Attention Reduce Residual Votes?

It remains possible that the changes in residual votes observed in the figures are due to increased voter interest in more recent elections (perhaps the counties that adopted new equipment are more prevalent in battleground states) or some local election administration practices, rather than (or in addition to) changes in voting technology. We need to take such factors into account in determining the effects of equipment on accuracy. To increase our confidence that voting equipment has increased accuracy, we also focus here more specifically on the types of new equipment that counties adopted, particularly on the presence of error prevention mechanisms.

In contests at the top of the ballot, such as presidential races, the key aspect of error prevention is helping voters avoid overvotes. Punch card ballots are notable for not offering much in the way of overvote prevention. In contrast, lever machines effectively prevent overvotes because they are programmed not to allow multiple votes in the same contest (e.g., the machines do not allow the voter to vote for more than the office specifies). Similarly, DRE machines (both full-face and scrolling varieties) are programmed so that overvotes are not possible. There is a key difference among optical scan systems. In precinct-count systems, the voter inserts the ballot into the scanner at the polling place and the scanners are usually programmed to alert the voter if there are overvotes on the ballot. Sometimes, systems are designed so as to alert a voter to undervotes, or if there are no votes cast on one side of a ballot. The central-count optical scan systems do not provide a comparable error prevention mechanism since the ballots are not scanned until they are brought to a central location after the polls close.

As noted in the previous chapter, the main change in voting equipment in the last ten years has been a shift away from punch cards and lever machines to optical scan systems and electronic voting machines. Based on the presence of error prevention mechanisms, we expect to observe a substantial reduction in residual votes in counties that switched from paper ballots or punch cards to DREs or precinct-count optical scan systems after the 2000 election. We do not expect much of a change in residual votes in counties that switched from punch cards or paper ballots to a central-count optical scan system. In addition, Table 2.1 noted that a significant number of counties replaced central-count optical scan systems with precinct-count systems or DREs. We expect residual votes to decline in these counties as well. We do not expect residual votes to decline in counties that replaced lever machines, since lever machines already prevent overvotes.

We follow an approach used by MIT Political Science Professor Charles Stewart to control for alternative sources of the decline in residual vote rates.[12] We estimate a fixed effects regression equation to model the impact of voting equipment on the change in residual votes from the 2000 election to later elections. In other words, we include all the counties in the analysis each year to take into account factors we cannot measure, but that are not as important to our central interest here, such as political culture or even changing administration or training. For example, if a county has a voter education program, with signs and instructions from poll workers to minimize voting errors, that should be captured by the fixed effect portion of the statistical model. Our central point is to examine whether the new equipment resulted in increased accuracy; so while these efforts could be important, knowing about them specifically will not help us evaluate equipment. Again, we evaluate accuracy using the dependent variable, the residual vote rate in a particular county in a particular year. We use a variable for each type of equipment: variables that specify whether the county used each type of equipment or not (scholars call them dummy variables). These dummy variables are used to capture the impact of switching to new voting systems between 2000 and a later election. In our research, we have discovered that the larger the turnout in a particular county, the higher the number of residual votes, which should not come as a great shock. However, with increasing numbers of voters, there is not a linear or comparable number of increased residual votes. In fact, previous analyses have shown that as voter turnout increases, residual votes also increase, but at a certain point, adding any more voters in the county will only mean that residual votes will increase only marginally. It is similar to saying that the first two or three hours of studying for a test will significantly increase your test score, but after a certain point, the studying might help a little more, but not very much. In our statistical analysis, we can represent that relationship by using the natural log of voter turnout as a control variable to estimate whether increasing turnout is associated with higher residual vote rates within a jurisdiction.

Finally, a dummy variable for the later election is included to assess whether the decline in residual votes occurred nationwide as a result of greater awareness of voting procedures and the potential for errors in elections that came after 2000.

Table 3.2 reports the results of a model of residual votes in the 2000 and 2004 elections, and the results reinforce the summary results seen in the previous figures and Table 3.1. The first model lumps together all counties that changed voting equipment. The results for the first model indicate that any county that changed its voting equipment between 2000 and 2004 produced an average reduction in the residual vote rate of 0.8 percentage points, quite a large reduction given that the nationwide residual vote rate was 1.8 percent in the 2000 election. We also find that, regardless of changes in equipment, residual vote rates

TABLE 3.2 The Impact of Voting Equipment Changes on Residual Vote Rate, 2000 and 2004 Presidential Elections (Fixed Effects Regression)

Explanatory Variable	Model 1	Model 2
	Coefficient (std. error)	Coefficient (std. error)
2004 Election	−.68** (.28)	−.68** (.28)
Ballots cast (natural log)	1.73 (1.60)	1.76 (1.64)
Any change in voting equipment	−.83*** (.21)	
Change from paper ballots or punch cards to DRE		−1.18** (.47)
Change from paper ballots or punch cards to precinct-count optical scan		−1.44*** (.46)
Change from paper ballots or punch cards to central-count optical scan		−.32* (.17)
Change from central-count optical scan to DRE		−.71** (.31)
Change from central-count optical scan to precinct-count optical scan		−1.00*** (.35)
All other changes in voting equipment		−.21 (.33)
Number of Cases	5910	5910
Root MSE	1.12	1.11
R^2	.70	.70

Notes:
The dependent variable is the residual vote rate (percent) in each county. Coefficients for county dummy variables are not shown. Each county is weighted by the number of ballots cast in the election. Robust standard errors are shown in parentheses.
***$p < .01$, two-tailed test
**$p < .05$, two-tailed test
*$p < .1$, two-tailed test

were, on average, almost 0.7 percentage points lower in 2004 than in 2000, even after controlling for changes in voting equipment and turnout and other unique county-level effects. This means that changes in voting equipment alone do not explain the decline in the residual vote rate from 2000 to 2004. Finally, the effect of increasing turnout is positive, as expected, but not statistically significant. This suggests that increases in turnout from 2000 to 2004 did not have much impact on residual votes.

The second model estimates in Table 3.2 distinguish between different voting systems and indicate that the different voting systems indeed have different impacts on residual votes. Changing from punch cards or paper ballots to DREs produced an average reduction in the residual vote rate of roughly 1.2 percentage points in 2004, while changing from paper ballots or punch cards to precinct-count optical scan produced an average reduction in the residual vote rate of approximately 1.4 percentage points. In contrast, changing from punch cards or paper ballots to central-count optical scan only produced an average reduction in the residual vote rate of 0.3 percentage points, an effect that is statistically weaker than the impact of touch-screen DREs and precinct-count optical scan (p<.01). Slightly more than 18 percent of ballots cast in 2004 were in counties that had replaced punch cards or paper ballots with optical scan systems or DREs, so those changes were responsible for a portion of the decline in residual votes.

In addition, upgrading from central-count optical scan systems made a difference in 2004. Changing from central-count optical scan to DREs or precinct-count optical scan reduced residual votes in 2004, with average reductions of 0.7 and 1.0 percentage points, respectively. These results indicate that central-count optical scan systems produce higher residual vote rates in presidential contests than touch-screen DREs or precinct-count optical scan systems.

Given that more widespread changes in voting equipment were made after 2004, we conducted a similar analysis of residual votes in the 2000 and 2008 elections. We estimate the same fixed effects regression model, this time with data from the 2000 and 2008 elections. This will help determine whether the improvement in residual votes in 2004 due to voting equipment was fleeting or durable. As Table 3.3 indicates, we observe a fair amount of continuity but also a few changes from the 2004 analysis. The results for the first model in Table 3.3 indicate that any county that changed its voting equipment between 2000 and 2008 produced an average reduction in the residual vote rate of almost 0.7 percentage points, a significant reduction that is a bit smaller than the 0.8 percentage point reduction observed in the 2004 election. We also find that the effect of increasing turnout in 2008 did not affect residual vote rates, even though the number of voters increased substantially between 2000 and 2008. Finally, after controlling for changes in voting equipment and turnout and other unique county-level effects, we observe no across-the-board drop in residual votes for president in 2008. If there was a universal increase in vigilance about residual votes in the 2004 election, that effect seems to have diminished by 2008.

The second model estimates in Table 3.3 distinguish between different voting systems and indicate that the different voting systems indeed have different impacts on residual votes. Changing from punch cards or paper ballots to DREs produced an average reduction in the residual vote rate of roughly 0.9 percentage points in 2008, while changing from paper ballots or punch cards to precinct-count optical scan produced an average reduction in the residual vote rate of approximately 1.7 percentage points. In contrast, changing from punch cards or paper ballots to central-count optical scan only produced a statistically insignificant reduction in the residual vote rate of 0.2 percentage points. Nevertheless, more than 28 percent of ballots cast in 2008 were in counties that had replaced punch cards or paper ballots with optical scan systems or DREs, so those changes were responsible for a significant portion of the decline in residual votes after 2000.

In addition, we find evidence that upgrading from central-count optical scan systems made a difference in 2008, but only when the change is to precinct-count

TABLE 3.3 The Impact of Voting Equipment Changes on Residual Vote Rate, 2000 and 2008 Presidential Elections (Fixed Effects Regression)

Explanatory Variable	Model 1 Coefficient (std. error)	Model 2 Coefficient (std. error)
2008 Election	−.19 (.18)	−.11 (.15)
Ballots cast (natural log)	−.55 (.83)	−.99 (.68)
Any change in voting equipment	−.66★★★ (.17)	
Change from paper ballots or punch cards to DRE		−.87★★ (.25)
Change from paper ballots or punch cards to precinct-count optical scan		−1.67★★★ (.36)
Change from paper ballots or punch cards to central-count optical scan		−.23 (.16)
Change from central-count optical scan to DRE		−.14 (.26)
Change from central-count optical scan to precinct-count optical scan		−.77★★★ (.20)
All other changes in voting equipment		.01 (.17)
Number of Cases	5891	5891
Root MSE	1.22	1.16
R^2	.58	.63

Notes:
The dependent variable is the residual vote rate (percent) in each county. Coefficients for county dummy variables are not shown. Each county is weighted by the number of ballots cast in the election. Robust standard errors are shown in parentheses.
★★★$p < .01$, two-tailed test
★★$p < .05$, two-tailed test

optical scan systems. Changing from a central count system in 2000 to a DRE in 2008 did not significantly reduce the rate of residual votes for president. Changing from a central-count optical scan system to a precinct-count optical scan system reduced residual votes in 2008, with an average reduction of 0.8 percentage points. Since roughly 12 percent of counties upgraded from central-count to precinct-count systems between 2000 and 2008, that change in technology also helps explain the decline in residual votes in 2008. Overall, the results indicate that voting technology with an error prevention mechanism (precinct-count optical scan systems or DREs) are most responsible for the contribution of voting equipment to the lower rate of residual votes in recent presidential elections. Slightly more than half of the counties in the United States had switched to voting equipment with an error correction feature by 2008. Thus, the United States is in a good position to minimize the number of residual votes in contests at the top of the ballot in elections going forward.

Voting Equipment and Reduced Variation within States in Residual Votes

Pragmatically speaking, these nationwide comparisons in the accuracy of voting equipment are important, but do not necessarily demonstrate the true nature of the problem of equal protection of voters. Consider this: if a voter in Missouri and a voter in Kansas use different technology from each other, the potential error difference between the two does not affect the outcome of the election, since our country uses an Electoral College system to elect the president. Each state's election is a separate one. As long as the Missouri voter is not disadvantaged compared to another Missouri voter, equal protection is not at stake. The Electoral College gives each state a fixed number of votes. The Missouri voter has no say in the Kansas election, or vice versa.

What would happen, however, if Florida voter John Q. Public voted in one county that used punch card vote tabulation, and in another county Joanna Q. Public used a precinct-count optical scan system? The chances of John's vote not being counted accurately are much higher than Joanna's, so Joanna has an advantage on John. The two voters are not provided "equal protection." Another way to evaluate voting equipment then, is to consider variation within states, across counties.

This is not just some made-up example for literary purposes. When residual votes are produced by some types of voting equipment, then variety in voting technology can produce significant variation in residual vote rates across counties. For example, in the 2000 election the six different voting systems listed in Table 3.1 were used in Florida's 67 counties. Counties using systems without an error prevention feature had significantly higher residual vote rates in the presidential election. Among counties using punch cards, the residual vote rate was as high as 9.6 percent. In Florida counties using central-count optical scan systems, the residual vote rate was as high as 12.4 percent. By comparison, in the one Florida county using lever machines, the residual vote rate was 0.9 percent in 2000. In the 24 counties using precinct-count optical scan systems, the residual vote rate was never higher than 3.9 percent. This high degree of variation suggests that voters in some counties are more likely to have their votes counted than voters in other counties.

The equal protection concern cited in the *Bush v. Gore* Supreme Court decision was similar in that it cited differing counting techniques for votes (e.g., counting hanging chads in punch card ballots or for optical scan ballots, counting ovals with X's in them, instead of those completely darkened). How should ballots with overvotes or undervotes be handled in a recount? What standard should be used to determine whether these ballots contain evidence of a valid vote for a particular candidate? Many states, including Florida, did not have clear answers to these questions in the 2000 election. For election officials, large variations in residual vote rates can create headaches in the event of a recount. The disparity in residual vote rates across counties is one key reason that prompted the infamous hand recount of ballots in some Florida counties in the 2000 election. The U.S. Supreme Court relied on an equal protection argument to halt the recount in the *Bush v. Gore* decision, noting inequities involved when different counties use different procedures and standards for recounting votes.

Regardless of one's position on the Florida recount debate, these controversies will be lessened if there is less variation in residual vote rates across local jurisdictions. Reducing the diversity of voting technology in the United States has moved us in that direction. One such measure is the standard deviation, which indicates the amount of variation around the mean, or average, of a set of numbers—here the "set" of numbers is the residual vote rate produced by each county. When we calculate the standard deviation of the residual vote rate in each presidential election for all counties in our data, we find that it declines from 1.6 percent in 2000 to 0.9 percent in 2004 and 0.8 percent in 2008. We also find that the standard deviation in residual vote rates has declined more in counties that switched to new voting equipment than in counties that did not make a change. Thus, the standard deviation in residual vote rates has been cut in half in eight years after 75 percent of American counties switched to new voting equipment.

Two states, which were quick to modernize their equipment, saw a lower amount of variation among counties. Georgia (which actually had a higher residual vote rate than Florida) saw its standard deviation fall from 2.0 in 2000 to 0.4 in 2008. Florida saw its standard deviation drop from 2.3 in 2000 to 0.3 in 2008.

Implications of New Voting Equipment for Equal Protection

Given the history of voting discrimination in our country, our concerns about equal protection are even more concerning when voting equipment performance is linked to race or class differences. Indeed, several studies have found that confusing or poorly designed voting systems produce larger residual vote rates that fall disproportionately on low-income and minority communities.[13] We provide some evidence of this from the 2000 election by examining the impact of voting technology across demographic groups. Table 3.4 shows residual vote rates in the 2000 presidential election in counties grouped by their racial or economic composition. The evidence indicates that voting systems without an error-prevention feature (punch card ballots and central-count optical scan ballots) produce a more dramatic increase in residual votes in counties with low median incomes and large percentages of African American residents. By comparison, systems with an error-prevention feature (DRE voting machines and precinct-count optical scan ballots) do not yield such a dramatic increase in residual votes in counties with large concentrations of low-income or African American citizens.

Fortunately, in this area, new voting equipment has made a difference: we find evidence that disparities in residual votes linked to race and income have diminished since the move to new voting equipment across the country.

TABLE 3.4 Racial and Economic Disparity in Residual Votes by Voting Technology 2000 Presidential Election

| Racial composition of county | *Percent of Residual votes in counties using:* | | | | |
	Votomatic punch cards	Optical scan–central	Optical scan–precinct	Lever machines	DREs
Less than 10% black	2.2	1.3	0.9	1.1	1.7
Between 10% and 30% black	3.1	2.3	0.7	1.7	1.7
Over 30% black	5.6	5.2	1.9	2.3	1.7
Median Income					
Less than $25,000	4.5	4.4	1.1	3.4	2.7
Between $25,000 and $32,499	3.2	2.1	1.3	2.0	2.2
Between $32,500 and $40,000	3.0	1.7	1.0	1.7	1.7
Over $40,000	2.2	1.0	0.8	1.1	1.3

Roughly 70 percent of the counties that adopted new voting equipment replaced systems without an error prevention feature (punch cards, paper ballots, and central-count optical scan systems). More than 80 percent of the counties that made a change after 2000 adopted new equipment that did have an error prevention mechanism. By sharply reducing the number of ballots cast on systems without an error prevention mechanism, the changes in voting equipment made after 2000 should reduce the racial and economic disparities indicated in Table 3.4.

On analyzing the evidence, that is indeed what we find. Figure 3.3 compares the residual vote rate in the last three presidential elections for counties with the largest and smallest concentrations of African American voters.[14] In the 2000 election, the residual vote rate in counties with a substantial African American population was double the residual vote rate in heavily white counties. By 2008, the racial disparity in residual votes had been eliminated. Some studies note that residual votes in African American communities tend to decline in elections when there is a viable African American candidate on the ballot.[15] Thus, the presidential candidacy of Barack Obama, and not just the change in voting equipment, may account for the lower residual vote rate in 2008 in counties with large African American populations. However, the racial disparity in residual votes was also reduced in the 2004 election, when there was no major-party African American candidate running for president. In addition, the racial gap in residual votes continued to narrow as more counties switched to new voting equipment between 2004 and 2008.

The pattern is similar with respect to income. In Figure 3.4 we compare the residual vote rate in the last three presidential elections for counties with

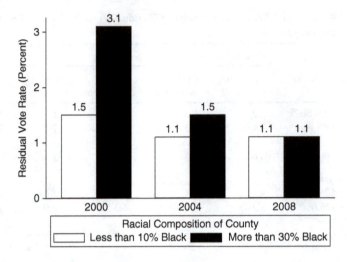

FIGURE 3.3 Residual Votes by Racial Composition of Counties, 2000–2008

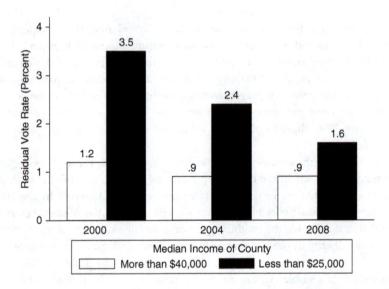

FIGURE 3.4 Residual Votes by Median Household Income of Counties, 2000–2008

the wealthiest and poorest families, as measured by median household income. In the 2000 election, the residual vote rate in the poorest counties was almost three times as high as the residual vote rate in the wealthiest counties. By 2008, the income disparity in residual votes had been reduced, although not completely eliminated. The income gap in residual votes has been narrowed by reducing the residual vote rate in the poorest counties. The residual vote rate has not changed much since 2000 in the wealthiest counties. We find a similar trend with the racial disparity in Figure 3.3. In any case, the widespread adoption of voting technology with error prevention mechanisms has reduced the racial and economic disparity in residual votes for presidential elections.

Limits of Modernizing Equipment: Two State Case Studies of Full-Face DREs

It is also important to consider the impact of voting technology on other contests on the ballot, not just the presidential race. Data from New Jersey and Louisiana indicate that is most definitely the case. However, some context will make this more clear and will help make the case that indeed, not all "modern technology" is created equal. Almost all studies of voting equipment and residual votes in the last ten years have focused on contests at the top of the ballot.[16] Indeed, examining the presidential contests over three elections, our evidence shows clearly that modern technology, particularly that which notifies the voter of an error, has reduced residual votes.

But, consider what happens when our investigation of voting equipment turns to analyzing down- ballot contests, such as initiatives and referendums, which are arguably two of the most important tools of democracy in our toolkit. In many states, almost all aspects of state government and public policy can be altered by such ballot measures. Certainly, there has been a significant proliferation of ballot measures in recent decades: the number of initiatives placed on state ballots by petition increased from 181 in the 1970s to 374 in the decade that just ended.[17] As a result, ballot issues have been used recently to shape state policies on many high-profile issues including taxes, abortion, minimum wage levels, and gay rights.

However, we present evidence that voting technology greatly influences the degree to which voters reveal their preferences on ballot measures. Sponsors of HAVA did not anticipate that some new voting equipment had fundamental usability problems for down-ballot contests. This involves an important distinction among electronic voting machines. Some DREs use a full-face layout in which all contests are visible on the computer screen at once. Other DREs use a scrolling layout with just one or two contests displayed on the computer screen at one time.

The problem is that voters are more likely to complete their voting session without recording any choices on ballot initiatives on full-face DREs. There was some reason to foresee this problem because full-face DREs were designed to mimic lever voting machines, and several studies show that lever machines produce higher rates of residual votes on ballot measures than other voting systems.[18]

There are two possible explanations for this phenomenon of high rates of residual votes on ballot measures when voting systems with full-face ballot layouts are used. One explanation is that placing all the contests before the voters at once may be overwhelming and cause them to stop voting before they have completed the ballot. In addition, it is easy to end the voting session before completing the ballot on full-face DREs because the button to end the session is prominently featured on the ballot.[19] In contrast, some models of scrolling DREs require the voter to scroll to the end of the ballot before one can end the voting session. However, optical scan systems list all contests on the printed ballots and these systems tend not to have the same problem with residual votes on ballot measures.

The second, and more likely, explanation is that voters are less likely to find the ballot measures on full-face DREs. As with many lever machines, many full-face DREs use a party bloc layout, a grid in which offices are listed in rows and candidates are listed in columns according to party affiliation. In theory, this should make it easier for voters to find all of the candidates from the same party since they will be located in the same column. However, in studying machine usability, a group of scholars led by Paul Herrnson at the University of Maryland found that voters are less satisfied with the party bloc layout and are more likely to require assistance when using full-face DREs.[20] Furthermore, ballot measures are not partisan contests that can be placed on an intuitive spot on the party grid. As a result, ballot measures are usually positioned below or next to the party bloc on full-face ballots, often in locations where voters are less likely to notice them.[21]

In a previous study, we examined the impact of voting equipment on residual votes for ballot measures across the country in the 2004 general election.[22] The impact of voting technology on voting for ballot measures is substantially larger than on voting in presidential elections. We found that the frequency of residual votes on ballot measures was 4 percentage points higher in counties using full-face DREs than in counties using other new voting systems. We can illustrate the impact of full-face DREs by more closely examining election returns in two states, since the same pattern exists within many states.

In states where some counties or voters use full-face DREs while the rest use other voting technology, a natural experiment is underway to gauge the impact on voting for ballot measures. One such state is New Jersey, where two counties, Salem and Sussex, use scrolling DREs. Since 2006, the remaining counties in New Jersey have used full-face DREs. For each of the last three general elections, we compare the residual vote rate on ballot measures in counties using full-face DREs to the rest of the state.[23] As Figure 3.5 shows, the comparisons are startling. In the two counties using scrolling DREs, the residual vote rate on ballot measures never exceeds 7 percent. In the counties using full-face DREs, the residual vote rate is never below 29 percent. The stark differences in voting on ballot measures are not present for other contests on the ballot in the same elections. For example, in the 2008 presidential election the residual vote rate was 1.0 percent on scrolling DREs and 1.1 percent on full-face DREs in New Jersey. It is only on ballot measures in New Jersey where the rate of residual voting on full-face DREs is six to ten times higher than on scrolling DREs. Thus, the voters

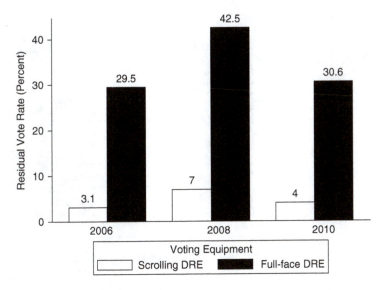

FIGURE 3.5 Residual Votes on New Jersey Ballot Measures by Voting Equipment, 2006–2010

of Salem and Sussex counties (where scrolling DREs are used) seem to have a disproportionate impact on the outcome of ballot questions in New Jersey.

Furthermore, voting equipment greatly exacerbates economic disparities in residual votes on ballot measures in New Jersey.[24] In municipalities using scrolling DREs in New Jersey, residual votes are no more common in high-poverty communities than in low-poverty communities. In contrast, in municipalities using full-face DREs the residual vote rate in communities with high levels of poverty is at least double the rate in communities with low rates of poverty. As a result, in much of the state using full-face DREs low-income communities have less impact on the results of ballot questions than their overall voting turnout would suggest.

Another natural experiment on the impact of voting technology is taking place in Louisiana. Since 2006, all counties in Louisiana have used full-face DREs for Election Day voting. However, scrolling DREs are used for the growing number of citizens who participate in early voting. For each of the last two general elections, we compare the residual vote rate among early voters and Election Day voters on the ballot measure with the closest outcome in the state (see Figure 3.6).[25] In both elections, the residual vote rate is 7 or 8 percentage points higher for voters using full-face DREs. It is possible that early voters in Louisiana are more interested in politics and more motivated to complete their ballot than Election Day voters. However, once again we do not observe such large differences in residual votes across voting equipment for other contests on the ballot in these

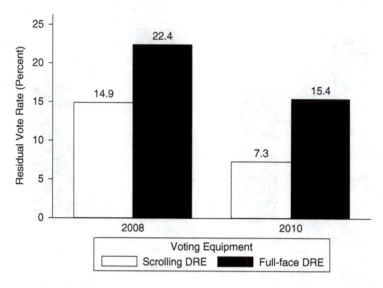

FIGURE 3.6 Residual Votes on Louisiana Ballot Measures by Voting Equipment, 2008–2010

two elections. If anything, residual votes in other contests tend to be less frequent among Election Day voters using the full-face DREs. For example, in the 2008 presidential election the residual vote rate was 1.9 percent on scrolling DREs and 0.9 percent on full-face DREs in Louisiana. As a result, early voters exert a disproportionate impact on constitutional amendments in Louisiana.

All of these findings indicate that voting equipment with a full-face ballot dramatically increases the number of voters who fail to record a vote on ballot measures. This is a challenge for direct democracy, but it is a manageable problem. As we show in Chapter 2, less than 10 percent of the nation's voters (from eight different states) live in jurisdictions where full-face DREs are used.

Limits of Modernizing Equipment: The Case of New York

New York did a good thing by replacing lever machines in 2010, but they designed the optical scan ballots to imitate the party grid layout on lever machines. Thus, public questions must be placed below the grid or on the back of the ballot, where voters are more likely to miss them. In the 2010 general election, New York City voters faced a ballot proposal to change the term limits for city officials. However, since the proposal was on the back of the optical scan ballot almost 30 percent of voters did not record a vote on the measure.

Some may argue that it is still the voter's responsibility to find all the contests on the ballot, and voters can choose to ignore some contests. However, voting is not supposed to be a game of hide-and-seek. In some cases, it would help if election officials and voting technology vendors took a customer-service approach to election administration. For example, if a bank discovers that some of its customers are having difficulty using an ATM, the bank is not likely to respond that it's the customer's responsibility to figure out how to use the ATM properly.

Conclusion

As some pointed out in the popular press, Floridians were definitely creative in spoiling their ballots in the 2000 election. It is also likely that some Floridians failed to cast a vote in the 2000 election and did so intentionally. However, news media reports made it clear that it was not just "creative" citizens or citizens failing to vote for president that were causing the crisis of the 2000 election. Indeed, we were voting on equipment that was not keeping pace with more current technology and modern technology gives us the means to warn someone if they do something they may not intend (much as a new mini-van will alert you if you are not turning the wheel correctly when sliding on the ice). Fortunately, policymakers defined the problem as voting equipment and some quickly began to address that problem. As this chapter indicates, changing to new voting equipment has helped reduce the frequency of residual votes in presidential elections. Overall, the results indicate that voting technology with an error prevention mechanism (precinct-count optical scan systems or DREs) is most responsible for the contribution of voting equipment to the lower rate of residual votes in recent presidential elections.

Yet unfortunately, when defining the problem largely as one of voting equipment, there are some unintended consequences amidst the good news. One limit of our election reform is noted by the team studying usability led by Maryland's Dr. Paul Herrnson. Their work, *Voting Technology: The Not-So-Simple Act of Casting a Ballot* shows that there are still some racial and socioeconomic disparities that remain with voting errors on newer types of voting equipment.

And, another limit is that some modern technology used today is made to be very similar to older technology. Only a few small municipalities in New York continue to use the lever machines to vote (until 2012). These machines were actually accurate by our accounting in contests at the top of the ballot. But the full-face feature offered by lever machines meant that ballot measures—which were often at the bottom of the ballot—were much harder to locate. Therefore, these machines produced much higher residual vote rates on ballot measures than other contests. And, certain DREs—in use in today's elections—share the full-face feature. Our evidence indicates that there are much higher levels of residual votes in the counties using these machines. Addressing the problem of elections by modernizing equipment has advantages in terms of accuracy, but jurisdictions should have been more careful about using old-style features on modern equipment.

Finally, our research indicates that slightly more than half of the counties in the United States switched to voting equipment with an error correction feature by 2008. These changes are very positive for accuracy (as we have defined it). However, these positive changes may be threatened by some new suggestions by those worried about ballot security. In the interest of greater ballot security, some suggest dropping DRE and precinct-count optical scan systems and returning to systems with central or hand-counted ballots. We think the evidence is clear that doing so will come with a cost of higher rates of residual votes on contests at the top of the ballot. Fortunately, such moves do not have to threaten equal protection, if the counties within any particular state are able to change their equipment yet again. We show in the next chapter that changing equipment—perhaps twice within a decade—begins to add up budget-wise and certainly will have financial implications. In the next chapter, we examine the cost implications of modernizing—and modernizing again to address security—as many jurisdictions did through defining the main problem of elections as voting equipment.

4

AT WHAT COST?

The Unintended Consequences of Reform

"Americans were hellbent, I would say insistent, that voting systems change and change immediately," says Rosemary Rodriguez, chairwoman of the U.S. Election Assistance Commission, created under federal law to guide state officials. "I think Congress responded to that."

(*USA Today*, October 29, 2008)

Following the 2000 election, several states moved quickly to adopt modern voting technology. Georgia became the first state to shift completely to direct recording electronic (DRE) voting machines. Florida moved to a mix of optical scan balloting and electronic machines to avoid "another Florida." By the time President Bush signed HAVA into law in 2002, still other states purchased new voting equipment. While other states such as New York, Idaho and Connecticut dragged their feet, as we showed in Chapter 2 most of the rest of the nation moved to modernize shortly after 2002, especially since HAVA imposed a 2006 deadline for states to replace old voting equipment. The data indicate a rapid policy response to the problem of inaccurate and old voting equipment.

The rapid move to new voting equipment became a source of controversy, particularly DRE voting machines. One by-product of HAVA and the move toward new voting equipment was a backlash against electronic voting machines. After 2002 some observers and journalists raised concerns about the durability and security of DRE voting machines. What happens if the computer equipment breaks down? Can voters be confident that their votes will be counted accurately? Are the computerized voting machines susceptible to hacking or voter fraud? In some cases, election officials bought new voting equipment without evaluating all of the features of the new voting systems or adopting adequate training and auditing systems for the new machines.[1] In response to many of these concerns, some states have scrapped the new DRE voting machines in favor of optical scan voting systems. Just five years after the passage of HAVA, Electionline. org characterized the backtracking as a "second overhaul."[2]

In addition, voting equipment purchases following the 2000 election were expensive. While HAVA was the largest investment in elections in the nation's history, in many cases the funds provided to the states were insufficient to cover the long-term costs of maintaining and upgrading the new voting equipment. In addition, states that backtracked on their initial voting equipment decisions incurred additional costs to switch voting equipment a second time. *USA Today* reported that, "[t]he U.S. government coughed up $3 billion, and states added some of their own money. More than $1 billion remains to be spent. Even so, states such as New Mexico and Ohio, where multiple systems were bought and discarded, soon ran out of federal money."[3]

One unintended consequence of HAVA is that it provides finite resources to implement mandates for new voting equipment and other new election procedures. Now, states and localities are paying the bill. Since the mandates are outliving the federal resources to implement them, this creates cost pressures as state and local governments struggle to pay for election administration. The recent economic recession has exacerbated this problem, since election administration tends to be a low priority for state and local government budgets. In this chapter, we examine these cost pressures in more detail. We first use a case study to show what the costs are. We also report the results of a national survey of local election officials, including their concerns about the costs imposed by HAVA. Election officials have sought ways to buy as few voting machines as possible. We consider one common local response to limit the cost of elections: reducing the number of precincts and polling places. This development coincides with a dramatic increase in early voting, absentee voting, and voting-by-mail in the United States. Some of these alternatives to traditional polling place voting on Election Day tend to reduce the cost of elections. However, as we discuss below, cutting the number of traditional polling places increases the distance to the voting booth for some voters and may reduce voter turnout.

The Security of Electronic Voting Machines

In the wake of HAVA, concerns about the security of DRE voting machines buffeted election officials as they were choosing new voting equipment for their state or local jurisdictions. While we do not assess the various concerns about the security of DRE machines, we briefly review some of the main security issues in these debates. This will provide an indication of the pressures facing election officials.

For some computer security experts, the major issue with electronic voting machines is the absence of a paper ballot. Other types of voting equipment, such as optical scan systems, leave behind paper ballots that can be recounted if necessary. Without tangible evidence of how a voter cast her ballot, there is a concern that electronic voting machines are more vulnerable to manipulation or a breakdown in the equipment.[4] If the DRE is outfitted with a paper trail, the voter may verify that his vote was cast as he intended; the paper prints and spools so the voter can see but not take the paper with him. Such a paper record may allow an audit after the election—an audit based on something the voter actually could verify. Not all DREs are so outfitted, but many could be retrofitted.

As Roy Saltman notes in his book, *The History and Politics of Voting Technology*, among computer scientists and election experts concerns about the security of computerized voting machines are not new.[5] Earlier concerns led to state laws requiring auditing procedures for computerized voting machines. In addition, the federal government adopted voluntary standards for the performance of the machines, including a recommendation that voting machines retain the electronic ballot image from each voter, a computer analog to the leftover paper ballot. Several states included the standards in state laws or election regulations. However, there was limited capacity to enforce these standards.

There is some evidence that voters using DRE machines are less confident that their votes will be counted as they intended than voters casting their ballots on other systems.[6] In addition, there have been incidents where electronic voting machines did not perform well. On the other hand, other voting systems have also performed poorly on occasion, and one field study of several different types of voting equipment found that voters were more confident in the ability of DRE machines to record their votes accurately than other voting systems.[7] In addition, it appears that public confidence in voting systems is based more on perceptions than objective measures of the performance of those systems.[8]

Nevertheless, concerns about DRE voting machines did not receive much attention shortly after the 2000 election when states began rapidly switching to new voting technology. It was not until after the passage of HAVA that a movement opposing computerized voting machines gained steam. Thus, from 2000 to 2004, much of the media coverage of electronic voting machines was positive, focusing, for example, on their ease of use for voters. Beginning in 2004, however, media coverage of electronic voting machines turned decidedly negative.[9] The changed perspective was fueled by organized opposition to DRE machines and reports by computer scientists noting how easy it was to tamper with the machines.[10] Some critics advocated that all electronic voting machines be fitted with a voter-verified paper trail, a paper receipt that could be checked by voters and by officials in a post-election audit.

Thus, for election officials there was an early period when the political environment was characterized by widespread acceptance of electronic voting machines, followed by a period of growing opposition. Election officials who initially purchased electronic voting equipment found themselves in a difficult position after 2004. In the wake of the 2000 election and HAVA, a few election officials had the foresight to temporarily lease new voting equipment while taking more time to evaluate a new system for purchase. Other states, such as Ohio, did not face such a smooth transition in voting equipment.

The case of Ohio is instructive because it illustrates that decisions about voting equipment took place in a changing political context. The policy choices concerning voting equipment cost Ohio and its various counties a significant amount of money. Not all states have followed the same twisting path as Ohio did where voting machines were concerned, but many have incurred significant costs.

Ohio

There's a delirium created by the Mad Chad Disease that the media has helped spread, and the resulting delusion is that the mechanism of our election system is tremendously flawed. It is not.[11]

By far, one of the most complicated and interesting cases of equipment changes comes from Ohio, and we believe it is important to trace this case in a certain amount of detail from the beginning of the decade. Ohio policy on voting equipment changed so many times over the past ten years that one Ohio newspaper characterized the changes as "whiplash."[12] Interestingly, after that comment was made in January of 2005, the whiplash continued and included several lawsuits.[13] The various pieces of the voting machine soap opera in Ohio demonstrate the peculiarities of the voting equipment solution. Largely defining the problem of elections in terms of voting equipment consumed a lot of time, effort, and resources for the state and county governments.

In the aftermath of the 2000 election Ohio reacted like many other states, with an election summit to analyze election procedures in the state. Ohio officials moved quickly to analyze the election situation following the 2000 election because 70 of the state's 88 counties used punch card voting. Yet, various political entanglements became evident at this early stage. During a February 2001 summit, county officials stated that they did not want a uniform voting system throughout the state. Ultimately, the state's chief election officers have moved toward a uniform system, even though it has not come to fruition.[14] After the February 2001 summit, Republican Secretary of State Kenneth Blackwell chaired a legislative study panel which was charged with making legislative recommendations. However, the panel was late with conclusions largely because it could not agree on voting technology issues. Some members of the panel apparently felt that punch card ballots were not such a problem.[15] Not all county officials wanted to keep punch cards. For example, Cuyahoga County (Cleveland) officials began to investigate conversion to DRE voting.[16] For part of 2001 and all of 2002, many of Ohio's counties ran tests on DREs.

In the meantime, the American Civil Liberties Union (ACLU) filed a lawsuit against four Ohio counties asking the counties to eliminate punch cards and in one case a central count optical scan system. Arguing that such ballots could not be checked for errors, the lawsuit cited the Supreme Court's *Bush v. Gore* decision to argue for new voting equipment on equal protection grounds.[17]

In October 2002, Congress passed HAVA, providing federal dollars for new voting equipment. At the same time, Cuyahoga County began to demonstrate its own unique set of election issues, negotiating a $300,000 contract to have someone help them *select* machines. Blackwell noted Cuyahoga County's difficulties in choosing voting equipment when he declared in February 2003 that his office would "negotiate and award contracts for new voting equipment in the state's 88 counties."[18] Blackwell said that counties might be able to select from a list of certified machines, but did not rule out the same manufacturer for all voting machines. Lucas County, which had just issued an RFP for new voting equipment, cried foul, but the plan to buy new equipment was stopped dead in its tracks.[19] However, Blackwell did note that the federal dollars were limited. Spokesperson for the Secretary, Carlo LoParo said the state would have to set priorities, because the federal dollars were not coming as quickly as expected. According to local papers, by April 2003, the state was only getting about half the $150 million expected federal dollars, so policymakers had to make choices. The secretary of state's office announced that counties which had not yet replaced punch cards and lever machines would get first priority for federal funds. Counties that had already bought electronic voting machines would be reimbursed later.[20]

Shortly after Blackwell's announcement, computer experts questioning DREs received more attention. A Johns Hopkins study noting security flaws in electronic voting machines made by Diebold was released just as Lucas County began to receive Diebold voting equipment it was leasing in preparation for a purchase. The reaction, as related in the local paper was instructive.

> The first of hundreds of the voting machines—which let voters use a touch screen or a[n] optical scan tabulating machine—arrived last week at the Lucas County Board of Elections. An additional 445 are expected by the end of the month... [Election Board Executive Director Joe] Kidd was shocked when told by *The Blade* last night about the study but expressed confidence in Diebold.[21]

As a result of the study, Blackwell delayed an announcement about venders from which counties could select new voting equipment.[22] However, by September 2003, firms who could sell in Ohio were announced and Diebold was on the list (it was an Ohio company after all).[23] At the same time, Blackwell had ordered a security review, which revealed flaws in the equipment that had been listed.[24] Blackwell expressed confidence that the firms could fix the problems. As a result, throughout the first quarter of 2004 counties began selecting voting machine venders.

Because of DRE security concerns, political support for an auditable paper trail on electronic voting machines began to grow. The state legislature created a Joint Committee on Ballot Security, which ultimately recommended that DREs include a paper trail. Soon, the state legislature mandated a paper trail for DREs used in Ohio, and also allowed 31 specified counties to select new voting equipment. However, none of the electronic voting machines on the state's list of acceptable vendors included a paper trail. As a result, if counties had purchased new voting equipment for the November 2004 election, they would have to retrofit their equipment after the election. Some counties opted to scrap relatively new DRE equipment. For example, Lake County bought DRE voting equipment in 1999 and then replaced it in 2006. Their story was related in the *Cleveland Plain Dealer*: "On Thursday, the commissioners sold them back to the manufacturer for $27,500. Even worse, commissioners still owe $800,000 to California-based Sequoia Voting Systems for the 549 machines."[25]

Meanwhile, most Ohio counties chose *not* to upgrade their equipment until the uncertainty about new machines was resolved. Thus, most counties continued using punch card ballots for the November 2004 general election. The presidential vote was close in Ohio, and the state proved decisive in the reelection of President Bush. The election results in Ohio were examined by many and challenged by some Democrats.[26] One problem involved long lines in some Ohio counties using electronic voting machines because election officials did not buy enough machines for some precincts.[27] Election officials reported they were barely equipped to handle increased voter registration, according to a report in the *Washington Post* shortly after the election:

> Earlier this year, state officials also decided to delay the purchase of touch-screen machines, citing worries about the security of the vote. That left many Ohio counties with too few machines. County boards are split evenly between Republicans and Democrats, and control the type of machines and their distribution. In Cuyahoga County, officials decided to quickly rent hundreds of additional voting machines.
>
> Other counties decided to muddle through. At Kenyon College, a surge of late registrations promised a record vote—but Knox County officials allocated two machines, just as in past elections. In voter-rich Franklin County, which encompasses the state capital of Columbus, election officials decided to make do with 2,866 machines, even though their analysis showed that the county needed 5,000 machines.[28]

While at least one study indicated that the misallocation of electronic voting machines in Franklin County cost John Kerry votes, the study noted it did not cost him the election.[29]

Shortly after Congress certified the reelection of President Bush and the Ohio Supreme Court dismissed a lawsuit challenging the results, Secretary of State

Blackwell changed course and announced that Ohio counties could no longer use DRE voting machines. He left in place the ability of counties to purchase them for use by disabled voters. The *Cleveland Plain Dealer* noted that reasons for the decision included public perception that the machines were "razor-toothed, vote-eating monsters prone to hacking," that security risks uncovered in 2003 had not been addressed, and that the state legislature had required an expensive paper-trail.[30] Furthermore, Blackwell expected optical scan machines to cost less, such that the cost of the machines would be covered by federal money. Blackwell imposed a tight deadline, asking counties to make a choice by February, 2005. State newspapers pointed out an interesting irony. In the year prior to the announcement, Blackwell had helped at least two county election boards break tie votes on voting equipment selection, and had done so by voting for DRE equipment. Quipped the *Toledo Blade* in an editorial:

> a number of counties that have recently invested millions of taxpayer dollars in touch-screen electronic voting machines will be faced with tossing them out and starting over with optical scan—all by Feb. 9. In fact, if the Lucas County Board of Elections had promptly complied with an order from Mr. Blackwell nine months ago to adopt touch-screen voting, it would now be reversing that process at great cost. Sometimes it pays to be dysfunctional.[31]

Franklin County Election Board Director Matt Damschroder warned his county commission they would have to come up with about $2.6 million for the upcoming election as a result of the change, and possibly $1 million a year after that.[32] Thus, the Election Board voted specifically to ignore Blackwell's directive and deadline.[33]

In other fall-out, Hart InterCivic sued Blackwell because they could no longer sell DREs in Ohio. Then the Ohio Attorney General issued a non-binding opinion that Blackwell could not prohibit counties from buying DREs.[34] In any case, more than 30 counties decided to purchase optical scan voting systems, and most of them did so before the deadline imposed by Blackwell. Then, on April 15, Blackwell announced that he was certifying one DRE system, negotiated with Diebold to be a little cheaper than first anticipated.[35] This prompted another lawsuit from rival manufacturers and counties that wanted more time to certify other voting machine options. A judge ruled against Blackwell in that case. Through all of this, most Ohio counties purchased new voting equipment. By January of 2006, 56 Ohio counties had selected touch screen voting machines and 32 selected optical scan systems. And, the "last remaining [voting machine] lawsuit challenging the process has been dismissed."[36] In the meantime, Diebold began having programming training classes for local officials: if the local officials could not figure out the programming, they would have to pay someone else, but of course, that is the issue for all computerized voting equipment.[37]

Then, in the May 2006 primary, Cuyahoga County was the only county to have problems with its new touch-screen voting machines. A report came out just two months before the 2006 general election, giving ammunition to the Democratic candidate for Secretary of State, Jennifer Brunner. The Election Science Institute (ESI) prepared the report paid for by Cuyahoga County. It included some damning findings involving the Diebold voting machines, according to the ESI Project Manager.

> Diebold machines are easier to use than the punch-ballot systems they replaced. However, use of the TSx equipment should currently be viewed as a calculated risk for the county, he warned. For example, the report said that 72 percent of the polling places demonstrated a discrepancy between the electronic record on memory cards and the paper ballots; 42 percent of the discrepancies involved problems with 25 votes or more.[38]

Newly elected Secretary of State Brunner called for an investigation of the election. In addition, Brunner placed the Cuyahoga County Election Board on administrative oversight until 2008 and asked each of the board members to resign.

Even though the November 2006 general election went much more smoothly than the primary, some Cuyahoga County Commissioners advocated getting rid of the DREs just a couple of weeks after the election, citing the great expense of training poll workers to use the DREs. The commissioners also worried that the machines could not handle the expected turnout for the 2008 election.[39]

Brunner called for a study of DRE equipment throughout the state. County election officials began to speak up about financial burdens of another potential change in voting equipment.[40] Brunner's report was a bombshell. It proposed that the State Legislature vote to return to optical scan voting machines with all optical scan ballots to be counted at a central location.[41] If her proposed legislation had passed, an error prevention mechanism would no longer be available to Ohio voters. As we note in Chapter 3, residual votes are more common on voting systems lacking an error prevention mechanism. The proposal met with opposition from county election officials and activists concerned about increased voting errors with the optical scan system.

Meanwhile, Brunner pressed the Cuyahoga County election board to replace its DRE voting equipment with a central count optical scan system. The board, however, deadlocked on the vote to replace the DRE equipment, leading Brunner to cast the tie-breaking vote in favor of the change in voting equipment. The ACLU filed yet another suit to stop the implementation of the central count scanners, which was later settled in favor of a precinct-count optical scan system.[42]

The critical election year 2008 witnessed more disagreements over voting equipment between Brunner, the Republican-controlled state legislature and county election officials. In January, Brunner announced that every precinct with DREs had to have some paper ballots on hand for voters who did not trust DRE machines. This plan, as well as the proposal for central count optical scan systems throughout the state, drew objections from county election officials largely because of the cost of another change in voting equipment.[43] In late January, county election officials voted at their annual meeting to oppose Brunner's plan.[44] The state legislature was not overly interested in spending more money on new voting equipment especially in March, when Brunner doubled her original cost estimate. The Speaker of the House, Jon Husted, called Brunner's bluff by asking her to decertify the DRE machines if she did not trust them. If she did decertify DRE machines, then she would leave more than half of Ohio's counties without voting equipment for the 2008 election. Ultimately, the legislature did not provide additional money for new voting equipment and Brunner did not decertify DREs in Ohio. Counties were able to keep the voting equipment they had. Only four counties in Ohio (including Cuyahoga) switched from electronic voting machines to optical scan systems before the 2008 election.

Brunner held several summits following the 2008 election to improve the administration of future Ohio elections. The follow-up report from one report noted concerns from county officials about the costs of implementing mandates from the secretary of state, particularly the requirement for paper ballots at every precinct with electronic voting machines.

> One county election official questioned how counties could afford to support two separate voting systems at every election. He reported that his county spent approximately $24,000 to provide and administer ballots. Under the required formula, they printed 14,700 ballots. Only 704 were used. While ballot printing would be reimbursed, other costs associated with paper ballot administration, e.g., poll worker time, would not.[45]

Indeed, following the 2008 election, several county election officials requested extra funds from their county commissions to cover the increasing cost of elections. In 2010, Jennifer Brunner ran unsuccessfully for Governor and Jon Husted, Brunner's nemesis in the legislature, was elected Secretary of State. Thus far, Husted is unwilling to push for new voting equipment in Ohio. As a result, no counties in Ohio have changed voting equipment since 2008. Nevertheless, the state and its counties spent a lot of time and money fighting over voting equipment for almost ten years. This was probably not the kind of election reform that most people had in mind after the 2000 election.

The twists and turns in Ohio were extreme, but several other states purchased DRE voting machines within the last ten years, only to abandon the technology a few years later. More generally, election officials in many states have struggled to cope with the rising costs of voting technology and election administration after the passage of HAVA. The cost issues extend beyond the technology issues we have covered so far. One concern involves the costs associated with maintenance and upgrades in voting technology. In particular, vendors may stop providing service for older equipment and software when upgrades are available.[46]

Furthermore, a number of mergers in the voting equipment industry have significantly reduced the number of competitors. This could prove costly to local election jurisdictions, as the lack of competition makes it possible for vendors to increase the price of their equipment. Eliza Newlin Carney reported on the 2009 sale of Premier Election Solutions to ES&S, two prominent voting equipment manufacturers.

> Still, state and local election officials are watching closely to see where legal challenges and a possible federal investigation may lead. Some have voiced concerns that consolidation in the industry could make it harder for election administrators to negotiate affordable contracts and will lessen both competition and innovation.[47]

The merger between Premier and ES&S was short-lived. In 2010 ES&S sold Premier to Dominion Voting Systems. However, in 2010 Dominion also acquired Sequoia Voting Systems, another voting equipment manufacturer. In any case, less competition among voting equipment vendors likely means fewer choices and higher costs for state and local governments.

Election Costs and Polling Place Consolidation

For election officials, a common response to these cost pressures is to consolidate the number of polling places. A report from Hawaii describes the issues in stark terms, noting that "voting equipment is the single greatest driver of costs" for the state's elections but that they can "reduce overall election costs by reducing the number of voting precincts and thereby the number of corresponding voting machines needed for the election."[48] Perhaps Hawaii seems like an isolated example and not indicative of a broader trend. However, we find evidence that many other states considered the same ideas as in Hawaii.

Following the 2004 election, we mailed surveys and requests for ballots to more than 1,800 jurisdictions which used optical scan or hand-counted paper ballots. We received a response from approximately 60 percent of the jurisdictions.[49] (Our examination of the ballots is in the next chapter.) In the survey, we asked election officials to comment on the impact of HAVA. The question was open-ended so officials could write down whatever was on their minds. We received more than 700 responses, and almost half of the comments about HAVA were negative. Of the comments mentioning budgets or costs, more than three-quarters were negative. This indicates that local election officials were concerned with the costs of administering elections after the passage of HAVA. In addition, 10 percent of the officials responding to the survey volunteered that they would need to consolidate the number of polling places in their jurisdiction in order to limit election costs.

Perhaps eliminating polling places was a way to cut costs in the face of all the expenses of election reform. While precinct voting on one day has been the law of the land since the mid to late 1800s,[50] over the last 15 years many states have moved toward alternatives to traditional polling place voting. Absentee voting, or voting by mail, has expanded in many states. According a survey of state and local election administrators conducted by the U.S. Election Assistance Commission, over 17 percent of voters in the 2008 presidential election cast absentee ballots. Another 13 percent of voters in 2008 cast their ballots up to several weeks before Election Day, at an election office or an early voting polling place.[51] In some states, a majority of votes were cast by absentee ballot or early voting. Finally, jurisdictions in a small number of states (particularly Colorado, Indiana, Nevada, and Texas) have experimented with voting centers as alternatives to traditional polling places. Voting centers are typically located in high-traffic areas such as shopping malls. They are typically configured so that any voter can vote at any voting center, rather than at one designated polling place.[52] Each of these alternatives provides a way to reduce the volume of Election Day voters and, ultimately, curtail the number of polling places that need to be operated on Election Day.

The terms precinct and polling place are slightly different, though often used interchangeably. Precincts are typically the smallest geographic units into which counties and townships are divided for the purposes of election administration. Each precinct typically has a designated polling place to vote. The polling place (a school, church, or community center, for example) is where people go to vote. However, there is no one-to-one correspondence between precincts and polling places, as many jurisdictions often have voters from multiple precincts vote at the same polling place. In any case, we find a substantial amount of both precinct and polling place consolidation. We are most concerned about polling place consolidation because it means that some voters must necessarily travel further— even out of their own neighborhoods or comfort zones—to vote. Furthermore, polling place consolidation may result in increased administrative error, because there is a greater possibility of the use of differing ballots within the polling place.

In order to get a good idea about whether there has been precinct/polling place consolidation over time, we gathered available data about the number of polling places in each county in the United States in the 2000, 2004 and 2008 elections. Where possible, some of these data come from the U.S. Election Assistance Commission's Election Day Survey, but often, our data derive from state and county election offices. We were able to obtain data for about two-thirds of U.S. counties.[53]

TABLE 4.1 Polling Place Consolidation, 2000–2008

Year	Mean Voters per Polling Place	Median Voters per Polling Place	Mean Polling Places per County[1]
2000	541 (342.7)	447	58 (191.0)
2004	625 (435.2)	506	49 (158.7)
2008	753 (530.8)	597	48[2] (158.1)

[1] Standard deviation in parentheses.
[2] If one only factors in the counties without early voting in 2008, the mean number of polling places per county drops to 56 in 2000 and 40 in 2008.

In order to standardize these data, we have calculated two variables of interest: the number of voters per polling place, and the number of polling places per county. As Table 4.1 indicates, the median number of voters per polling place increased from 447 in 2000 to 597 in 2008. Increases in the number of voters per polling place could simply reflect increased turnout in 2004 and 2008. Thus, the last column in Table 4.1 reports the mean number of polling places in each election. We see that even with increasing turnout, the number of polling places has dropped.

Between 2000 and 2008 the mean number of polling places per county declined by ten polling places. The average polling place had 200 more voters in 2008 than in 2000. These changes were fairly consistent. Of the 31 states in our sample, 20 states saw a decline in the number of polling places per county from 2000 to 2008. Almost every state had more voters per polling place in 2008. In addition, polling place consolidation was not confined to states with early voting. In early voting states, the mean number of polling places per county declined by 8.9, while in states without early voting the decline was 15.6 polling places.[54] Overall, the evidence of a reduction in the number of polling places between 2000 and 2008 is clear.

The Impact of Polling Place Consolidation on Voter Turnout

Despite the budgetary pressures fueling the reduction in polling places, a growing body of research suggests that consolidating polling places reduces voter turnout. Some research uses a cost–benefit framework to understand voting participation. Laws or administrative features that increase the cost of voting are likely to reduce voter turnout.

Henry Brady and John McNulty outline two different costs imposed on voters when polling places are consolidated. One cost is a "transportation" effect, due to the fact that some voters will have more distance to travel to their polling place. The second is a "search" cost, which includes the effort needed to locate a new polling place and uncertainty about the new polling location.[55] Brady and

McNulty examine the 2003 California gubernatorial recall election in Los Angeles County. In order to reduce the costs of the election, the county reduced the number of precincts by almost two-thirds and changed the polling locations for two-thirds of the registered voters. They find that polling place consolidation reduced turnout almost two percentage points.

The Brady and McNulty study is consistent with others which found that increasing the distance and effort needed to get to a polling place reduces an individual's likelihood of voting.[56] In addition, as distance to a polling place increases, absentee voting increases. However, other research suggests that the relationship between polling place location and turnout is more complicated. Robert Stein and Greg Vonnahme examine voting centers in Larimer County, Colorado and conclude that, because of their proximity to high-traffic areas, voting centers increase turnout for infrequent voters.[57] However, the experience with voting centers in Denver in 2008 was less positive.[58]

To examine the potential impact of polling place consolidation on voter turnout, we combine our data on polling places with county-level turnout data for the 2000 and 2008 elections. For our measure of consolidation, we create a binary variable indicating whether or not the number of polling places in a county declined between 2000 and 2008. We have polling place data in both elections for 2,171 counties, slightly more than two-thirds of the counties in the United States. We find that slightly more than 40 percent of the counties in our sample cut the number of polling places between 2000 and 2008.

We measure turnout as the number of ballots cast as a percentage of the voting age population. We obtained estimates of the voting age population for each county for the relevant election years from the Census Bureau. We also include data on changes in voting equipment from Chapters 2 and 3. We estimate a fixed effects regression equation to model the impact of polling place consolidation and new voting equipment on the change in voter turnout from the 2000 election to the 2008 election. This allows us to examine whether turnout was lower in counties that consolidated polling places. We also examine whether switching to new voting equipment affected voter turnout, if for example, some voters were scared away by new voting technology.[59] Other characteristics of a county that might influence voter turnout, such as its political culture or other areas of election administration, should be captured by the fixed effect portion of the statistical model. Our statistical model includes the natural log of the voting age population, to determine whether turnout drops when there is a large influx of new residents. Other studies indicate that people who move to a new address are less likely to vote than people who stay in the same residence.[60] Finally, a dummy variable for the 2008 election is included to assess whether the change in turnout occurred nationwide as a result of greater awareness of the election and increased efforts to mobilize voters in 2008.

Table 4.2 reports the model estimates for our analysis of voter turnout in the 2000 and 2008 elections. The results indicate that polling place consolidation reduced voter turnout in 2008. Counties that consolidated polling places

TABLE 4.2 The Impact of Polling Place Consolidation on Voter Turnout, 2000 and 2008 Presidential Elections (Fixed Effects Regression)

Explanatory Variable	Coefficient (std. error)
2008 Election	7.68★★★ (.40)
Voting age population (natural log)	−2.02 (1.81)
Any change in voting equipment	.40 (.37)
Polling place consolidation	−.88★★ (.41)
Number of Cases	4342
Root MSE	2.59
R^2	.96

Notes:
The dependent variable is voter turnout (as a percent of voting age population) in each county. Coefficients for county dummy variables are not shown. Each county is weighted by the voting age population. Robust standard errors are shown in parentheses.
★★★$p < .01$, two-tailed test
★★$p < .05$, two-tailed test

experienced a drop in voter turnout of almost 0.9 percentage points, on average, compared to counties that did not consolidate. Meanwhile, the widespread adoption of new voting technology between 2000 and 2008 did not have much of an impact on voter turnout. Interestingly, polling place consolidation was just as common among counties that adopted new voting technology as in counties that kept the same voting equipment. From this, one might conclude that voting equipment change (and the related costs) do not affect voter turnout. Among counties that made no switch in technology, 37.6 percent consolidated. Among counties that made one change in technology, 41.2 percent consolidated. However, we find that among counties that switched technology more than once, 45.4 percent consolidated. We do not want to overstate our results; but it does appear that those jurisdictions that switched equipment twice have consolidated somewhat more than others.

We also find that turnout was, on average, almost 7.7 percentage points higher in 2008 than in 2000, even after controlling for changes in voting equipment and polling places and other unique county-level effects. This estimated effect is similar to the overall increase in the nation's voter turnout from 2000 (50.0 percent) to 2008 (56.9 percent).[61] To put these findings in perspective, heightened interest in politics in 2008 had a much bigger impact on voter turnout than polling place consolidation, yet we must remember that not all elections elicit the kind of interest that a presidential election does—or the 2008 election more generally. Finally, the effect of increasing voting age population on turnout is negative, as expected, but not statistically significant. This suggests that changes in the voting age population did not have much impact on turnout in these elections.

Conclusion

Our country focused on voting equipment and moved quickly to modern equipment in the wake of the 2000 election. However, many policymakers and citizens have been concerned about electronic voting equipment, particularly its integrity. It should be noted that the headlong rush into electronic equipment has made state legislatures, such as Florida's, regret their decisions—yet another unintended consequence of reforms designed to increase the accuracy of elections. While simply the initial replacement of equipment after the 2000 election was expensive, it was the backtracking and second-guessing that made the process even more expensive. Administrative costs of holding elections have been rising, partly due to HAVA mandates and partly due to other factors. These expenses have weighed on state and local election officials, leading to one noticeable change, a reduction in the number of polling places. While the evidence we present is certainly not the last word, it indicates that cutting the number of polling places reduces voter turnout. Perhaps the rapid growth in early and absentee voting will eventually make polling place consolidation irrelevant, yet we are cautious about that. Perhaps voting centers will prove to be superior alternatives to neighborhood polling places. Right now, however, these are largely untested hypotheses. It is important that changes in election administration be supported by evidence to help ensure that those changes don't make matters worse.

In the book *Electronic Elections*, Mike Alvarez and Thad Hall argue that voting technology, particularly electronic voting machines, should be evaluated based on evidence rather than perceptions. We agree, and this chapter shows that sometimes election officials and policy makers have too quickly yielded to perceptions about voting equipment. Rather than figuring out how to get the best performance out of DRE voting machines, some policymakers backed away from them at the first sign of trouble. This encourages further conspiracy theories about voting equipment and it encourages losing candidates in close elections to blame the voting machines.

One recent example illustrates this point. Inexplicably, political unknown (not the singer) Al Greene won the 2010 Democratic primary for U.S. Senate in South Carolina, defeating an experienced opponent. What made the result more puzzling was that at the time of Greene's primary victory, he was facing a felony obscenity charge, for allegedly showing a University of South Carolina coed some pornography in a computer lab. Democrats immediately gave up on any chance of winning the seat, as Greene trailed incumbent Jim DeMint by huge margins in summer polling.[62]

Naturally, some blamed the election outcome on the electronic voting machines in South Carolina.[63] We have seen no evidence to implicate the voting machines. More likely explanations include the fact that Greene's name was listed first on the ballot, a significant aid in a low-intensity, low-turnout primary election. This was not the first time an oddball candidate defeated a party favorite in a primary election. In other similar instances the oddball was also listed first on the ballot.[64] It also didn't hurt that Greene shared the same name as a famous soul singer.

Nevertheless, we expect that the second-guessing of voting equipment will continue. As long as we have peculiar results such as an unknown, silent, non-campaigning candidate winning an election in a state with no paper trail and electronic equipment, some will question the results. One wonders how a more carefully considered implementation of electronic equipment might have worked. Or, alternatively, how would the implementation of electronic equipment have worked in the presence of other systemic reforms, such as taking the administration of elections out of the hands of partisan officials? We address this question in Chapter 6.

5

WE MOSTLY ELIMINATED THE BUTTERFLY BALLOT...ISN'T THAT ENOUGH?

Palm Beach County has a lot of elderly voters. I was trying to make the ballot so that it would be easier for the voters to read, which is why we went to the two-page, now known as the butterfly ballot.
(Palm Beach County Election Supervisor, Theresa LePore speaking to ABC News, December 21, 2000)[1]

We decided to use the arrow because it was easier for voters to draw a line than to fill in the bubble as per a lot of studies that are out there.
(LePore speaking to NPR on her ballot design choice for absentee ballots, August 26, 2004)[2]

As the previous chapters indicate, much of the energy and attention of election reform in the past ten years has been driven by questions surrounding voting equipment. Which voting machines produce more voting errors? What are the costs of new voting equipment? How secure is each system? However, the focus on voting equipment has drawn attention away from broader issues of the design and usability of ballots and voting procedures. In the middle of all the controversy about elections, some states have eliminated the most obvious ballot design problem, butterfly ballots. Yet, beyond the butterfly, there are ways to improve the usability of ballots to make it easier for voters to communicate their electoral preferences. That is to say, election accuracy may be affected by more than simply the technology. The ease or difficulty of using the ballot itself may determine how accurate the election count is. In this chapter we examine the impact of ballot design on residual votes in contests at different places on the ballot.

In order to illustrate the importance of ballot design, we first revisit Florida's 2000 election to show our analysis that indicates that ballot design perhaps should have received as much legislative attention as voting technology. In the official vote count, George W. Bush defeated Al Gore in Florida by just 537 votes. However, there were more than 175,000 residual votes in the presidential contest, roughly 2.9 percent of the ballots cast in Florida (one of the highest rates among the states in that election). Furthermore, more than 100,000 of the residual votes for president were overvotes (where voters mistakenly cast votes for more than one candidate). This is a much higher frequency of overvotes than observed in other states that released data on overvotes, and the overvoted ballots were a source of controversy in the presidential recount in Florida.

Twenty-four Florida counties (including the state's most populated counties) used punch card machines in the 2000 general election, while another 17 Florida counties used optically scanned ballots counted at a central location. Almost all of the remaining Florida counties used precinct-count optical scan voting systems in the 2000 election. As we noted in Chapter 3, precinct-count optical scan systems have an error prevention mechanism that is lacking in punch cards and central-count optical scan systems. Thus, we expect higher rates of residual votes, and overvotes in particular, in Florida counties that used punch card ballots or central-count optical scan voting equipment. We examine data on overvotes and undervotes in the 2000 presidential election from each Florida voting precinct gathered by a consortium of newspapers and provided by *USA Today*.[3] As Figure 5.1 indicates, overvotes, and residual votes more generally, were more common in Florida counties using punch cards and central-count optical scans. In counties using precinct-count optical scan systems, the overvote rate was

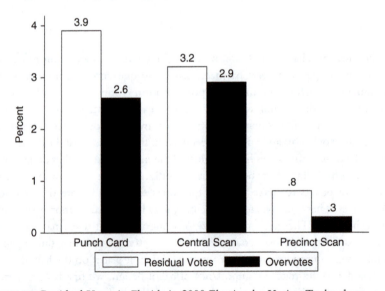

FIGURE 5.1 Residual Votes in Florida in 2000 Election by Voting Technology

approximately 2.5 percentage points lower than in the rest of the state. This pattern is consistent with our findings in Chapter 3.

However, voting equipment was not the most potent source of problematic ballots in the 2000 election in Florida. Because of a change in state law that eased ballot access requirements for minor parties, ten presidential candidates qualified for the Florida ballot in 2000, which posed a challenge for election officials to fit all the presidential candidates on the ballot. Much attention has been devoted to the infamous "butterfly" ballot in Palm Beach County, which listed the presidential candidates on two facing pages (see Figure 5.2).[4] This confusing layout generated an unusually high number of voting mistakes in Palm Beach County. These mistakes included overvotes as well as votes cast for the wrong candidate.[5] What is perhaps forgotten is that 18 other Florida counties also listed the presidential candidates on multiple pages or multiple columns in the 2000 election. As a result, almost 20 percent of Florida voters in 2000 voted on ballots that listed the presidential candidates in more than one column. As we explain in more detail below, listing candidates for the same office in multiple columns tends to confuse voters. If voters mistakenly believe that each new column indicates a new contest, then they may overvote by selecting a candidate from each column.

Figure 5.3 indicates the consequences of what may seem like a trivial decision about the way presidential candidates are listed on the ballot. In Florida counties

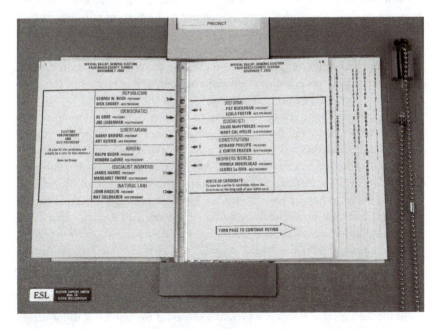

FIGURE 5.2 Palm Beach County "Butterfly" Ballot Used in the 2000 Presidential Election
Source: Smithsonian National Museum of American History

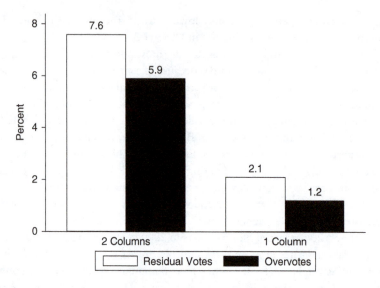

FIGURE 5.3 Residual Votes in Florida in 2000 Election by Ballot Design

where candidates were listed in one column, 2.1 percent of the ballots contained residual votes for president. In counties where candidates were listed in more than one column, the residual vote rate jumped to 7.6 percent of ballots cast. In addition, the overvote rate was almost five percentage points higher in counties with the confusing two-column ballot design than in counties with candidates listed in one column. Comparing the disparities in the two figures indicates that ballot design had a greater impact on residual votes and overvotes in the 2000 election in Florida than voting equipment.[6]

As in our analysis of voting equipment in Chapter 3, we find an interaction between ballot design and demographic variables. In Florida counties with the two-column presidential ballot design, high rates of overvotes and residual votes were concentrated in precincts with large African American or low-income populations. In counties that adopted the confusing ballot design, well over one of every ten voters in heavily poor or African American precincts mistakenly voted for more than one presidential candidate. In contrast, in counties that listed presidential candidates in a single column, overvotes remained below 4 percent even in precincts with the largest concentrations of low income or African American residents. Thus, poorly designed ballots, like inferior voting equipment, generate higher rates of voting errors that tend to occur disproportionately in disadvantaged communities.

In the sections that follow we present a theory of the impact of ballot design on voting behavior, as well as evidence to support that theory. Our framework likens voting to completing a public opinion survey. We argue that residual votes are similar to the situation where someone fails to answer a question on a public opinion survey (survey non-response). Researchers and election administrators can draw from studies of questionnaire design and layout in self-administered surveys (surveys that are mailed and those given to a group in person) to identify ballot features that may simplify or complicate the voting process. Based on this approach, we identify several ballot features that we think lead to lower (or higher) rates of voting mistakes. (Another way of putting it is that some features may make the ballot more or less "usable." We define usability features that reduce residual votes.) We test these hypotheses based on an analysis of actual ballots used in five states in the 2002 mid-term elections, as well as a much larger sample of ballots used in more than 1,100 counties in the 2004 presidential election. Finally, we discuss additional examples of consequential ballot designs in more recent elections. Our results indicate that ballot design has a significant impact on the ability of people to record their votes. Yet, beyond the butterfly, it seems that ballot design did not receive attention as a policy "problem" that lawmakers needed to expend significant resources to address.

Voting is Like Completing a Public Opinion Survey

There is a small but growing body of scholarly work[7] evaluating ballot design and the usability of voting systems, yet until recently, the federal government spent few resources to ensure ballots were designed well, and certainly nothing like the resources expended on voting equipment. While federal legislators did implicitly consider the issue of ballot design in HAVA, there were little more than voluntary standards enacted and ultimately issued by the Election Assistance Commission. In 2007, the EAC issued federal guidelines concerning ballot design and election administration design more generally (e.g., voter materials such as signs posted at the precinct as well as various ballot designs and DRE screen design and usability suggestions).[8] The EAC report stemmed from the initiatives of the AIGA's Design for Democracy initiatives[9] (see Lausen, 2007). However, a report from the Brennan Center for Justice notes that Voluntary Voting System Guidelines have not "required vendors to fully support the ballot design recommendations made in *Effective Designs for the Administration of Federal Elections*."[10]

Contrast that with the Census forms in the 1990s where the federal government spent the better part of a decade redesigning Census forms to encourage response to the 2000 Census, and tested design alternatives in the field and in the laboratory.[11] One of the main consultants on the Census redesign was a survey methodologist from Washington State University named Don Dillman.[12] Instead of saying, "why don't we spend that much money designing something arguably as important?" we decided to borrow the usability research (and other elements of Dillman's and his colleagues' work) and see if it applied to ballots.[13] In applying such a framework, we argue that a residual vote is much like the situation when someone does not answer a question on a public opinion survey: there are some cases where people intend not to answer questions (people often skip the question, "what is your household income?"). Yet, many times, people do not even realize they have failed to answer a question. Ballots and self-administered questionnaires have many features in common, especially when voting involves making written marks on a paper ballot, which we have already noted, the majority of Americans do. As a result, we argue that several rules of survey graphic design can be applied to ballots.[14]

Applying Survey Design Techniques to Ballots

In general, the text and graphics on a ballot should be arranged so that all voters follow the same efficient path in navigating the contests on each page of a ballot. Several of the ballot features described below are based on Gestalt psychology's law of proximity: placing items of text or graphics close together encourages the reader to understand that those items are related or go together. By the same token, placing barriers or areas of separation between different items of text encourages the reader to see that those items do not go together.[15] Some desirable ballot features are specific to the instructions, such as their location and readability. Other features are specific to the layout of the candidates and choices, such as where voters mark the ballot, shading and bolding of candidate names and office titles, and clutter around candidate names. Finally, there are still other ballot features that assist the voter in completing the entire ballot.[16]

Ballot Instructions and Text

In terms of ballot instructions, our first concern is the location of the instructions. Survey methodology research indicates that instructions should appear just before the first response task to which the instructions apply. Thus, ballot instructions should be near the top of the ballot, just above the first contest. Since people in the United States read from left to right and typically glance first at the top left corner of any text, the ideal location for instructions is the upper left-hand corner of the ballot.[17]

The next concern is with the readability of ballot instructions—they should be easy to read and be written in an active and affirmative style. Ballot instructions and other text written at a low-grade level should be easier for voters to understand. Another readability concern involves the appearance of the text. Lowercase text is quicker and easier to read than text in all capital letters.[18] Thus, ballot instructions, candidate names, and ballot measures should appear on the ballot in "sentence case," that is, with names and other proper nouns capitalized, along with the first letter of sentences. All other letters should be in lower case.

Finally, ballot instructions should indicate the consequences of a spoiled ballot as well as what voters should do if they spoil their ballot. Our culturally based norms often lead voters to try to correct a mistake when they make an incorrect mark on the ballot, which often produces a spoiled ballot (i.e., a residual vote).

In addition, HAVA requires jurisdictions with paper ballots to include instructions on the effect of multiple votes for a single office and how to correct a spoiled ballot.[19]

The Choices on the Ballot

We also hypothesize that the layout of the offices and candidate names affect the level of residual votes. One important ballot feature involves the use of shading and clear lines to help distinguish one contest from the next. A reader's eye is drawn to "high contrast areas" where one portion of text stands out from the rest.[20] Thus, shading each office or groups of similar offices can help guide the voter from one task to the next.[21] Bold-faced text and indentation are additional mechanisms for creating contrast in text. Bolded text may be used to highlight each office, while non-bolded or indented text may be used for candidate names to help draw the voter's attention to the response task for each contest.[22] Ballots created with these design features should be easier for voters to follow because these features follow the law of proximity in grouping candidates for the same office together.

The law of proximity also helps explain why it is a bad idea to list candidates for the same office in multiple columns or pages. When candidates for the same office are printed in the same column, voters see that they are grouped together for the same voting task. When candidates for the same office are listed in two columns, the design encourages voters to see the candidates in the second column as part of a separate voting task, which then leads to overvotes and spoiled ballots.

Another concern with the layout of candidate names is whether there is ambiguity in the box, circle or arrow to mark for the voter's candidate of choice. This issue has several dimensions. In order to limit the number of ballot pages, ballots often divide a page into two or three columns of offices and candidate names. As a result, confusion may arise if spots for marking a vote appear on both sides of a candidate's name. Clear lines or borders should be used to keep each contest separate from the other contests on the ballot in the eyes of the voter. Furthermore, there is less voter confusion if a candidate's name and the place for marking the ballot for that candidate are very close together.[23] Ideally, the candidate names should be left-justified with the oval, square, or arrow appearing just to the left of the candidate's name. This is the most common format used in written surveys.

In order to cast a vote, many ballots ask voters to darken an oval or mark a square or circle. In contrast, other ballots ask voters to draw a line to connect the base and point of an arrow. However, some studies indicate that the "complete the arrow" ballot format generates substantially higher rates of residual votes.[24] Even though drawing a line may be a simpler fine-motor skill than coloring inside an oval (which is probably the reason LePore suggested that the connect-the-arrow ballot was a good choice for absentee ballots in Palm Beach County in 2004), there are other design elements that make ballots with the arrow format confusing. First, ballots with the arrow format often feature arrows appearing on either side of a candidate's name. It is not intuitive to voters whether the point or base of the arrow should be next to the candidate's name. Second, on many connect-the-arrow ballots the candidate is some distance from the arrow that needs to be marked. As a result, there can be some confusion about which arrow to mark. Finally, we believe that voters are generally less familiar with the arrow format than the oval format (which is common on surveys, standardized tests, government forms, and lottery tickets). In fact, we are not aware of instances of any other form or survey that uses the connect-the-arrow design. In any case, the manner in which the voter is asked to mark the ballot is another design element that can generate confusion.

It is also important to consider whether there is clutter around the candidate's names, which can also confuse voters. A study of reading and eye movement finds that when there is more cluttered information on a page competing for the reader's attention, people spend less time reading and learn less of the material.[25] State laws sometimes require that ballots include extra detail (such as a candidate's occupation or hometown, or the names of the presidential electors for each candidate). Survey researchers advise against putting any extraneous text near the response options on a questionnaire.[26] Richard Niemi and Paul Herrnson have applied this logic in a broad critique of ballots in the United States, arguing that many ballots include too much information. The only candidate information needed on a ballot is the candidate's name and party affiliation.[27]

Navigation among Offices

There are some additional ballot features that are particularly important for down-ballot contests in terms of guiding the voter through the ballot, so they do not unintentionally fail to cast a vote for a particular office. First, many down-ballot races or ballot measures appear on a second page, after many other contests. In situations where there are more contests on the following pages, there should be instructions to turn the ballot over to continue voting. In keeping with the law of proximity, directions to turn the ballot over should appear just after the office on a page.

A second important ballot feature is a straight-party mechanism that allows voters to select all candidates of a particular party in one ballot mark. Seventeen states in our sample included a straight-party feature on the ballot in 2004. This is a feature that may simplify the voting task for partisan races. Some studies suggest that the straight-party option reduces the frequency of residual votes in partisan contests at the top of the ballot.[28] However, ballot propositions and other non-partisan races are not covered by the straight-party device, even though voters may believe they have completed their ballot once they use the straight-party feature. Thus, we expect that a straight-party mechanism will increase the rate of residual votes, and undervotes in particular, on ballot measures.[29]

A third and related ballot design feature that is important for down-ballot contests involves the arrangement of candidate names and party labels. Most jurisdictions use an "office block" layout in which each office has its own section of the ballot, with candidates running for a particular office listed below the name of the office. However, slightly less than 10 percent of jurisdictions instead use a "party column" layout in which party labels and candidates are arranged in a grid. In a typical party column layout, candidates running for the same office are listed in the same row of the grid while candidates from the same political party are listed in the same column. As Chapter 3 notes, the party column layout is commonly used on lever machines and full-face DRE voting systems. It is seen by some as an efficient way to allow for straight-ticket voting, by selecting all of the candidates in the same party column. However, the party column layout poses a problem for ballot measures and other nonpartisan contests, which must be listed on a separate page or away from the party column grid. By the law of proximity, voters may reason that any material that is not on the party column grid is not part of the ballot, and they may inadvertently miss those contests. Thus, we expect that residual votes, and more specifically, undervotes, are more common on ballot measures when the party column layout is used.

Evidence from Actual Ballots

To test the hypothesized ballot design effects, we gathered ballots and examined whether the ballots had the design features the survey design literature suggests make for more usable forms. We obtained ballots used in the 2002 and 2004 general elections. We focus on paper-based ballots (hand-counted paper ballots and optically scanned ballots), which are most similar to the written questionnaires upon which we base our theory of ballot design. In addition, paper-based ballots are the most common type of ballot in general elections in the United States. Thus, we exclude other voting methods from this analysis (punch cards, lever machines, and DREs). Elections are administered (and ballots are often designed and printed) at the county level in most states and at the municipal level in a handful of other states. We use these local jurisdictions as our unit of analysis.[30] The informed reader will ask whether we are obtaining every single ballot that could be used in any particular county, as some counties have a great number of ballots used. For our analysis, we obtained one ballot per county, preferably from the largest precinct in the county. We analyze the accuracy of voting on races that everyone in the state faces when they cast their votes, so we do not focus on school board elections, which may be selected by district. This matches the types of residual vote analyses and ballot analyses that have been conducted in the past.

In the 2002 election we sought ballots from counties using paper-based ballots in five states (Florida, Illinois, Iowa, Kansas, and Tennessee) that had a

gubernatorial election. Of the 261 counties in those five states, we obtained ballots from 250 counties, which included approximately 4.3 million voters in the
2002 general election.

In the 2004 election, we attempted to gather ballots from every state using
paper-based ballots. In New England states where decisions about voting equipment and ballot design are made by town clerks, we randomly selected a number
of towns proportional to the total number of jurisdictions in the state. This produced a sampling frame of 1,816 election jurisdictions using paper-based ballots in
the November 2004 election. From each jurisdiction, we requested a copy of the
November 2004 ballot, and election results, including overvotes and undervotes,
in the presidential contest, another partisan statewide race, and a ballot measure (if
there were any on the ballot).[31] We received a copy of the ballot and election data
from 1,139 counties and municipalities, a response rate of 63 percent. These jurisdictions account for roughly 32.5 million voters in the 2004 election.

We examined each ballot we received to see if it did or did not have the ballot
features we identified in the previous section.[32] Most ballot features were coded
in a binary fashion (either the feature was present or absent—yes/no). One exception is readability: in order to measure the readability of ballot instructions, we
typed instructions into Microsoft Word and computed Flesch reading ease scores
and Flesch–Kincaid grade level scores. The Flesch reading ease scores place texts
on a 100-point scale. Higher scores indicate documents that are easier to read.
The Flesch–Kincaid scores indicate the grade level needed to understand the
text.[33] Higher scores indicate documents that are harder to read. The two measures of readability are strongly correlated ($r = -.93$). Therefore we combined the
measures to create a readability index: we standardized both measures, reversed
the scale of the grade level score, and averaged the two measures. We use a
similar method to code the readability of the ballot measures. Previous research
suggests that more difficult to read propositions garner higher rates of residual
votes.[34]

What Features Do the Ballots Have?

Given the decentralized nature of election administration in the United States,
readers should not be surprised that we find a great deal of variety in ballot design,
even within the same state. Table 5.1 indicates how often we observe many of
the desirable features described above in our sample of ballots in the 2002 and
2004 elections. In examining the table, it is important to note that we had many
more ballots from many more states in the 2004 election; the differences in the
percentages of ballots with each design feature from each year should not be
taken to mean that "more ballots or fewer ballots in 2002 had a certain feature
than in 2004."

On the positive side, it is very rare to find ballots with the sin of listing the
presidential candidates in more than one column (although we do find 13

TABLE 5.1 Frequency of Desirable Ballot Features in Sample Counties, 2002 and 2004

Ballot Feature	2002	2004
Instructions in top left corner of ballot	56%	45%
Sentence-case text for instructions	—	80%
Mean grade level of instructions (standard deviation)	8.2 (1.9)	7.9 (3.3)
Instructions mention how to correct a spoiled ballot	90%	38%
Instructions note the consequences of a spoiled ballot	22%	12%
Sentence case text for candidate names	—	39%
Shading to identify different offices	36%	34%
Bolded text to differentiate offices from candidates	40%	39%
Candidates for top office appear in one column	100%	99%
Clear about where to mark ballot for top office	78%	70%
No clutter around candidate names	36%	49%
Candidate names left-justified	86%	72%
Instructions to turn over ballot after last contest	—	71%
Lower-case text for ballot measures	—	90%
Mean index of ballot features (standard deviation)	1.1 (1.7)	1.3 (1.5)
Number of counties in sample	250	1,139

instances of that in the 2004 election). Most ballots use sentence-case text for instructions and ballot measures, and most ballots left-justify the placement of candidate names and the space for marking the ballot. In addition, most ballots avoid confusion over where to mark the ballot, although it may be troubling that roughly 20 to 30 percent of the ballots in our sample may confuse voters on this fundamental aspect of design.

We see other instances where many ballots fail to adopt some of the appealing design features we describe above. For example, less than half of the ballots use shading to help identify different contests or bolded text to distinguish office titles from candidate names. In addition, less than half of the ballots we observe list candidates in sentence-case text or avoid cluttered information around the candidate names. Roughly half of the ballots place instructions at the top left portion of the page, where voters are most likely to notice the instructions. Finally, the instructions on the average ballot are written at an eighth-grade reading level, although more than 20 percent of the ballots in our sample are written at or above a twelfth-grade reading level.

An Index of Ballot Features

We believe that each of the ballot features described above and listed in Table 5.1 derive from the same basic design principles. Thus, for each local jurisdiction in our sample, we compute an overall index of ballot features. Not only do these features measure good (or bad) ballots as a group, but using such an index in the analyses that follow will make it easier to interpret them. Since each ballot feature except for the readability of ballot instructions is measured as a yes/no variable, the index is a count of the number of simplifying and the complicating features on a ballot. In creating the ballot index, we add variables hypothesized to simplify the voting process and subtract variables hypothesized to make voting more difficult. Our readability scale is divided by two, so that it runs from −1 to +1, and so it too is added. (If a theoretical ballot had no good feature and no bad features, it would have a score of zero.) None of the ballots in our sample was perfect on all indicators (which would be an index score of +5 in 2002 and +6 in 2004), and none of the ballots in our sample failed on all of the features (which would be an index score of −4 in 2002 and −5 in 2004). The ballot index values in our data range from −3 to +4 in 2002 and from −3 to +5 in 2004. The mean ballot score is 1.1 in 2002 and 1.3 in 2004. This indicates that the average ballot in our sample contains roughly half of the desirable ballot features outlined above. Nevertheless, as the standard deviation measures at the bottom of Table 5.1 indicate, there is substantial variation around the mean score on our ballot index. We expect ballots that score highly on our ballot design index should produce lower rates of residual votes.

Ballot Design and Accuracy at the Top of the Ticket

From looking at the multiple column ballot in Florida, it seems easy to see that ballot design does affect accuracy. However, the survey methodology framework suggests that all these features may work together to make for more usable ballots. Thus, for each of the local jurisdictions in our study, we also gathered data on turnout and candidate totals to compute the number of residual votes. We also asked local election officials for data on overvotes and undervotes in the contests we examine. Recall that residual votes are the difference between the total number of ballots cast in an election and the number of votes cast for candidates running for a particular office. The distribution of residual votes across local jurisdictions is somewhat skewed; that is, there are a few counties which have particularly high levels of residual votes. In general, residual votes are substantially more common on ballot measures than in presidential and gubernatorial races that appear at the top of the ballot. In our sample of counties from the 2002 gubernatorial elections, the mean residual vote rate was 1.0 percent of ballots cast and the standard deviation was 0.8 percent. Residual vote percentages for the 2004 presidential contests in our sample yield a mean of 1.0 percent, and a standard deviation of 1.1 percent (very similar to the data on the entire nation presented in Chapter 3).

As a preliminary step, we examined the correlation between the residual vote rate and our ballot design index. Each of the bivariate relationships is in the expected direction: residual vote rates are higher when a confusing ballot feature is present and lower when a simplifying feature is present. In the 2002 sample, the correlation between the ballot design index and residual votes for governor is −0.61 (p < .001). In the 2004 sample, the correlations are weaker, −0.28 for the presidential contest and −0.26 for ballot measures, but still in the expected direction (p < .001 in both cases).

Explanations Other Than the Ballot Index

Many of the same factors we analyzed in Chapter 3 are also relevant in an analysis of the effect of ballot design on residual votes. In the same way as the earlier analyses, a variety of factors other than ballot design features could affect the residual vote rate. If we want to understand how ballot design affects the number of residual votes, then we must consider other factors that may affect the number in any given election jurisdiction.

Thus, we focus on other ballot design features that are not included in the index (for various reasons noted below), voting technology, and demographic variables commonly associated with residual votes. With respect to other ballot features, we include a separate variable indicating whether candidates are listed in two columns. We control for this separately because of the dramatic effects of this design flaw observed in the 2000 election in Florida. No ballots in our sample from the 2002 election listed gubernatorial candidates in two columns. However, 13 local jurisdictions in the 2004 sample placed the presidential candidates in two columns. We also include separate controls for a straight-party ballot feature and for the connect-the-arrow format. Previous studies suggest that these ballot features affect residual votes and we want to examine whether they do so independently of the other design elements in this study. The straight-party feature in particular has been a source of political controversy and partisan argument, given the fact that having such a feature is determined by state law.[35]

Additionally, a straight-party feature can be good for accuracy or bad, depending on the office: we expect residual votes to be less common in partisan contests when the straight-party option is on the ballot, but on non-partisan contests, since people believe they have completed their ballot when they cast the straight party vote, it can be bad.[36] Our tests of the 2002 ballot features have shown that the connect-the-arrow feature has a uniquely high error rate associated with it. Its effect on residual votes is so strong that it may bias our findings on the other ballot features if we included it in the ballot index.

We also consider the type of technology (or not) used to count the paper ballots. The jurisdictions in this analysis use one of three types of voting equipment: hand-counted paper ballots, optical scan ballots counted at a central location, and optical scan ballots counted at the voting precinct. The central-count system is the most common of the three systems in our data. For example, in the 2004 sample, 47 percent of jurisdictions use central-count optical scan systems, 41 percent use precinct-count optical scan systems, and 12 percent use hand-counted paper ballots. Our statistical models include dummy variables for the other two systems to compare their effect to the central-count system. As Chapter 3 indicates, the precinct-count optical scan systems have an error prevention feature that allows voters to detect and fix mistakes that the other two systems lack. Thus, we expect lower residual vote rates on the precinct-count optical scan systems, as voters would be more likely to catch the mistakes that they made due to ballot design with a precinct notification system.

As control variables, we include the percentage of a county's residents who are African American, the percentage over the age of 65, the percentage of adults with at least a high school degree, and the natural log of the number of ballots cast in the jurisdiction. (Recall from Chapter 3 that we use the natural log of ballots cast because, while the number of residual votes may increase as turnout increases, after some point increasing turnout has less of an effect.) The demographic variables come from the Census Bureau and were measured in the 2000 census. Based on previous studies, we expect residual votes to be positively correlated with the size of the African American and elderly populations, and negatively correlated with education. As for votes cast in the jurisdiction, previous studies indicate that the smaller the county, the larger the number of residual votes.[37] This finding may be due to election administration—larger urban counties tend to have more professional operations than smaller rural counties. Thus, we expect the natural log of the number of ballots cast to be negatively correlated with residual votes.

Analyzing Residual Votes

For the statistical analyses that follow, we are analyzing residual votes: the number of ballots cast in each county that fail to record a valid vote for a particular contest. We also will examine why the number of overvotes and undervotes may vary across jurisdictions.[38] For our analysis here, we analyze these outcome variables (dependent variables) using a type of statistical analysis called negative binomial regression, a technique that factors in the idea that residual votes can be concentrated in particular locations (because of poorly designed ballots, for example).[39] Using the results of these regressions,[40] we compute the percent change in the number of residual votes, given a change in a particular variable. Of particular interest is the ballot index because that percent change will show how much easier (harder) good (or bad) ballot design makes casting a valid vote for citizens. The percent change calculations for the ballot design and voting technology measures of interest are reported in Table 5.2. The first column reports the estimates for the 2002 gubernatorial election and the second column provides estimates for the 2004 presidential election.

The results indicate that residual votes indeed are less common when more usable ballots are used. The impact of the ballot design index is slightly stronger in the 2002 election. In the 2002 sample, increasing the ballot design index by two standard deviations reduces the expected number of residual votes by 56 percent. The comparable effect of the ballot design scale in the 2004 sample is

TABLE 5.2 Impact of Institutional Factors on Residual Votes: 2002 and 2004 General Elections

Explanatory Variable	2002 Governor Percent Change	2004 President Percent Change
Ballot Design		
Index of ballot features	−56	−48
Candidates listed in two columns	—	+373
Straight-party option	−10	−45
Connect-the-arrow format	+15	+21
Voting Technology		
Precinct count optical scan	−30	−38
Hand-counted paper ballot	+3	+14
Demographic Controls		
Percent black	+28	−4
Percent 65 or older	−1	−6
Percent w/high school degree	−7	−30
Ballots cast (natural log)	−50	−24

Note: Cell entries are the expected percent change in the number of residual votes due to a particular variable, while holding other variables constant.

a 48 percent reduction in the expected number of residual votes. These figures suggest that serious improvements in ballot design can cut the number of residual votes in half in partisan contests at the top of the ballot. Comparing the percent change estimates in Table 5.2 also indicates that the impact of the ballot design measure is larger than almost all of the other factors that we take into account in our analyses.

Our results also reaffirm the Florida analysis we presented at the beginning of the chapter. In the 2004 election, the residual votes in jurisdictions that placed the presidential candidates in two columns were a whopping 373 percent higher than in the rest of the jurisdictions in our sample. The jurisdictions that committed this design faux pas in 2004 tend to be small rural counties, so they did not confuse a large number of voters or affect the outcome of the presidential election. Nevertheless, before ballots are printed, election officials should be warned not to list candidates for the same office in more than one column!

As expected, we also find that the straight-party option tends to reduce residual votes in partisan contests at the top of the ballot. In addition, even after controlling for many other ballot design features, residual votes are more common on ballots with the connect-the-arrow format for marking the ballot. Finally, our findings mimic the results in Chapter 3 in that we consistently find that voting equipment with an error correction feature reduces the frequency of residual votes. Precinct-count optical scan systems reduce the expected number of residual votes by 30–40 percent, when compared with ballots that are scanned at a central location.

Analyzing Overvotes and Undervotes

Residual votes may be one of the best measures of accuracy that scholars have. Most jurisdictions have it and it is easy to compute; but it is also a rough measure, especially since it includes people who did not cast a vote in a contest on purpose. Thus, we also attempted to gather the number of overvotes and undervotes from each jurisdiction. So, we also examine the impact of ballot features on overvotes and undervotes. We were able to gather data on overvotes and undervotes for more than half of the jurisdictions in our sample (many counties do not keep track of these data). Overvotes are almost always unintentional, whereas undervotes may be intentional. Put differently, overvotes are almost always the result of voting errors, while undervotes may result from voting errors or the voter's intent to skip a contest. Since overvotes are errors of commission and undervotes may be errors of omission, the impact of ballot design and other factors on overvotes and undervotes may be different. While our conclusions about the predictors of overvotes and undervotes are more tentative due to the smaller sample, the results support our ballot design hypotheses.

The dependent variables are the number of ballots cast with overvotes or undervotes for a particular contest. Typically, undervotes are more common than overvotes. In our sample of counties from the 2002 gubernatorial elections, the mean overvote rate was 0.1 percent (with a standard deviation of 0.2 percent), and the mean undervote rate was 0.7 percent (and a standard deviation of 0.5 percent). In the 2004 presidential election, our sample produces a mean overvote rate of 0.2 percent (with a standard deviation of 0.8 percent) and a mean undervote rate of 0.6 percent (and a standard deviation of 0.4 percent).

We use the same type of regression technique (negative binomial regression) to examine overvotes and undervotes as we did for residual votes. Table 5.3 shows the percent change in the expected number of overvotes or undervotes due to the independent variables in the model. The first two columns focus on overvoting and undervoting in the 2002 election. The last two columns focus on the 2004 election. In each case, we find that better designed ballots reduce the frequency of both overvotes and undervotes.

The ballot index measure appears to have a stronger effect on overvotes than on undervotes, which should not be surprising, since undervotes are sometimes intentional. For example, in the 2004 election, increasing the ballot design index by two standard deviations reduces the expected number of overvotes by 66 percent. The same change in the ballot design index reduces undervotes by roughly 48 percent. A similar pattern holds for the 2002 election.

In terms of overvotes, the ideal outcome of an election would be if there were no overvotes. That would suggest minimal voting errors and fewer

TABLE 5.3 Impact of Institutional Factors on Overvotes and Undervotes: 2002 and 2004 General Elections

Explanatory Variable	2002 Governor		2004 President	
	Overvotes Percent change	Undervotes Percent change	Overvotes Percent change	Undervotes Percent change
Ballot Design				
Index of ballot features	−75	−37	−66	−48
Candidates listed in two columns	—	—	+955	+63
Straight-party option	−48	+7	−62	−39
Connect-the-arrow format	+417	−1	+38	+32
Voting Technology				
Precinct count optical scan	−76	−20	−75	−16
Hand-counted paper ballot	—	—	+2	+26
Demographic Controls				
Percent Black	−1	+23	−18	−14
Percent 65 or older	+15	−1	+12	+2
Percent w/high school degree	−18	+1	−82	−22
Ballots cast (natural log)	−27	−52	−4	−11

Note: Cell entries are the expected percent change in the number of overvotes or undervotes due to a particular variable, while holding other variables constant.

problematic ballots for election officials to sort out. So, what is the probability of having this ideal outcome? We use our regression results to compute the probability of zero overvotes for different types of ballots, holding other factors constant. In 2002 and in 2004, switching from a poorly designed ballot (with low scores on the ballot index) to a well-designed ballot (with a high ballot index score) increases the probability of zero overvotes by more than 30 percent.

As expected, other ballot and voting technology features are also strongly associated with overvotes. In the 2004 election, jurisdictions that printed the presidential candidates in two columns increased by expected number of overvotes by a shocking 955 percent. We observe a weaker, though still positive, effect of the two-column design on undervotes. This suggests that listing candidates in two columns leads many voters to mistakenly select a candidate in both columns. In the 2002 election the connect-the-arrow format increases the expected number of overvotes by a massive 413 percent, although we observe a weaker effect of the arrow format in the 2004 election.

Furthermore, a straight-party punch tends to reduce the expected number of overvotes and undervotes in candidate contests. As with others, this feature has a stronger effect on overvotes than undervotes.

Correcting That Mistake?

We also find that overvotes and undervotes are less common in counties using the error-correction feature on precinct-count optical scan ballots. We think it is important here to make a point related to our decision to use the negative binomial regression technique. We said we used this technique because residual votes (and overvotes and undervotes) tend to be concentrated in some jurisdictions: in statistical language, this concentration is known as overdispersion. A statistic in the model which indicates how "bad" the overdispersion is indicates that, as expected, overvotes are more likely than undervotes to be concentrated in a relatively small number of jurisdictions. The reason overvotes tend to spike in a few jurisdictions is likely a poorly designed ballot. In comparing the two sets of effects in Table 5.3, it appears that various ballot features and the precinct-count mechanism have a stronger impact on overvotes than on undervotes. This is consistent with the view that overvotes are voting mistakes caused by voting technology and ballot design while some undervotes are intentional and thus unaffected by election administration. However, the fact that ballot design measures and the error-correction features of precinct-count optical scan balloting are significant determinants of undervotes suggests that some undervotes are unintentional as well. We expect that when people get a chance they do fix errors.

Compared to other races on the same ballot, contests for president and governor tend to receive the most attention in terms of media coverage, campaign spending, and voter mobilization. In turn, voters are likely to know the most about candidates in those contests, including their own preferred choice for the office. As a result, voters should be highly motivated to cast a vote in those contests, and they should be less influenced by the design of the voting procedures in those races. Thus, by examining top-of-the-ballot contests we have provided a difficult test for the impact of design features, and yet we still find that ballot design matters. As we showed in Chapter 3, we suspect that ballot design can have an even greater impact in down-ballot contests, which we turn to next.

Ballot Design and Residual Votes on Ballot Measures

Using the same sample of jurisdictions from the 2004 election, we examine the impact of ballot design on voting for ballot measures, which tend to appear farther down the ballot. For each state in our sample with more than one issue on the ballot in 2004, we selected for closer analysis a ballot measure that was both salient (i.e., it was the subject of substantial news coverage and organized campaigning) and competitive (a result within a 60 percent to 40 percent margin).

If none of the state measures satisfied both criteria, then we picked one that was salient even if not competitive (as happened in several states with gay marriage amendments that passed easily). If multiple measures satisfied both criteria, then we picked the most salient ballot measure. See Table 5.4 for a list of ballot issues included in our data.[41] The measures range from hot-button issues such as gay marriage, marijuana legalization, and immigration to more mundane topics such as bond issues.

We again calculate the number of residual votes as the difference between the total ballots cast and the number of votes cast on the ballot measure. We do not examine overvotes and undervotes separately since there are almost no overvotes on the ballot measures we examine. Since ballot measures have only two response options (yes/no), there is less opportunity for the type of confusion that leads to overvotes. Since ballot measures tend to appear after several candidate races on the ballot, residual votes are more frequent for ballot measures. In the same sample of localities from the 2004 election, residual vote percentages for ballot issues range from 0.9 percent to 42.7 percent, with a mean of 8.2 percent, and a standard deviation of 6.0 percent.

As above, we created a ballot design index for the ballot propositions. The index is based on the same design features in Table 5.1, but analyzed according to the design of the portion of the ballot where the measure is located. In addition, the ballot design index for ballot measures includes factors measuring the location of instructions to turn the ballot over, and the location of the ballot question (top or bottom half of page). Since ballot measures often appear after the first page of the ballot, it is important that the ballot include instructions to continue voting on the next page. Those instructions should appear just after the last contest on the page. Those who do research on questionnaire design and layout say that directions should be placed where they are needed.[42] As soon as the voter finishes the first page of the ballot, he may forget to turn the ballot over to the other side, if that information is placed with other directions at the beginning of the ballot. In addition, we hypothesize that ballot measures on the top half of the page are more likely to be noticed (and voted on) than measures listed on the bottom half of the page.

The correlation between the ballot index and residual votes for ballot propositions in our sample is −0.26, which suggests that well-designed ballots may also reduce the frequency of residual votes on ballot measures.

Explanations Other Than the Ballot Index

We run similar analyses as we did for the residual votes at the top of the ballot. However, there are a couple of factors unique to ballot measures that we must take into consideration. As we explain above, we expect that voters are more likely to inadvertently miss ballot measures when a party column (or grid) layout is used for partisan contests rather than an office block format. Our model includes

TABLE 5.4 Ballot Initiatives and Referendums Examined in 2004

State	Title	Topic
Alabama	Amendment 2★	Repeal sections on race and education in the Alabama Constitution
Alaska	Measure Number 2	Legalize marijuana
Arizona	Proposition 200	Policies to combat illegal immigration
Arkansas	Amendment 3	Ban gay marriage
California	Proposition 71	$3 billion bond issue for stem cell research
Colorado	Amendment 37	Require more renewable energy
Florida	Amendment 4	Gaming in Broward and Miami-Dade counties
Hawaii	Amendment 3★	Confidentiality of communication between crime victim and doctor
Indiana	Public Question 1★	Allow General Assembly to exempt certain property from property taxes
Kentucky	Amendment 1★	Ban gay marriage
Maine	Question 2	Ban bear hunting with bait, traps, or dogs
Michigan	State Proposal 04–1	Require state and local approval for new gambling facilities
Mississippi	Amendment 1	Ban gay marriage
Missouri	Amendment 3	Allocation of fuel taxes
Montana	Initiative 147	Allow cyanide in mining
Nebraska	Measure 417	Initiative can allow new casinos
New Hampshire	Amendment Question	Clarify legislative and court powers
New Mexico	Bond Question C★	$16.3 million bond for libraries
North Carolina	Amendment 1★	Bonds for local development
North Dakota	Amendment 1	Ban gay marriage
Ohio	Issue 1	Bay gay marriage
Oklahoma	State Question 707★	Local government bond payments
Oregon	State Measure 35	Limit pain and suffering awards in medical malpractice suits
Rhode Island	State Question 9★	$14 million bond for library at URI
South Carolina	Amendment 1★	End requirement that alcohol be sold in mini-bottles
South Dakota	Amendment B★	State food and transportation funding to religious schools
Utah	Amendment 3★	Ban gay marriage
Virginia	Amendment 1★	Redistricting only done every 10 years
Washington	Referendum Measure 55	Repeal law creating charter schools
West Virginia	Amendment 1★	$8 million bond for veterans
Wyoming	Amendment C★	Alternative dispute resolution before suit filed against health care provider

Source: Initiative and Referendum Institute
★ Proposed by legislature

a variable indicating whether the office block design is used. Less than ten percent of the ballots in our sample used the party column design. As above, our model includes a measure indicating the presence of a straight-party option on the ballot. However, in this case we expect residual votes on ballot measures to be more common when the straight-party feature is available. Some voters may use the straight-party feature and then believe that their voting session is complete without considering other contests, such as ballot measures. In our sample, 39 percent of the jurisdictions have a straight-party mechanism on the ballot. None of the ballots in our sample listed ballot questions (and the approve/disapprove or yes/no) in more than one column, so that predictor is dropped from our model of voting on ballot measures.

It is not relevant to contests at the top of the ballot, but scholars have suggested that people do not vote on contests toward the end of the ballot because they are tired—maybe they did not have time to become more informed about more contests or they just plain do not want to waste time voting on issues they do not perceive as important. Since this so-called "ballot fatigue" may be an issue which contributes to residual votes on ballot issues, the analyses in this part of the chapter include a variable indicating how many contests come before the measure on the ballot.[43] We expect more frequent residual votes on ballot measures when the measures appear farther down the ballot. For this study, we consider how many offices appear on the ballot before the ballot measure as well as the number of the page where the ballot measure is located.

We also consider the complexity of the text of the ballot measures. A comprehensive study of ballot questions by Shauna Reilly and Sean Richey finds that residual votes are more common when the language of the ballot measure is more difficult to understand.[44] We measure the readability of each ballot measure in our sample using the Flesch reading score described above. We expect that residual votes are less common when ballot measures are easier to read.

Finally, we control for the salience of the ballot issue. Some measures in our sample involve controversial issues like gay marriage that may attract a lot of campaign and media attention. Other issues on more obscure topics like bonds for local development may not receive much attention from the press. More salient issues may attract more voters. We have three measures of issue salience. One measure counts the number of articles covering the issue in the state's largest newspaper during the fall campaign. A second measure counts the number of words in newspaper coverage of the issue. The third measure indicates whether the issue was placed on the ballot by citizen petition or by the legislature. Since petition drives tend to attract media coverage, issues placed on the ballot by petition are more salient to voters. We create a salience index by standardizing each of these three measures and averaging them together.[45] We expect fewer residual votes on more salient issues.

In Table 5.5, as with previous analyses in this chapter, we report the percent change in the expected number of residual votes due to the independent variables

TABLE 5.5 Predictors of Residual Votes on Ballot Measures in the 2004 Election

Explanatory Variable	Percent Change
Ballot Features	
Index of ballot features	−8
Office block layout	−57
Straight-party option	+66
Ballot position	+18
Readability of ballot measure	−46
Connect-the-arrow format	+1
Issue Specific	
Issue salience	−28
Voting Technology	
Precinct-count optical scan	+23
Hand-counted paper ballots	−25
Demographic Controls	
Percent black	+10
Percent 65 or older	+6
Percent with a high school degree	−14
Ballots cast (natural log)	−8

Note: Cell entries are the expected percent change in the number of residual votes due to a particular variable, while holding other variables constant.

we consider.[46] We again find evidence that ballot design influences voting behavior. The ballot index measure has the expected negative effect on residual votes for ballot measures, but the effect is weaker than in previous analyses and fails to reach conventional levels of statistical significance. However, other design features have a substantial effect on voting behavior. The number of residual votes on ballot measures is 57 percent lower when ballots have an office block layout rather than a party column design.

Our evidence also confirms findings from other studies. For example, we find that residual votes are less common when the ballot measure is easier to read. Using less forbidding language for ballot issues encourages more voter participation. In addition, we find evidence of ballot fatigue. Residual votes are more common when more contests appear before measures on the ballot. Finally, we find that residual votes are less common for ballot measures that receive a lot of media attention.

The Straight-Party Feature: A Paradox

Another ballot feature that matters is the straight-party option. The expected number of residual votes on ballot measures is 66 percent higher when a straight-party mechanism is on the ballot. When it comes to residual votes, the straight-party feature is something of a paradox. As we expect, this feature tends to reduce residual votes on partisan contests at the top of the ballot but it substantially increases residual votes on ballot measures. The relative importance one attaches to ballot measures versus partisan contests might influence whether the straight-party feature should remain on ballots. It is important to consider other evidence in making that assessment. For example, Paul Herrnson and his colleagues conducted a large field study testing the usability of various types of voting equipment. They found that when a straight-party feature was included on the ballot, voters were more likely to seek assistance with the ballot and voters were more likely to make mistakes.[47] In fact, the straight-party option was one of the most potent sources of voting problems in their study. Thus, a wider body of evidence supports removing the straight-party option from ballots for the sake of keeping ballots as simple as possible.

Design Applies to Voting Equipment Too

While our evidence to this point comes from the design of paper-based ballots, it is important to note that design principles also apply to computerized voting equipment. A recent large-scale study by Paul Herrnson and colleagues tested the usability of several types of DRE machines and optical scan systems. They identified many design features that can make these systems easier to use.[48] Keeping in mind that optical scan equipment has an electronic user interface, we provide two additional examples from recent elections to illustrate the point of Herrnson and his colleagues. A prominent example of this was seen in the election for Florida's 13th congressional district in 2006. The outcome of the contest was decided by a mere 369 votes, and the election drew additional scrutiny because of an unusually high rate of undervotes, almost 10 percent of ballots cast in the district.[49] The 13th district contained all or parts of five counties, and the primary source of undervotes was Sarasota County. This was a surprise to some, because Sarasota County was using scrolling DRE voting machines, modern equipment that was expected to reduce voting errors. However, in Sarasota County the screen with the House contest also included the race for governor and lieutenant governor. Because of the large number of candidates for governor and lieutenant governor, as well as the use of shaded text that highlighted the statewide race but not the House race, many voters simply missed the House contest on that page. Among Sarasota County voters who cast their ballots on scrolling DREs with this ballot layout, roughly 15 percent failed to cast a vote for the House contest. Thus, one design lesson from this election is it may be best to simply list one contest per page for scrolling DRE voting machines.

Partly in response to the design flaw in Sarasota County in 2006, Florida required all counties using DRE voting machines to switch to precinct-count optical scan voting equipment by the 2008 election. When viewed from a distance, shifting between two types of voting equipment that both provide an error prevention mechanism should not substantially affect voting behavior. However, the switch in Florida did not go off without reason, and design features seemed to play a key role.

The number of overvotes in the presidential election in Florida increased from approximately 4,000 in the 2004 election to more than 23,000 in the 2008 election.[50] When the switch in Florida took place, different counties chose different types of optical scanning equipment. All of the scanners were required to notify voters if a ballot had any overvotes. However, there was variation in how scanners were designed to carry out this error prevention function. In some systems, if there were overvotes then the scanner immediately returned the ballot to the voter with a message about which office has too many votes. In other systems, the scanner held the overvoted ballot and then let the voter choose whether to get the ballot back to make corrections or have the machine accept the overvoted ballot anyway. Overvotes were more common in Florida counties using the latter systems than the former systems.[51]

In addition, one of the latter systems (the DS 200 scanner) had poor design features on the screen notifying voters about their ballot. The screen reports that the ballot is "over voted" (which some voters may not understand) but does not say that there are too many votes for a particular contest. In addition, the screen does not mention that the person's vote for that office will not count unless the ballot is corrected. Finally, the button to "accept" the overvoted ballot has a bright-green check mark on it and is in a larger font than the other text on the screen. These features appear to encourage voters to go ahead and cast the overvoted ballot without making any corrections. Indeed, the overvote rate on DS 200 scanners was higher than for other optical scan systems used in Florida in the 2008 election.

Conclusion

The accuracy problem of elections in 2000 was not just a voting equipment problem. All in all, the evidence indicates that ballot design matters in terms of helping to increase the accuracy of election results. Building on the idea that voting a ballot is much like completing a public opinion survey a person receives in the mail, we are able to advance a series of suggestions for creating better ballots. Our research on actual ballots indicates that these suggestions can improve the accuracy of voting. We create a ballot index comprised of several of the features suggested by those researching better survey forms. The impact of the ballot design index is slightly stronger among ballots used in the 2002 election than in the 2004 election, but nevertheless, these improvements can cut the number of residual votes in half in partisan contests at the top of the ballot.

When we are able to break down residual votes into overvotes (usually unintentional) and undervotes (often intentional), we see that the ballot changes we suggest have a stronger effect on overvotes than on undervotes, consistent with the idea that voters are making unintended mistakes.[52] For example, in the 2004 election, increasing the ballot design index by two standard deviations reduces the expected number of overvotes by 66 percent. The same change in the ballot design index reduces undervotes by roughly 48 percent. A similar pattern holds for the 2002 election. While the ballot index we suggest does not have such a strong effect on the ballot measures part of the ballot, there are a number of additional design elements that have an effect on candidate contests, placing contests in multiple columns and using connect-the-arrow ballots.

Palm Beach County, Florida's Theresa LePore probably wished she had the benefit of hindsight in designing the ballots she used in 2000 and in 2004. By her comments in the media, those ballots were intended to benefit the elderly and others who commonly have problems seeing ballots and carrying out fine motor tasks. She had no idea at the time that research studies would indicate the enormous effect that these designs have on residual ballots, but especially on overvotes. Yet she had very little advice to go on and the federal government, unfortunately, did not provide much in the way of advice to help her when it passed the Help America Vote Act of 2002. The bulk of the funding went to new voting equipment. This is a good outcome in terms of the number of precincts which now have equipment that to a certain extent, allows voters to check for mistakes that they make because of poorly designed ballots. And of course, in 2007, the federal government released the design report in *Effective Designs for the Administration of Federal Elections*. However, these standards are voluntary and should be integrated with voting equipment changes. *If elections are supposed to reflect the voice of the people, then well-designed voting **systems** are a must.*

In recent years, experts in design and usability have made an effort to educate election officials and policy makers about ballot design issues. We think this is a positive development. For example, the Brennan Center released a report detailing good ballot design practices called *Better Ballots*, and held a number of seminars for election officials all over the country giving them information about what ballot design changes they could make within the constraints of their own existing state law. The EAC did release its voluntary guidelines, and made designs and prints widely available to election officials. And, in some cases we are happy to report that election officials have consulted with design experts to produce more usable ballots. However, it is not clear that election officials have made progress toward better ballots, or that they are using the EAC guidelines.[53] It remains to be seen whether good design principles are more fully incorporated into ballots and voting systems.

6

DEFINING THE PROBLEM
IN HUMAN TERMS

Who Implements Reform?

Who's watching the watchdog?
(Stephen Colbert, Colbert Report, June 3, 2010)[1]

While we have provided evidence indicating that voting technology and ballot design influence voting behavior and have contributed to past election controversies, other aspects of election administration are important too. In thousands of jurisdictions all over the country, local election officials must manage the everyday details of making an election happen. The decentralization of election administration in the United States affords a great deal of discretion and autonomy to local officials.[2] The individuals who administer elections are human beings with political views of their own, including a party affiliation. For example, in several states, local election officials are recruited for the job by one of the major political parties. The decentralization does not end with the local election officials. In most elections, polling places are staffed by local volunteers. In determining who is eligible to vote these volunteers also have considerable discretion in how they treat the people who come into their polling place on Election Day. The bottom line is that humans run elections, not machines. However, in defining the problem of elections, the human element has not received the same amount of attention as has voting equipment, especially from those with the formal power to change election policy (e.g., the U.S. Congress, state legislatures and ironically, partisan state chief election officers who engage in formal rulemaking).

Election officials have not completely escaped notice in recent elections. State election authorities tend to receive the most attention. In 2000, Florida's elected Secretary of State, Katherine Harris, also served as co-chair of George W. Bush's campaign in Florida. Some accused Harris of using her elected position to help the Bush campaign, especially after she oversaw a controversial purge of the registered voter database in Florida.[3] In 2004, Ohio Secretary of State Kenneth Blackwell was similarly accused because he co-chaired President Bush's re-election campaign and made some controversial decisions regarding voting procedures for the presidential election.[4] Blackwell's successor, Democrat Jennifer Brunner, was also criticized for managing elections in a partisan manner.[5] In addition, California's former Secretary of State Kevin Shelley, a Democrat, resigned from office because of suspicions he had mishandled federal election administration funds, which a federal investigation later revealed to be the case.[6]

While state-level officials such as Harris, Blackwell, Brunner, and Shelley tend to receive more attention, local election officials also make many important decisions in managing elections, conducting such tasks as buying and maintaining voting equipment, registering voters, designing and printing ballots, hiring election workers, and choosing polling places. While these individuals must follow state and federal laws, local officials may interpret and implement those laws in different ways. Daniel P. Tokaji writes that discretion is sometimes written into election law and "also exists where it is unclear what the law prescribes and where there are no effective means to ensure that the law's prescription is followed."[7] For example, the infamous "butterfly ballot" used in Palm Beach County, Florida in the 2000 presidential election was designed by the local election supervisor, apparently in violation of state law.[8] Thus, local discretion in administering elections may extend beyond the letter of the law.

Furthermore, as politics has become more polarized in the United States, there is increasing partisan conflict over election laws and procedures.[9] Partisan disputes over election administration can often be boiled down to two political facts. First, socioeconomic status is strongly associated with voter turnout. That is, highly educated and wealthy people are more likely to vote than low-income citizens and those with little formal education. Second, among voters, socioeconomic status is strongly associated with party preference. Low-income voters and less-educated voters are more likely to support Democratic candidates than wealthy and highly educated voters. These two facts fuel a common belief that increased voter turnout is likely to benefit the Democratic Party while decreased voter turnout will benefit the Republican Party. As a result, Republicans tend to promote efforts to combat voter fraud, which may reduce turnout, while Democrats tend to support measures to reduce barriers to voting and increase turnout.[10] In addition, debates about election reform frequently include competing efforts to frame the issue in terms of integrity (rooting out fraud) versus access (removing barriers to voting).

The combination of state and local discretion and partisan disputes over election administration evokes concern that election officials may manipulate election rules and procedures to favor a political party or to advance their own election prospects. Partisan or biased election administration may occur in a couple of ways. First, election officials may have strong views about the role of government in elections and the appropriate balance between the values of integrity and access. Their own opinions about election administration may affect how they implement election laws. Second, as we show below, many election officials are themselves elected. Thus, election officials may feel somewhat beholden to their party for help in their own elections. Similarly, election officials may receive pressure from their party to manage elections a certain way. Finally, partisan election officials may feel the need to act as representatives or agents of their political party.

We are certainly not the first to raise these issues. Election administration in the United States has been a political—and local—affair for a long time.[11] Many observers have proposed reforms in the way election officials are chosen, with the aim of removing partisanship and producing more independent, nonpartisan, or bipartisan election administration.[12] There is also evidence that the public prefers nonpartisan election administrators.[13] Yet, most of the reforms have been advanced with very little firm evidence about the behavior of partisan election administrators (other than to suggest that it is never a good idea to have foxes guard henhouses).

In this chapter we provide an evidence-based examination of state and local election officials. First, we explain how election officials are chosen in the United States. We provide evidence about what most election observers already have suspected; there is a patchwork of methods used to select the people who administer our elections. Thus, it is perfectly logical to look more closely at the people who manage elections. Second, we examine some of the political attitudes and behavior of election officials. We show that election officials are nowhere near agreement on how elections should be administered or reformed. We also examine the degree to which the opinions and behavior of election officials are related to their party affiliation. We focus in particular on the implementation of provisional voting, a program mandated by HAVA where state and local officials have a considerable amount of discretion. In some situations, we indeed find partisan differences in the way elections are administered in the United States. The human side of election administration deserves more consideration, and we should think more seriously about how we choose the people who manage elections.

How Are Election Officials Selected?

We begin with state election officials, where there is a bit more uniformity in the method of selection. Thirty-five states use partisan elections to choose a secretary of state, whose duties include election administration. The rest of the states appoint an individual or board to manage elections. Nevertheless, in the states with an appointed election authority a majority of those officials are Democrats or Republicans. As a result, only five states have bipartisan or nonpartisan election administration. The top election office in nine out of ten states is controlled by someone affiliated with a major political party.

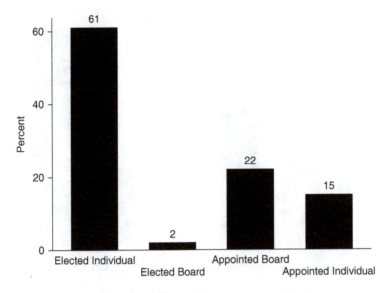

FIGURE 6.1 Methods of Selecting Local Election Officials in 2004
Source: Kimball and Kropf (2006)

In a previous study, we compiled information about the selection methods and party affiliation of all local officials who oversee election operations in the United States.[14] We summarize some of that data here. Looking first at the method of selection for local officials, we see that a majority of local election authorities are elected (see Figure 6.1). However, a significant number of localities have an appointed individual (15 percent) or an appointed board (22 percent) running elections. Mississippi stands apart as the only state in which local election boards are selected by voters (roughly half are partisan and half are nonpartisan). Our data indicate the least common type of local election authority in the United States is an elected nonpartisan board of elections.

The variation in selection methods occurs throughout the country. That is, each region of the country has instances of appointed and elected local officials. However, the method of selection is related to population density. It is more common to find appointed election authorities in heavily populated urban and suburban jurisdictions. Meanwhile, elected clerks are more frequently found administering elections in rural, less populated counties and towns. As a result, roughly half of the voters in the United States are served by elected officials and half are served by appointed officials.

The methods by which election officials are chosen are only one source of variation among local jurisdictions. The party affiliation of local election officials is another source of variation. As Figure 6.2 indicates, partisan election authorities serve almost half of the local jurisdictions in the United States. Among partisan election officials Democrats slightly outnumber Republicans, especially in the

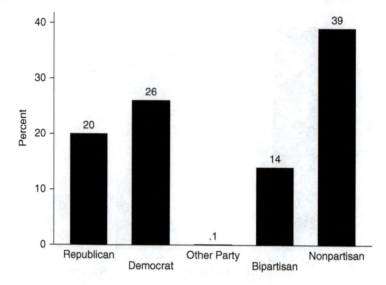

FIGURE 6.2 Party Affiliation of Local Election Officials in 2004
Source: Kimball and Kropf (2006)

South. In addition, the method of selection is not entirely predictive of the partisanship of local authorities. Roughly one-third of appointed election officials are partisan, while two-thirds of elected officials are partisan.

One important reform of the Progressive movement in the early twentieth century was an effort to adopt nonpartisan elections to choose local government officials. It is somewhat ironic that this electoral feature became more firmly established among city councils, where approximately 77 percent of officials are nonpartisan, than among the authorities who manage local elections.[15] Among local election authorities, bipartisan boards serve roughly 15 percent of local jurisdictions, and nonpartisan officials administer elections in approximately one-third of the localities in the United States. Nonpartisan and bipartisan election authorities dominate the Northeast, while a majority of election officials in the rest of the country are Democrats or Republicans. All in all, there is considerable variation in the political affiliation and method of selection of local election officials.

The Political Views of Election Officials

Scholars have recently begun to take an interest in the policy attitudes of election officials in the United States. These studies indicate considerable disagreement over a variety of reform proposals. In addition, policy disagreement tends to fall along party lines on proposals to increase access to voting or reduce fraud. Other policies that do not tap into the access-versus-integrity debate do not generate partisan disagreement among election officials. For example, a recent survey of state election officials finds that Democrats more strongly support policies (such as Election Day registration) that make voter registration easier.[16] At the same time, Republican state election officials are more likely to support policies (such as photo identification requirements) that combat election fraud. However, there are no partisan differences in support for new voting methods, such as early voting or Internet voting.

Two surveys of local election officials conducted by Donald Moynihan and Carol Silva found substantive differences in their attitudes toward the role of government and specific policies. While the surveys did not assess the partisan identification of local election officials, it should not come as a surprise that the election officials do vary in terms of political ideology. Moynihan and Silva find the officials lean toward conservatism—with 49 percent rating themselves as either slightly conservative (19.7 percent), conservative (25.2 percent) or strongly conservative (3.8 percent). Sixteen percent labeled themselves as liberals while roughly one-third of local officials claimed to be "middle of the road."[17] Compared to the general public, then, a greater number of local election officials think of themselves as conservative and about equal numbers thought of themselves as political moderates. According to Gallup polls, in 2004, 40 percent of Americans reported being conservative, 38 percent reported being moderate, and 19 percent reported being liberal—and the numbers have remained roughly similar in the last six years.[18] It is worth noting that on ideology alone, the individuals who run elections in our country are somewhat more conservative than other government bureaucrats. James C. Garand, Catherine T. Parkhurst, and Rusanne Jourdan Seoud analyzed a group of individuals who self-identified on the American National Election Study as government employees. Garand and his colleagues found that state and local employees were much more liberal than the general population (and federal government employees) on a variety of measures, including self-placement on the ideology scale.[19]

Moynihan and Silva also examined the attitudes of local election officials toward HAVA, which is arguably more important than ideology. They make an important point in noting that local officials who support the policy goals of HAVA may work harder to implement those parts of the law. Moynihan and Silva find substantial variation in assessments of HAVA by local election officials. More specifically, local officials who believe that election administration costs have increased are less likely to express positive attitudes toward HAVA.[20] This finding echoes the concerns about the costs imposed by HAVA that we reported in Chapter 4. In addition, Moynihan and Silva find that local officials who believe the federal government has had too much influence over voting equipment decisions tend to have more negative evaluations of HAVA. Thus, some local election officials are less enthusiastic than others about implementing HAVA.

While these surveys do not assess the party affiliations of local officials, they do shed some light on the effect of partisanship. One report on these surveys notes that most local election officials (LEOs) "believe that election administration in their state is independent of partisan politics" but ironically, "more than half of elected LEOs (57 percent) indicated that they communicated their party affiliation during their election."[21] This is consistent with the evidence presented above on the partisan affiliation of local officials.

Knowing that LEOs are communicating their partisanship does not necessarily tell us whether partisanship affects their attitudes about job-related policies. Fortunately, some other surveys of local election officials address this question. One study examines attitudes toward provisional voting, a policy mandated by HAVA.[22] Section 302 of HAVA requires states to provide provisional ballots to voters who believe they are registered but whose names do not appear on the voter list at their polling place. If the voter's eligibility is confirmed, then the provisional ballot is counted. If the voter's eligibility is not verified, then the provisional ballot is not counted. While some states offered provisional ballots before passage of HAVA, the new federal law required most states to change voting procedures to accommodate provisional voting.

Survey evidence indicates that Democratic local election officials' attitudes vary depending on the partisan make-up of their constituencies. The more Democratic the jurisdiction in terms of voting in presidential elections, the more likely the Democratic official would support the provisional voting policy. Interestingly, Republicans did not feel any more or less strongly about provisional voting than did non-partisan election officials. This relationship holds controlling for a number of other factors, including organizational norms as measured through years served and whether the jurisdiction had used provisional voting before the federal law passed.[23] The results suggest that Democratic election officials might provide greater access to provisional voting in jurisdictions where the additional provisional ballots are more likely to provide votes for Democratic candidates.

It is important to note whether or not election policies stoke partisan fights over the values of integrity versus access. Some policies, such as photo identification requirements and aggressive purges of voter registration lists, are offered to strengthen the integrity of elections. Other policies, such as automatic or Election Day registration, are designed to increase access to the voting booth. Both sets of policies tend to provoke disputes about voting access versus voting integrity. In contrast, some proposals for new ways of voting (by mail, or at early voting centers, or over the Internet) tend not to devolve into partisan disputes.

Another study provides evidence of partisan differences in support for different election-related policies, in addition to provisional voting. A recent survey of local election officials finds considerable variation among election officials in their support for different election reform proposals.[24] There are significant differences between Republican and Democratic local officials in terms of support for policies intended to reduce fraud or ease access to voter registration, but not for proposed new methods of voting. As expected, Republicans are more supportive of anti-fraud policies (like photo identification requirements) and Democrats are more supportive of policies to make registration easier. Furthermore, partisan polarization among local election officials is largely confined to officials who serve large jurisdictions (more than 16,000 voters). Thus, partisan differences in the attitudes of election officials are most evident in places that serve the most voters (at the state level and in large local jurisdictions).

Given that there are some differences in the policy attitudes of Democratic and Republican election officials, there is a concern that partisanship may affect the way elections are administered. Perhaps local election officials are able to set aside partisanship and their policy preferences when managing elections. Perhaps professionalism and nonpartisanship are such important values in election administration that the policy views of officials are not important. Perhaps local budgets and other features of local government explain differences in election administration. In the next section we examine the behavior of election officials to determine whether election outcomes are affected by partisanship.

The Behavior of Election Officials

There are a number of studies in public administration indicating that bureaucrats may represent particular groups with which they identify, in addition to serving the public as a whole.[25] It is possible that some election officials may seek to represent their political party's point of view on election administration. To test this hypothesis, we examine the role of state and local officials in the administration of provisional voting in the 2004 presidential election. One critical feature of the provisional voting requirement in HAVA is that it is silent about several key elements of the provisional voting process. For example, what information is required to verify someone's voter registration? Who is responsible for finding that information? What happens if a voter casts a provisional ballot in the wrong voting precinct based on the voter's most recent address? Since HAVA does not answer these questions, state and local election officials have broad discretion over the manner in which provisional voting is implemented. It is possible that officials might use their discretion to administer provisional voting in a way that benefits their political party.

At first glance, provisional voting appears to be a meaningful election reform. In the 2004 election, 1.9 million voters cast provisional ballots and more than 1.2 million provisional ballots counted as valid ballots. However, provisional votes in the 2004 election were not evenly distributed across the country. In some states more than 5 percent of ballots cast were provisional votes. In other states less than one-tenth of 1 percent of the ballots were provisional ballots. In some states the vast majority of provisional ballots were counted as valid ballots. In other states the vast majority of provisional ballots were rejected. There is even more variation in the disposition of provisional ballots across jurisdictions within the same state.[26] This begs the question of why provisional voting was more common, and more successful, in some jurisdictions.

Allowing someone to vote provisionally takes some measure of discretion—but that may be more discretion of the pollworker at the polling place, though under the oversight or following the training of the LEOs. The second step of actually counting the provisional ballot would be more likely to be judged under the direct observation/direction of the local election official. If the partisanship of local election officials matters to election administration, we may see it manifested in how many provisional votes are cast, but most especially in the number counted. If there is evidence of partisanship in election administration, the implementation of provisional voting should offer a good chance of finding some.

Provisional Voting Rule Making at the State Level

Another reason to suspect partisan administration of provisional voting is because, prior to the 2004 election, provisional balloting was a source of partisan conflict in several states, particularly over the location in which provisional ballots needed to be cast. There were legal challenges in a few states over whether to count provisional ballots cast in the wrong precinct.[27] Five of the cases involved liberal or Democratic interests suing a Republican state election official. The other case involved Republican candidates suing the state board of elections (controlled by a Democratic majority).

Under a partisan theory of election administration we might expect Democratic election officials at the state level to promulgate more permissive rules for provisional ballots than Republican officials. State rules for counting provisional ballots varied in 2004. Seventeen states chose to count provisional ballots cast outside the correct precinct and 27 states chose not to count provisional ballots cast at the wrong precinct. In almost every case, the top election authority in the state chose the rule for counting provisional ballots.

We find some evidence suggesting that states with Democratic election officials are more likely than states with Republican officials to adopt a rule allowing provisional ballots cast outside the correct precinct, although the evidence is not strong. Nine out of 20 states with Democratic election officials adopted the more permissive standard, allowing provisional ballots cast in the wrong precinct, while only seven of 21 states with GOP election officials counted provisional ballots cast in the wrong precinct. The evidence of partisanship is stronger when we only consider "battleground" states where the outcome of the presidential election was in doubt. Six out of seven battleground states with Republican election officials chose to disallow provisional ballots cast in the wrong precinct, while four out of six battleground states with Democratic officials chose to allow provisional ballots cast in the wrong precinct.

Provisional Voting at the Local Level

While some states passed legislation to codify the provisional ballot requirement in HAVA, many states left the implementation of provisional voting to state and local election officials.[28] Thus, one might observe partisanship in the administration of provisional voting at the local level. A party operative might view provisional ballots as an extra pile of votes that could be included in the final tally. As a result, we expect that partisan administration of provisional voting is conditioned by the political leaning of the local constituency. That is, each party may prefer higher turnout if that means more of its own voters going to the polls, and each party may dislike higher turnout if it means more of the other party's voters going to the polls. For example, Republican officials may be more permissive with rules for casting and counting provisional ballots in a heavily Republican local jurisdiction. Similarly, if a Democratic official oversees a heavily Republican jurisdiction, he or she may be tempted to tighten rules for casting and counting provisional votes. This partisan dynamic played out in the Florida recount controversy in the 2000 presidential election. The Gore campaign, in trying to find more Democratic votes, asked for a manual recount in only four heavily Democratic counties run by Democratic election commissions.[29] Similarly, the Bush campaign pushed for more permissive standards for counting overseas absentee ballots in heavily Republican counties.[30] Thus, local party competition may interact with the partisanship of the local election official in the implementation of procedures that affect voter turnout.

We examined the impact of partisanship on the casting and counting of provisional ballots in the 2004 presidential election while controlling for a variety of legal, institutional, and demographic factors that also affect provisional balloting. We found evidence of a conditional effect of the partisanship of the local election official on the number of provisional ballots cast by voters and on the number of provisional votes counted by election authorities. For example, in heavily Republican jurisdictions, more provisional ballots were likely to be cast and counted under a Republican election official than a Democratic election official. Similarly, provisional ballots were more likely to be cast and counted in heavily Democratic jurisdictions if the local election authority was a Democrat.

The partisan effects we found are substantial. Based on our analysis, we estimated the number of provisional votes counted in a medium-sized local jurisdiction in the 2004 election under different circumstances depending on the party affiliation of the local election official and the political leaning of the jurisdiction. As Figure 6.3 indicates, in a heavily Republican county, over 100 additional provisional ballots would be counted if the election was administered by a Republican rather than a Democrat. Similarly, in a heavily Democratic locality, more than 100 additional provisional ballots would be counted if the election official was a Democrat rather than a Republican. Meanwhile, the party affiliation of the election official had little effect on provisional voting in a competitive local jurisdiction with an equal number of voters from each party. The results are consistent with a theory that local election officials may work to influence voter turnout in ways that benefit their political party.

There is other evidence of a relationship between the partisanship of election officials and election outcomes. Anna Bassi, Rebecca Morton and Jessica Troustine

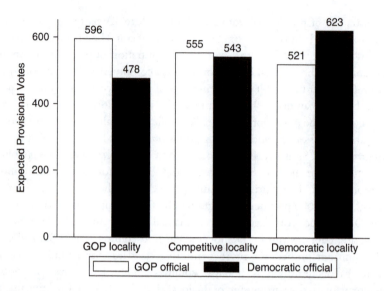

FIGURE 6.3 Expected Number of Accepted Provisional Ballots in the 2004 General Election by Partisanship of Local Official and Jurisdiction's Voters
Source: Kimball, Kropf, and Battles (2005)

examine voting in gubernatorial elections from 1990–2000. As they report, the impact of local election officials on turnout exhibits a pattern similar to our study.

> We find that when the local registrar changes parties turnout declines over-all but the effect is much larger for new Republican registrars than for Democratic registrars. Additionally, new Republican registrars decrease Democratic turnout to a greater extent than new Democratic registrars decrease Republican turnout. We find that both parties' registrars affect the margin of victory in their counties.[31]

In addition, Bassi and her colleagues examine mechanisms by which state governments might limit the discretion of local election officials. They focus on two state institutions: (1) whether the state purchases voting equipment for all local jurisdictions; and (2) whether the state appoints a bipartisan board to monitor election administration at the local level. Both mechanisms tend to reduce the variation in voter turnout across local jurisdictions within a state. This suggests that there are effective options available to states to reduce the discretion of local election officials.

Some other studies that examine elections within a particular state also find evidence of partisan election administration. For example, Guy Stuart analyzes the use of centralized lists to purge felons from the voting rolls in Florida before the 2000 presidential election.[32] Despite the fact that the felon lists contained many errors, Stuart finds that counties with Republican election administrators purged voter rolls more aggressively than counties with Democratic election administrators. The results are consistent with partisan self-interest in that Democrats are thought to benefit (and Republicans suffer) from expanded voter rolls. Similarly, James T. Hamilton and Helen F. Ladd find evidence that Republican county election boards strategically manipulated ballot formats to influence straight-party voting in the 1992 election in North Carolina.[33] Other studies note efforts of partisan manipulation of election laws and procedures within particular states.[34]

Another recent study provides evidence about the impact of partisan local election officials on election outcomes. Josh Dyck and Nicholas R. Seabrook (2009) examine Oregon, which has held vote-by-mail elections for many years.[35] Local election officials mail ballots only to those individuals whose registration is considered active. The purpose of the program seems relatively straightforward, yet state laws and regulations provide little direction about which voters should be considered inactive. As a result, local election officials have autonomy in moving voters to inactive status. Dyck and Seabrook find bias in the inactivation assignment in that "Democratic registrants in counties with Republican clerks are significantly more likely to be moved to inactive status than other registrants."[36] However, they find no evidence that Democratic county clerks differ from non-partisan clerks. One interesting feature of the study is that county clerks in Oregon do not run under a partisan label, but the authors argue that just because an official is elected as a nonpartisan does not necessarily make one nonpartisan. Dyck and Seabrook examine the Oregon voter registration database to determine the party registration of each election official. In any case, the study finds that the behavior of election administrators is partly explained by their party affiliation.

However, not all differences in election outcomes are due to partisan election administration. For example, variation in local treatment of absentee ballots formed the basis for Norm Coleman's challenge of Al Franken's win in the 2008 U.S. Senate election in Minnesota. During the recount, some absentee ballots provided additional votes for Al Franken, and different counties used different procedures and standards for determining which absentee ballots were returned in time to be counted.[37] We examined data on the number of absentee ballots rejected in each county in Minnesota in the 2008 Senate election. However, we found no evidence that the party affiliation of the county auditor accounted for differences in the number of rejected absentee votes in the Minnesota Senate election.

Nevertheless, there is a growing body of evidence that election officials from different political parties have different ideas about how elections should be administered. Furthermore, several studies have observed that Democratic and Republican election officials behave differently when implementing election laws. Below we consider some reform proposals designed to minimize the impact of partisanship in election management.

A Solution is Part of the Problem Definition

As noted above, a number of election observers have advocated proposals intended to produce more nonpartisan election administration. A prominent example is from Richard Hasen.[38] Under his plan, the top election official in each state would be appointed by the governor and require approval from a 75 percent supermajority in the legislature to be confirmed to the post. Hasen argues that the supermajority requirement would ensure that the person selected would be respected by both political parties. In some circumstances, Hasen would use the same confirmation process to select local election officials. On the state level, Hasen would like election chiefs to be long-term employees whose office would have a guaranteed budget in order to insulate them as much as possible from politics. He argues that these reforms would lead to more professionalized election administration at both the state and local level. One disadvantage of this approach is that it is much more likely that a local government appointing body will be completely dominated by a single party so that the proposed 75 percent supermajority approval requirement will not necessarily ensure a consensus, bipartisan candidate.

Other reform proposals focus on a code of ethics for election officials. The Center for Democracy and Election Management (CDEM) at American University goes a bit further and suggests in model legislation that the state election official may not:

(1) either directly or indirectly engage in any political campaign or in any partisan political activity except to vote;
(2) serve as an officer of any political party or any partisan organization;
(3) publicly support or oppose any candidate, including a candidate for any local, state, or federal office, or partisan organization; or allow his or her name to be used in connection with any activity of a political organization;
(4) make speeches on behalf of a political organization or any candidate;
(5) attend political gatherings;
(6) take a public position for or against or participate in a campaign to support or oppose any ballot initiative or ballot measure; and
(7) make any contribution to, or solicit funds on behalf of, any candidate, including a candidate for any local, state, or federal office, political party or partisan organization.[39]

Other groups such as Common Cause have also suggested similar restrictions in model state legislation.[40]

If these reforms are enacted, election officials may begin to look more like appointed judges. However, as with judges, it may be futile to try to wring partisan or other political beliefs and biases out of election officials. Hasen admits that judges sometimes hand down decisions that appear to be decidedly partisan.[41] Hasen suggests that while many scholars propose a bipartisan election commission so that the political parties can balance each other, this solution is simply not adequate, as a bipartisan election board may turn out to be as weak and ineffective as the Federal Election Commission. Professor Kenneth R. Mayer notes other arguments against nonpartisan election administration. He argues that long-term appointment of the chief election officer inhibits the public's ability to hold the person accountable and remove poorly performing officials from office in an election.[42] As Mayer notes, these are issues long discussed in studies of public administration and proposals for nonpartisan election administration "may be a case where perfection is the enemy of good enough."[43]

In addition, switching to nonpartisan election administration on the state and local level would prove difficult. Supporters would need to expend a great deal of political capital in order to see such a solution passed into law. Why? First, it would send the large number of partisan officials looking for a new line of work or force them to compete for their job in a new system. The National Association of Secretaries of State (an organization that includes most state election officials) recently defended the practice of partisan officials administering elections and continues to uphold that position.[44] Second, some states have home rule provisions that leave decisions about the structure of local government to towns or cities. These states tend to be in New England, which already has nonpartisan local election officials in most jurisdictions.[45] However, in other states home rule provisions may complicate efforts by the state government to change the way local election administrators are chosen. Beyond the practical issues, it seems clear that most policy is adopted when some sort of focusing event makes it possible. At a minimum, there would have to be an election catastrophe so large that it would be impossible for members of Congress or state legislators NOT to pass implementing legislation. The election of 2000 did not produce a fundamental shift in the way our country chooses election administrators. Thus, it would take a much bigger legitimacy crisis for people to take notice, or those beyond a few law professors, even influential law professors.

Conclusion

Election officials all over the United States have broadly varying partisan attitudes and attitudes about how elections should be administered. Additionally, election administration is hyper-decentralized, making oversight of such officials very difficult. Such conditions increase the possibility that local officials will use discretion in a partisan manner, influencing elections for one political party over another. Given these two conditions, perhaps it is somewhat difficult to understand why policymakers did not define at least part of the problem of elections as one of excessive discretion, what we call the human problem. Yet, consider the most direct answer to the problem: creating legislation to make all election officials non-partisan. For so many reasons, this solution to the problem is not tractable, nor is it a terribly politically popular position to take. Federal legislation to say all the states must have a non-partisan chief election officer who appoints all the officials is counter to the political culture of federalism in our country. Having 50 separate state legislatures makes such a large change unlikely. Defining the problem of elections as localism and partisanship, with a solution such as non-partisanship is impractical. Yet without considering the problem in this way, one almost guarantees some inequality.

This is a limit to election reform. Perhaps such solutions hold too many challenges for passage, not the least among which is active defense of current officials and practices by professional associations such as the National Association of Secretaries of State.[46] Not only that, non-partisan election administration would need to be passed by a large number of state legislatures who do not currently practice such administration, and a federal constitutional change to centralize elections would require three-quarters of the states to agree. As Heather Gerken points out, "if you are the party in control, what incentive do you have to abandon this important weapon in your political arsenal? It's not a coincidence that election reform proposals tend to come from the party out of power, which loses interest in reform the moment it gains a majority of seats."[47]

Creative academic scholars such as Gerken have suggested ways around those pathologies. We describe her Democracy Index in the concluding chapter, which requires no constitutional change and only a few federal statutory changes.[48]

Assuming that LEOs are sincere in efforts to implement election laws in a neutral manner, report after report indicates that pollworkers do not implement state laws in a neutral manner or consistently with the desires of the principals, in this case, the LEOs who hired them. Things become even more difficult to analyze when one considers what Alvarez and Hall call the principal–agent relationship between the local election official and the pollworkers he or she hires (or has someone hire, depending on the jurisdiction size). Since it has been so controversial in the last few years, voter identification has been the source of excellent and revealing research. While pollworkers have a great deal of discretion, especially in the largest jurisdictions where it is difficult to observe their actions, ultimately, the person who runs the election in the jurisdiction has the final say for policies, including the level and type of training and the amount of constraint he or she wishes to place on the pollworkers.

All this being said, we respect the position of those who must direct elections in our country. Among scholars who research elections, there are probably very few who would say that local officials do not find themselves in a nearly impossible situation. They are asked to implement national, state and local election policy with very little funding or support for training on the part of state or county officials who serve as their direct supervisors. Scholars such as Gerken seem to suggest that deferred maintenance occurs because of partisanship and localism, which is true to a certain extent, yet some is due to county budget processes and constraints. Localities have vastly different levels of capacity to run elections, as do the individuals who run the elections. While the work of local officials may affect capacity, many times such problems are beyond their control.[49] Report after report notes that states and localities consistently under-fund elections. Funding may be more important than partisanship for proper administration of elections and is mentioned in many of the scholarly treatments of bureaucrats. For example, many election officials in Missouri have opposed early voting simply because they cannot afford to implement it, according to Wendy Noren, formerly the Legislative Co-Chair Missouri County Clerks Association.[50] She observed that there are many innovations that local election officials would like to make, but could not afford them.[51] County governments are not likely to fund election improvements. "I've got county commissioners that don't mind spending one million dollars on a road that will serve 1,000 people. But the thought of needing a million dollars for election equipment that'll serve 60,000 people is just beyond comprehension to them," Noren said.

Let us be more clear. We have talked to dozens of election officials (many are stated partisans) who run elections professionally, and take every opportunity to help voters learn how to use new equipment and educate them about how to make choices. Some argue that partisanship is only a matter of convenience for them. In fact, one local official told one of us that she switches her party affiliation whenever a new governor of a different party is elected. We have attended state-level training seminars where election officials are eager to learn more about what they can do to improve elections. Some, such as Mecklenburg County, North Carolina's Election Director Michael Dickerson, who works under a Democratically-led bipartisan board, has reached out to academics and other experts to help him gather and analyze data to improve election procedures. He sends his staff to state seminars. County data are available for download on the Mecklenburg County Board of Elections website.

Richard H. Pildes wrote before the renewal of the Voting Rights Act in 2006,

> "[w]e are still in the early stages of reverse engineering ourselves out of the pathological decentralization of American elections, even national elections, that is a path-dependent product of America's unique political history—including, ironically, the fact that American democracy was established over 200 years ago and has endured since."[52]

Another scholar, Alec Ewald argues that we have incrementally moved toward more federal control of elections to the point we have "overlapping and shared authority" over many areas of elections.[53] Yet, even with the most recent change—the Help America Vote Act of 2002—we are seeing partisan effects in election administration, as shown by the evidence in this chapter. HAVA accomplished quite a bit. However, without defining at least part of the problem of elections as a lack of oversight over officials who have partisan attitudes that affect administration, any solution to problems in election administration is only a partial solution.

7

CONCLUSION

What Have Reforms Accomplished?

> Even if it is questionable whether governmental officials have solved a problem, they sometimes feel that they have addressed it by passing legislation or making an administrative decision. If they have, they turn their attention elsewhere, and then that subject drops from their agendas.
>
> (John S. Kingdon, *Agendas, Alternatives and Public Policies*)

The 2000 election controversy provided a focusing event that led to significant election reforms in the United States. Michael Traugott once likened election administration to planning for floods. In describing the 2000 election he noted, "They have this concept of designing for a 50-year-flood or a 100-year-flood. This was a once-in-a-lifetime election."[1] The "once-in-a-lifetime election" sparked changes in states and in federal legislation. In HAVA, federal lawmakers largely defined the problem as a voting equipment issue to be addressed via an infusion of funds to the states for new voting equipment. The political culture of federalism in our country, and the feeling that new voting equipment addressed concerns about voting access and election integrity made this approach the most viable.

More than ten years have elapsed since the 2000 presidential election, and more than eight years have transpired since the passage of the Help America Vote Act (HAVA). Enough time has passed that we are now in a position to assess the impact of the election reforms in HAVA. It is important to make such an evaluation since HAVA involves significant changes in election administration in the United States. Furthermore, the United States holds more elections, and elects more public officials, than other countries.[2] If elections are going to accurately reflect the voice of the people, then it is also important to apply a critical eye to election administration to continue to improve the way elections are managed.

As we noted in the first two chapters, HAVA largely defines the problem of elections in terms of voting technology. Not surprisingly, the biggest impact of HAVA is a substantial change in the voting equipment Americans use to cast their ballots. In 2010, most Americans voted on equipment that was not available in their jurisdiction ten years earlier. Lever voting machines appear to be extinct in the United States (except for a few remaining in New York for use in local elections, where we predict they won't last long), and with the exception of a handful of counties in Idaho, punch card ballots are no longer used. The vast majority of American voters now cast their ballots on electronic voting machines or optically scanned ballots.

The change in voting equipment has produced positive returns by reducing the frequency of residual votes, as we demonstrate in Chapter 3. The widespread adoption of voting technology with an error prevention feature has substantially reduced the number of residual votes in presidential elections. In addition, the replacement of all lever machines and some full-face electronic voting machines has reduced the number of undervotes on ballot measures. New voting equipment has improved the accuracy of voting.

One way to view this progress is to consider the major disputed election outcomes in recent years. In the 2000 presidential election in Florida, residual votes (due to the two-column ballot design and the use of punch cards in many counties) were the main source of controversy. However, in more recent election recount disputes, since the change in voting technology, other issues have supplanted residual votes as the primary object of litigation and conflict. For example, in the drawn-out recount of votes in the 2008 U.S. Senate race in Minnesota between Norm Coleman and Al Franken, absentee ballots were the main source of conflict.[3] In the race for a Senate seat from Alaska in 2010, the main issue involved write-in votes for incumbent Lisa Murkowski.[4] A disputed election for juvenile court judge in Hamilton County, Ohio in 2010 appears to hinge on the disposition of provisional ballots.[5] The most recent election recount involves a Wisconsin Supreme Court election in April of 2011. The main source of controversy in that election is a county clerk's failure to include results from one town in the canvass of votes on the day after the election.[6] Unlike Florida in 2000, the more recent election disputes did not focus heavily on residual votes.

Edward Foley notes that election recount controversies tend to focus on "uncounted ballots" in which the voter's intent or the ballot's legitimacy may not be firmly established on Election Day. Uncounted ballots can include residual votes, provisional ballots, and rejected or late-arriving absentee ballots.[7] Since residual votes have been reduced due to new voting technology, other sources of uncounted ballots are now more likely to be the focus of election disputes. For example, in the 2008 presidential election residual votes (approximately 1.4 million) were exceeded by provisional ballots (almost 1.8 million) and rejected or uncertain absentee ballots (over 2.4 million).[8] Another election such as Florida in 2000 is less likely to happen. Future post-election disputes are more likely to focus on absentee and provisional ballots than residual votes. By reducing one source of post-election controversy, HAVA has made some progress in improving elections.

While new voting technology has produced some positive outcomes, there also is a downside to defining election reform primarily in terms of technology. After the 2000 election and the passage of HAVA, many election officials and policymakers quickly adopted new voting equipment, without considering all features or how the new equipment would be used. When criticism of electronic voting machines increased beginning in 2004, some of the same policymakers quickly replaced recently purchased DRE machines with something else. The whiplash in equipment changes increased the cost of election administration and did little to improve voter confidence.

Furthermore, despite the substantial federal funding provided to purchase new equipment and implement other reforms, HAVA increased the cost of administering elections. Particularly during the recent economic recession, election officials have struggled to find ways to reduce administrative costs. A fairly common solution is to consolidate polling places, which reduces the number of voting machines that need to be purchased and the number of poll workers that need to be hired, trained, and paid. Unfortunately, some evidence indicates that consolidating polling places reduces voter turnout. This may be one of the unintended consequences of HAVA.

The focus on equipment has also deflected attention from broader concerns about the design of ballots and other election supplies. As we showed in Chapter 5, ballot design is a key source of voting errors. Furthermore, compared to the costs of new technology, creating more usable election materials is a relatively inexpensive reform. The good news is that the EAC and several design professionals have made clear design recommendations for a variety of election materials, including ballots, voting instructions, and registration forms. It remains to be seen whether election officials follow those recommendations.

The largest blind spot in election reform since the 2000 election involves the human side of election administration. The decentralized nature of election administration in the United States is remarkable, and it affords state and local officials considerable discretion when they manage elections. While decentralized election administration provides tremendous opportunities for innovation, it should provoke a closer examination of the people who administer elections. We find that many election officials are partisans. In addition, Republican and Democratic election officials have different policy preferences on proposals to increase access to voting and combat fraud, especially in jurisdictions with many voters (where the political stakes are the highest). Finally, there is growing evidence that partisan election officials can put their thumb on the scale of administration to help their political party. This should be troubling to anyone interested in fair elections.

Election officials have been compared to umpires or referees in sports, making sure the game is played fairly.[9] Consider umpires in professional baseball.

Umpires go through lengthy and rigorous training to advance in their profession. Like the athletes they observe, umpires must prove through their performance that they are the best in order to make it to the big leagues. Even when they reach the height of their profession, league officials carefully monitor the performance of umpires and inform them about areas where improvement is needed. The same degree of professional development, monitoring and feedback is lacking for election officials. Having such systems does not ensure that an umpire will never make a bad call. In 2010, for example, umpire Jim Joyce acknowledged that he made a bad call, ending Detroit Tigers pitcher Armando Galarraga's chance for a perfect game. However, Galarraga did not complain and promptly got the next batter out.[10] Good sportsmanship helped, but so did having an umpire whose skill had been tested over and over—a "legitimate" umpire, who simply made a mistake.

If election administration is going to be like the big leagues, then greater attention should be given to the manner in which election officials are selected, the ways in which they carry out their duties, and who is responsible for oversight of their performance. In Chapter 6 we described some proposed changes in the selection methods and codes of ethics for election officials. These ideas should receive more attention. A stronger code of ethics, drawing a brighter line between election administration and political activities, seems more feasible and more urgent in the short term. Within the past two years at least five secretaries of state (Democrat Debra Bowen in California, Democrat Robin Carnahan in Missouri, Republican Todd Rokita in Indiana, Democrat Jennifer Brunner in Ohio, and Democrat Natalie Tennant in West Virginia) have run for another office while continuing to serve as the top election administrator in their state. This presents a clear conflict of interest, between winning one's own election and overseeing fair elections. Voters should be skeptical of election officials who claim to pursue both goals at the same time.

While HAVA has produced a mix of intended and unintended consequences, it also illustrates the limits of election reform. Despite the heavy reliance on elections in American democracy, election administration is usually not a priority for policymakers or the public. Without a focusing crisis, the impetus for serious election reform is usually lacking. Election systems are really only tested when we have a very close election. When election reform is attempted, the issue is typically defined in limited terms (for example, as a technology problem) which rules out other areas in need of improvement. Partisan conflicts over the goals of election reform stymie meaningful changes. Local administration of elections means that national and state election laws are sometimes implemented in ways not intended by lawmakers. Finally, the lack of resources for election administration diminishes the appetite for reform.

For all of these reasons, another large-scale election reform like HAVA is unlikely. The ballot design flaw in the 2006 election in Sarasota County, Florida caused some states to replace electronic voting machines, but action by the federal government has been limited. The most significant federal legislation since

HAVA is the Military and Overseas Voter Empowerment (MOVE) Act of 2010, which provides more time for military and overseas voters to receive absentee ballots and participate in elections. Legislation has been introduced to require a paper record on all electronic voting machines, but it has not received much consideration in Congress. Meanwhile, incremental changes continue, primarily at the state and local level, and there are growing efforts to gather and examine data on election administration. We close by considering some of these efforts.

The Future of Election Administration

Until the next election crisis serves as a focusing event, election reform in the United States is likely to be incrementally adopted at the state and local level. One incremental change that has spread quickly is the move toward non-precinct place voting. Since the late 1990s, more states and jurisdictions have allowed early voting and unexcused absentee voting. According to the National Conference of State Legislatures, about two-thirds of states and the District of Columbia offered early in-person voting before the 2010 midterm election. Approximately 30 states and DC offer no-excuse absentee voting.[11] These reforms are often appealing to election officials as a way to reduce the costs for voting equipment and poll workers. Perhaps such moves were originally thought to increase voter turnout, but scholars now recognize that early and no-excuse absentee voting mostly allow those who were planning to vote anyway a convenient alternative to voting in the precinct. And this alternative seems even more attractive when we are faced with long lines on Election Day because of fewer pieces of expensive voting equipment. While more non-precinct place voting is not necessarily the direct result of HAVA, there is the possibility of some unintended consequences.

Voting by mail may introduce some error one would not see with Election Day voting. In July of 2010, the *Cleveland Plain Dealer* reported that there were many errors in returned absentee ballots, disqualifying many of the ballots in Ohio. In the May primary,

> [s]ome forgot to include the form necessary to change political parties for that primary. Some forgot their social security or driver's license numbers. Others forgot to sign the required 'identification envelope,' seal that envelope, fill in other required lines or ... include the identification envelope at all when they mailed in their ballots.

Still others completely forgot to include the ballot itself! The Election Board reported that only about one-quarter of voters fixed their errors when notified.[12] Absentee ballots are typically counted at a central location. Thus, absentee voting lacks the error prevention mechanism available on most of the newer types of voting equipment used for in-person voting. This contributes to more voting mistakes on absentee ballots.

Evidence indicates that early voting does not provide much of a boost in voter turnout, and there is some concern about a long-term decrease in turnout with the demise of traditional neighborhood polling places.[13] One explanation for the long-term reduction in turnout may be that early voting negatively affects the civic exercise of Election Day. Dennis Thompson argues that the simultaneous nature of voting on the same day not only expresses the will of the majority but also gives all voters equal access to available information. Civic engagement in his view is also greatly decreased when the electorate is no longer voting at the same time. He points out that early voting contributes to a loss of civic engagement noting that "[v]oting alone may be worse than bowling alone."[14] One recent study conducted over a short period of time (from the 2000 to the 2004 elections) finds evidence of declining social capital as a result of moving to non-precinct place voting.[15] Despite these concerns, all signs indicate that early voting, voting centers, and other alternatives to Election Day voting will continue to grow. While conclusions about the impact of non-precinct voting are tentative, it would be unwise to uncritically accept the current reduction in the number of traditional neighborhood polling places. More evidence needs to be examined on the performance of alternatives in the timing and location of voting.

Alec Ewald has written a recent book arguing that local election administration has proven much more durable than federal policymakers could have imagined; understanding local administration holds the key to understanding our "right to vote."[16] Since local election officials understand the needs and behavior of voters in their constituency, innovations in election practices that enhance democracy tend to emerge at the local level. However, if innovations in election administration are most likely to emerge at the state and local level, then it is critical to have reliable data to compare the performance of elections in different state and local jurisdictions. For example, where are voting lines the longest? Which states or counties reject the most absentee ballots? Which jurisdictions have the most bloated registration rolls?

It is a positive sign that more election officials, lawmakers, advocacy groups, and other observers are tackling these issues. For example, Heather Gerken suggests a "Democracy Index" to rank state and local jurisdictions according to the degree to which they meet three election administration goals: (1) whether eligible citizens are able to register to vote; (2) whether registered voters are able to cast a ballot; and (3) whether all ballots are counted properly.[17] The measures would identify places where elections run smoothly and places in need of improvement, allowing voters in those jurisdictions to press for changes. Gerken also notes many examples where officials used performance data to improve election practices. In a related vein, other observers advocate regular audits of election counts, to verify that votes are counted accurately.[18]

Some advocate a bargain to simultaneously advance the interests of election administrators and reformers—provide federal funding to state and local jurisdictions for election administration in exchange for data on election practices.[19] Legislation was proposed by former Senators Barack Obama and Hillary Clinton to provide grants to create the Democracy Index.[20] Several organizations, including the Election Assistance Commission (EAC), the Pew Center on the States, the Caltech/MIT Voting Technology Project, and the Ohio State University Moritz College of Law, compile data and reports on election administration. The EAC, under part of its mandate from HAVA, has provided grants for studies of election administration and better data collection. All of these efforts support evidence-based democracy in the United States.

In an ominous sign, there are threats to the existence of the EAC. In the current period of large federal budget deficits, the EAC faces cuts in its annual budget. The National Association of Secretaries of State, chafing under the enhanced role of the federal government in elections since the passage of HAVA, has called for dissolving the EAC since 2005.[21] More recently, Representative Gregg Harper, the Republican chairperson of the House Elections Subcommittee, has introduced legislation to eliminate the Election Assistance Commission.[22] Under Harper's legislation, testing and certification of voting equipment would be transferred to the National Institute of Standards and Technology, and other reporting duties would be moved to the Federal Election Commission. In the current environment of divided government and partisan disagreement about the direction of election reform, the legislation is unlikely to pass during this session of Congress. However, two hearings have been held on the bill, which is more attention than many policy proposals receive in Congress.[23]

It strikes us as counterproductive to terminate the EAC. As we have argued in these pages, reliable evidence is needed to evaluate and improve election administration. Others have made a similar argument that a variety of data must be available for the purposes of transparency and measuring the performance of local election officials.[24] The EAC serves as an important central location for election administration data, particularly through the Election Administration and Voting Surveys (commonly known as the Election Day Surveys). Since 2004, the Election Day Surveys have gathered information about key features of elections in each local jurisdiction. The data collected in the surveys include information about registration, turnout, absentee voting, provisional voting, polling places, and poll workers. In addition, the information in the surveys has become more complete and more reliable over time.[25] It is important that these efforts continue. Election administration and election reforms are more successful when supported by reliable evidence.

NOTES ON THE TEXT

1 Introduction: The Context of Election Reform

1 See "2004 Governor's Race," www.secstate.wa.gov/elections/2004gov_race.aspx (accessed December 2, 2008).

2 Gary Fineout, "Voting Change Irks Supervisors," *Miami Herald*, May 24, 2007, 58.

3 Mark Songini, "Florida Bans Touch-Screen Voting Machines," *PC World*, May 22, 2007, http://www.pcworld.com/article/132138/florida_bans_touchscreen_voting_machines.html.

4 Laurin Frisina, Michael C. Herron, James Honaker, and Jeffrey B. Lewis, "Ballot Formats, Touchscreens, and Undervotes: A Study of the 2006 Midterm Elections in Florida," *Election Law Journal* 7(2008):25–47.

5 "Many Question Bush or Gore as Legitimate Winner," *Pew Research Center for People and the Press*, December 1, 2000, http://people-press.org/reports/display.php3?ReportID=22 (accessed July 29, 2007).

6 R. Michael Alvarez, Thad E. Hall and Morgan H. Llewellyn, "Are Americans Confident Their Ballots Are Counted?" *Journal of Politics* 70(2008):754–766.

7 *Reynolds v. Sims*, 377 U.S. 533. See also Richard L. Hasen, "After the Storm: The Uses, Normative Implications, and Unintended Consequences of Voting Reform Research in Post-*Bush v. Gore* Equal Protection Challenges," in Ann N. Crigler, Marion R. Just, and Edward J. McCaffery (eds.), *Rethinking the Vote: The Politics and Prospects of American Election Reform* (New York: Oxford University Press, 2004), 185–199.

8 Michael Traugott, "Why Electoral Reform Has Failed: If You Build It, Will They Come?" Ann N. Crigler, Marion R. Just, and Edward J. McCaffery (eds.), *Rethinking the Vote: The Politics and Prospects of American Election Reform* (New York: Oxford University Press, 2004), 167–184. See also Adam Berinsky, "The Perverse Consequences of Electoral Reform in the United States," *American Politics Research* 31(2004):1–21.

9 Alexander Keyssar, *The Right to Vote: The Contested History of Democracy in the United States* (New York: Basic Books, 2000).

10 Berinsky, "Perverse Consequences of Electoral Reform." Martha Kropf, Janine Parry, Jay Barth and E. Terrence Jones, "Pursuing the Early Voter: Does the Early Bird Get the Worm?" *Journal of Political Marketing* 7(2008):131–150.

11 In North Carolina, even the position of one's bedroom (one's "bedroom or usual sleeping area") determines one's voting precinct. Interestingly, if a couple is fighting and the husband sleeping in the guestroom, it is theoretically possible that two spouses may vote in different precincts! (NC §163–57); Wright, Don (General Counsel, State Board of Elections). 2007. "Residency Issues." Packet presented at "Two Days of Elections." School of Government, University of North Carolina at Chapel Hill.

12 Keyssar, *Right to Vote*, 151–159. See also, Roy Saltman, *The History and Politics of Voting Technology in the United States* (New York: Palgrave/Macmillan, 2006), 72, 134.

13 Keyssar, *Right to Vote*.

14 Despite the conventional wisdom, there is scholarly disagreement over the hypothesis that higher turnout helps Democrats. For example, see Michael D. Martinez and Jeff Gill, "The Effects of Turnout on Partisan Outcomes in U.S. Presidential Elections 1960–2000," *Journal of Politics* 67(2005):1248–1274.

15 John Fund, *Stealing Elections: How Voter Fraud Threatens Our Democracy* (New York: Encounter Books, 2004).

16 Frances Fox Piven and Richard A. Cloward, *Why Americans Don't Vote* (New York: Pantheon Books, 1988).

17 For a timeline of the events of November and December 2000, see http://archives. cnn.com/2000/ALLPOLITICS/stories/12/13/got.here/index.html (accessed June 26, 2007).

18 Al Gore, "Vice President Al Gore Delivers Remarks," December 13, 2000, http:// archives.cnn.com/2000/ALLPOLITICS/stories/12/13/gore.ends.campaign/index. html.

19 Jonathan N. Wand, et al., "The Butterfly Did It: The Aberrant Vote for Buchanan in Palm Beach County, Florida," *American Political Science Review* 95(2001):793–810.

20 Peter Whoriskey, "Protests Put West Palm 'On the Map' for Once...Focus is not on Glitter across the Bay," *Miami Herald*, November 10, 2000 (accessed via Newsbank, July 23, 2007).

21 See for example, Kirk Wolter, Diana Jergovic, Whitney Moore, Joe Murphy, and Colm O'Muircheartaigh, "Reliability of the Uncertified Ballots in the 2000 Presidential Election in Florida," *American Statistician* 57(2003):1–14.

22 Saltman, *History and Politics of Voting Technology*, 36.

23 Stephen Knack and Martha Kropf, "Who Uses Inferior Voting Technology?" *PS: Political Science and Politics* 35(2002):542 (Table 1).

24 Knack and Kropf, "Who Uses Inferior Voting Technology?"

25 *Bush v. Gore* 531 U.S. 98 (2000). end of Section IIA, 104. www.law.cornell.edu/ supct/html/00-949.ZPC.html (accessed July 29, 2007).

26 See William Raspberry, "Post-Traumatic Suggestions," *Washington Post*, January 1, 2001 (accessed via Lexis/Nexis).

27 Knack and Kropf, "Who Uses Inferior Voting Technology?"

28 Stephen Knack and Martha Kropf, "Voided Ballots in the 1996 Presidential Election: A County-Level Analysis," *Journal of Politics* 65(2003):881–897; D. E. "Betsy" Sinclair and R. Michael Alvarez, "Who Overvotes, Who Undervotes, Using Punchcards? Evidence from Los Angeles County," *Political Research Quarterly* 57(2004):15–25.

29 Caltech/MIT Voting Technology Project, *Voting: What Is, What Could Be*, July, 2001. http://www.vote.caltech.edu/drupal/node/10 (accessed December 15, 2001); Stephen Knack and Martha Kropf, "Roll-Off at the Top of the Ballot: Intentional Undervoting in American Presidential Elections," *Politics & Policy* 31(2003): 575–594.

30 U.S. Commission on Civil Rights, Office of Civil Rights Evaluation, "Is America Ready to Vote? Election Readiness Briefing Paper," 2004. www.law.umaryland.edu/ Marshall/usccr/documents/isamerreadyvote.pdf (accessed July 29, 2007).

31 The U.S. Commission on Civil Rights, "Voting Irregularities in Florida During the 2000 Presidential Election," June 2001. www.usccr.gov/pubs/vote2000/report/main. htm (accessed July 29, 2007).

32 Felons who live in Florida were not accorded the right to vote, even after their sentence was over.

33 In several states, convicted felons serving their sentences cannot vote, but also many states disenfranchise those who have served their prison terms. States often systematically purged voter registration rolls, leading to lawsuits contesting the practice in four states. See Kevin Johnson, "States Grapple with Voting Status of Felons," *USA Today*, November 3, 2008. www.usatoday.com/news/politics/election2008/2008-11-02-prison-vote_N.htm (accessed December 2, 2008).

34 Tova Andrea Wang, "Missouri Miseries." Century Foundation, 2004. http://tcf.org/commentary/2004/no757.

35 Christopher S. Bond, "'Motor Voter' Out of Control," *Washington Post*, June 27, 2001 (accessed via Lexis/Nexis, July 2, 2007).

36 Matt Blunt, "Mandate for Reform: Election Turmoil in St. Louis," November 7, 2000, Missouri Secretary of State's Office, July 24, 2001.

37 Carolyn Tuft, "Bond Wants Federal Investigation of Problems at City Polls," *St. Louis Post-Dispatch*, November 10, 2000 (accessed via Newsbank August 7, 2007).

38 But see R. Michael Alvarez, Thad Hall and Susan Hyde, eds., *Election Fraud: Detecting and Deterring Electoral Manipulation* (Washington, DC: Brookings Institution Press, 2008).

39 Daniel J. Palazzolo, "Election Reform After the 2000 Election," in Daniel J. Palazzolo and James W. Ceaser (eds.), *Election Reform: Politics and Policy* (Lanham, MD: Lexington Books, 2005), 3–15, 4.

40 Randall Strahan and Mathew Gunning, "Entrepreneurial Leadership and Election Reform in Georgia: 2001 to 2003," in Daniel J. Palazzolo and James W. Ceaser (eds.), *Election Reform: Politics and Policy* (Lanham, MD: Lexington Books, 2005), 59–73.

41 Gimpel and Dyck argue such changes were not necessarily the result of the 2000 election, but of events that had their genesis in the 1994 gubernatorial race. See James Gimpel and Joshua J. Dyck, "Maryland: Policy Entrepreneurship in a One-Party State," in Daniel J. Palazzolo and James W. Ceaser (eds.), *Election Reform: Politics and Policy* (Lanham, MD: Lexington Books, 2005), 74–89.

42 Century Foundation Working Group on State Implementation of Election Reform, *Balancing Access and Integrity* (New York: Century Foundation Press, 2005), 1–2.

43 Edward Walsh, "Election Reform Bill Is Passed by Senate; $3.86 Billion Allotted for Improvements," *Washington Post*, October 17, 2002 (accessed via Lexis/Nexis, July 2, 2007).

44 Ibid.

45 See for example, Steven M. Gillon, *"That's Not What We Meant to Do": Reform and Its Unintended Consequences in 20th Century America* (New York: Norton, 2000).

46 Bryan D. Jones and Frank R. Baumgartner, *The Politics of Attention: How Government Prioritizes Problems* (Chicago: University of Chicago Press, 2005), 14.

47 Ibid., 14.

48 Roger W. Cobb and Charles D. Elder, *Participation in American Politics: The Dynamics of Agenda Building* (Boston: Allyn and Bacon, 1972); John W. Kingdon, *Agendas, Alternatives and Public Policies*, 2nd ed. (New York: Harper Collins, 1995). Deborah Stone, *Policy Paradox: The Art of Political Decision Making*, revised edition (New York: Norton, 2002).

49 Stephen Ansolabehere and Charles Stewart, III, "Residual Votes Attributable to Technology," *Journal of Politics* 67(2005):365–389.

50 Saltman, *History and Politics of Voting Technology*.

51 Ibid., 155.
52 Roy G. Saltman, "Accuracy, Integrity and Security in Computerized Vote-Tallying," *Communications of the Association for Computing Machinery* 31(1988):1184–1191, 1218; Roy G. Saltman, *Accuracy, Integrity and Security in Computerized Vote-Tallying.* NBS Special Publication 500-158, 1988. www.itl.nist.gov/lab/specpubs/500–158.htm (accessed July 23, 2007).
53 Commission on Federal Election Reform, *Building Confidence in U.S. Elections,* September 2005, 19 www.tcf.org/publications/2001/7/pb246 (accessed June 19, 2007).

2 How Does Definition of the Problem Affect the Solution?

1 "Antiquated Voting System Needs Permanent Upgrade," *Atlanta Journal-Constitution,* A12, November 13, 2000.
2 Peter S. Goodman, "An Outcome Driven by Technology, High and Low," *Washington Post,* November 10, 2000, E1.
3 Deborah Zabarenko, "A Chad is Born: Debuting in 1890, It Stuck Around," *Washington Post,* November 24, 2000, A41.
4 Knack and Kropf, "Who Uses Inferior Voting Technology?" Saltman, *Accuracy, Integrity and Security*; Federal Election Commission, *Voting System Standards: A Report to the Congress on the Development of Voluntary Engineering and Procedural Performance Standards for Voting Systems.* Washington, DC: National Clearinghouse on Election Administration of the Federal Election Commission, 1982.
5 Saltman, *History and Politics of Voting Technology,* 28.
6 Caltech/MIT Voting Technology Project, *Voting: What Is, What Could Be*; Knack and Kropf, "Voided Ballots in the 1996 Presidential Election."
7 Knack and Kropf, "Voided Ballots in the 1996 Presidential Election"; Michael Tomz and Robert P. Van Houweling, "How Does Voting Equipment Affect the Racial Gap in Voided Ballots?" *American Journal of Political Science* 47(2003):46–60; R. Darcy and Anne Schneider, "Confusing Ballots, Roll-Off, and the Black Vote," *Western Political Quarterly* 42(1989):347–364.
8 *Bush v. Gore,* 531 U.S. 98 (2000).
9 John Conyers, "Voting Rights in Peril," *New York Times,* January 30, 2002.
10 Hasen, "After the Storm: The Uses, Normative Implications, and Unintended Consequences of Voting Reform Research in Post-*Bush v. Gore* Equal Protection Challenges."
11 For more on the federal government's legal role in election administration, see Trevor Potter and Marianne Holt Viray, "Federal Election Authority: Jurisdiction and Mandates," in Crigler et al., *Rethinking the Vote*; General Accounting Office, "The Scope of Congressional Authority in Election Administration," March 2001. www.gao.gov/new.items/d01470.pdf (accessed July 27, 2007).
12 Alex C. Ewald chronicles the level of control that localities have had over elections. He argues that "local administration of elections has proved far more durable than many reformers suspected" (*The Way We Vote: The Local Dimension of American Suffrage* (Nashville: Vanderbilt University Press, 2009)), 6.
13 David Broder, "Election Report Delivered to Bush." *Washington Post,* August 1, 2001.
14 Guy Stuart, "Databases, Felons, and Voting: Bias and Partisanship of the Florida Felons List in the 2000 Elections," *Political Science Quarterly* 119(2004):453–475.
15 Caltech/MIT Voting Technology Project, *Voting: What Is, What Could Be.*
16 Christopher S. Bond, "'Motor Voter' Out of Control."
17 Associated Press, "California Sued Over Ballots," *Miami Herald,* April 18, 2001, A16.
18 Strahan and Gunning, "Entrepreneurial Leadership and Election Reform."

19 Palazzolo, Daniel J. 2005. "Election Reform After the 2000 Election," in Daniel J. Palazzolo and James W. Ceaser (eds.), *Election Reform: Politics and Policy* (Lanham, MD: Lexington Books), 4.

20 Steve Bousquet, "Florida's Best Buy for Better Elections Not Clear," *Miami Herald,* January 20, 2001, A1.

21 Mark Silva, "Lawmakers Negotiating Election-Reform Bill," *Miami Herald,* May 1, 2001, B6.

22 Mark Silva and Steve Bousquet, "Punch-Card Ballots Banished as of 2002," *Miami Herald,* May 5, 2001, A19.

23 Bill Rankin, "Cox: State's Vote Gap Nearly Twice U.S. Norm," *Atlanta Journal-Constitution,* December 29, 2000, D1.

24 Strahan and Gunning, "Entrepreneurial Leadership and Election Reform."

25 Bill Rankin, "Uniform Voting System May Meet Opposition—2001 Georgia Legislature," *Atlanta Journal-Constitution,* January 3, 2001, B6.

26 Aviel D. Rubin, *Brave New Ballot: The Battle to Safeguard Democracy in the Age of Electronic Voting* (New York: Morgan Road Books, 2006), 29.

27 Brigid Schulte, "Jolted Over Electronic Voting," *Washington Post,* August 11, 2003, sec. A1.

28 Kim Zetter, "Maryland E-Voting Passes Muster," *Wired News,* September 25, 2003.

29 Douglas W. Jones, "Confusion of Myth and Fact in Maryland," University of Iowa, Department of Computer Science. www.divms.uiowa.edu/~jones/voting/myth-fact-md.html (accessed August 18, 2004).

30 "Testing the System," *Sioux City Journal,* November 4, 2001 (accessed via Newsbank, June 15, 2010).

31 Associated Press, "Task Force Decides Against Unified Voting System," *Dubuque Telegraph Herald,* May 15, 2001, A5 (accessed via Newsbank, June 15, 2010).

32 James Q. Lynch, "Old Voting Machines on Way Out," *Gazette,* October 15, 2002 (accessed via Newsbank, June 15, 2010).

33 Warren Christopher, "The Stalling of Election Reform," *New York Times* September 15, 2002.

34 Century Foundation, *Balancing Access and Integrity.*

35 Remarks of Senator Christopher Bond (R-MO), "Help America Vote Act of 2002—Conference Report," S10488, October 16, 2002.

36 Remarks of Senator Edward Kennedy (D-MA), "Help America Vote Act of 2002—Conference Report," S10488, October 16, 2002.

37 Robert Montjoy, "HAVA and the States," in Palazzolo and Ceaser, *Election Reform.*

38 The National Voter Registration Act specified that states should have failsafe measures in the case of moving voters. However, by the 2008 election, scholars found that as many as three million people did not cast votes because of registration problems. See R. Michael Alvarez, et al., "2008 Survey of the Performance of American Elections: Final Report," www.pewcenteronthestates.org/uploadedFiles/Final%20report20090218.pdf.

39 Timothy Vercellotti, "Embracing Change at the Polls: Election Administrators and the Provisional Ballot in 2004," paper presented at the 2007 Midwest Political Science Association Meeting, Chicago, IL, 2.

40 Eagleton Institute of Politics, Report to the U.S. Election Assistance Commission On Best Practices to Improve Provisional Voting: Pursuant to the HELP AMERICA VOTE ACT OF 2002, Public Law 107-252. Submitted by the Eagleton Institute of Politics, Rutgers, State University of New Jersey; and the Moritz College of Law, Ohio State University, June 28, 2006. In the interests of full disclosure, Kropf assisted as a peer reviewer on this study.

41 Sarah F. Liebschutz and Daniel J. Palazzolo, "HAVA and the States," *Publius* 35(2005):497–514.

42 HAVA, Section 303a1B.

43 Electionline.org, "Assorted Rolls: Statewide Voter Registration Databases Under HAVA," June 1, 2005, www.pewcenteronthestates.org/report_detail.aspx?id=35430 (accessed May 17, 2011).

44 Eagleton Institute of Politics, Report to the U.S. Election Assistance Commission On Best Practices to Improve Provisional Voting, page 5.

45 "EAC Requests Review of Voter ID, Vote Fraud and Voter Intimidation Research Projects." April 16, 2007 (www.eac.gov, last accessed June 18, 2007).

46 David C. Kimball and Martha Kropf. "Assessing Election Reform Four Years After Florida." Paper presented at the Annual Meeting of the Southern Political Science Association, New Orleans, LA, January 2005.

47 Kimball and Kropf, "Assessing Election Reform."

48 In some counties, mainly in New England and in areas with heavy absentee or early voting, not all ballots are cast using the same technology. In those cases, we code the voting technology as the equipment used by at least 75 percent of the voters. If no single method was used by at least 75 percent of the voters, the county's voting technology is coded as a "mixed" system.

49 Precinct scanners are typically programmed to alert voters of overvotes, but are often not programmed to identify undervotes.

50 Some counties have precinct-count optical scan balloting but do not activate the error correction feature when scanning the ballots. These counties are coded as central-count systems.

51 The Justice Department had to file suit against the state of New York because of its delays in transitioning to newer machines, especially those accessible to the disabled. A court order in 2009 stated that the state must acquire technology usable for the disabled in 2009, and replace all the lever machines. The reason for New York's delays are rather complicated, but include partisanship and trying to fit new technology into the framework of New York's election laws. For example, state law requires the entire ballot to be shown at once. Then, the state legislature allowed the use of DRE machines. See Eric Lipton, "Vote Machine Replacement Lags, Despite Age," *New York Times*, October 20, 2003, A1. Interestingly, in 2010, the New York General Assembly passed a law allowing the use of lever machines in school district elections and ballot questions, to end at the conclusion of 2012 (Consolidated Laws of New York, Education Law § 2035, Use of voting machines at school district meetings). In 2011, the State Assembly was considering similar laws for village, special district, library district or fire district elections (see http://assembly.state.ny.us/, last accessed February 5, 2011).

52 As Table 2.1 indicates, the number of mixed voting systems has increased somewhat in recent years. This is due to the significant growth of early voting (in-person or by absentee ballot). Some states and counties use different voting equipment for early voting than for Election Day voting.

3 Did the Reforms Increase Accuracy?

1 Martin Merzer, "Review Shows Ballots Say Bush Floridians Zany, Creative in Spoiling Their Ballots," *Miami Herald*, April 4, 2001, A1. (Accessed via Newsbank, February 5, 2011).

2 David C. Kimball and Martha Kropf, "Ballot Design and Unrecorded Votes on Paper-Based Ballots," *Public Opinion Quarterly*, 69 (2005):508–529.

3 Ansolabehere and Stewart, III, "Residual Votes Attributable to Technology"; Caltech/MIT Voting Technology Project, *Voting: What Is, What Could Be*, July.

4 Some of the studies which show this variation among types of voting equipment include Charles Bullock and Richard E. Dunn, "Election Roll-Off: A Test of Three Explanations," *Urban Affairs Review*, 32 (1996):71–86; Knack and Kropf, "Voided Ballots in the 1996 Presidential Elections,"; David C. Kimball, Chris T. Owens, and Katherine M. Keeney, "Unrecorded Votes and Election Reform," *Spectrum: The Journal of State Government*, 76(2003):34–37; and Martin P. Wattenberg, Ian McAllister, and Anthony Salvanto, "How Voting Is Like Taking an SAT Test: An Analysis of American Voter Roll-off," *American Politics Quarterly*, 28(2000): 234–250.

5 An example is Knack and Kropf, "Roll-Off at the Top of the Ballot."

6 See Charles Stewart, III, "Residual Vote in the 2004 Election," *Election Law Journal*, 5(2006):158–169; R. Michael Alvarez, Stephen Ansolabehere, and Charles Stewart, III, "Studying Elections: Data Quality and Pitfalls in Measuring of Effects of Voting Technologies," *Policy Studies Journal*, 33(2005):15–24.

7 A word of thanks is in order for many election officials that assisted us, as well as Lindsay Battles, Cassie Gross, Matt McLaughlin, Susan Mason, Jeremiah Olson, and Chris Owens for research assistance.

8 For a comparison, see Stewart, "Residual Vote in the 2004 Election," Alvarez, et al., "Studying Elections,"; and CalTech/MIT, "Voting."

9 Knack and Kropf, "Voided Ballots in the 1996 Presidential Election"; Sinclair and Alvarez, "Who Overvotes, Who Undervotes, Using Punchcards? Evidence from Los Angeles County"; and Wattenberg, et al., "How Voting Is Like Taking an SAT Test."

10 R. Michael Alvarez and Thad E. Hall, *Electronic Elections: The Perils and Promises of Digital Democracy* (Princeton, NJ: Princeton University Press, 2008).

11 A similar approach is used in some other work in this area. Examples are Stewart, "Residual Vote in the 2004 Election," and Michael J. Hanmer, et al., "Losing Fewer Votes: The Impact of Changing Voting Systems on Residual Votes," *Political Research Quarterly* 63(2010):129–142.

12 See Stewart, "Residual Vote in the 2004 Election."

13 Tomz and Houweling, "How Does Voting Equipment Affect the Racial Gap in Voided Ballots?"; Michael C. Herron and Jasjeet S. Sekhon, "Overvoting and Representation: An Examination of Overvoted Presidential Ballots in Broward and Miami-Dade Counties," *Electoral Studies*, 22(2003):21–47; Kimball and Kropf, "Ballot Design and Unrecorded Votes on Paper-Based Ballots," 522–524; Knack and Kropf, "Voided Ballots in the 1996 Presidential Election,"; Stephen M. Nichols, "State Referendum Voting, Ballot Roll-Off, and the Effect of New Electoral Technology," *State and Local Government Review*, 30(1998):106–117; David C. Kimball, Chris T. Owens, and Katherine M. Keeney, "Unrecorded Votes and Political Representation," in Robert P. Watson, (ed.), *Counting Votes: Lessons from the 2000 Presidential Election in Florida* (Gainesville, FL: University Press of Florida, 2004), 135–150; Robert Darcy and Anne Schneider, "Confusing Ballots, Roll-Off, and the Black Vote,"; Justin Buchler, Matthew Jarvis, and John E. McNulty, "Punch Card Technology and the Racial Gap in Residual Votes," *Perspectives on Politics*, 2 (2004):517–524; Paul Moke and Richard B. Saphire, "The Voting Rights Act and the Racial Gap in Lost Votes," *Hastings Law Journal* 58 (2006):1–59.

14 For ease of presentation, we leave the middle groups out of the graphs in Figures 3.3 and 3.4. The middle groups have residual vote rates in between the extremes shown in the graphs.

15 See Bullock and Dunn, "Election Roll-Off,"; James M. Vanderleeuw and Glenn H. Utter, "Voter Roll-Off and the Electoral Context: A Test of Two Theses," *Social Science Quarterly*, 74(1993):664–673; Michael C. Herron and Jasjeet S. Sekhon, "Black

Candidates and Black Voters: Assessing the Impact of Candidate Race on Uncounted Vote Rates," *Journal of Politics*, 67(2005):154–177.

16 Two recent exceptions are Michael J. Hanmer and Michael W. Traugott, "The Impact of Vote-By-Mail on Voter Behavior," *American Politics Research*, 32(2004):375–405; and Sinclair and Alvarez, "Who Overvotes, Who Undervotes, Using Punchcards?"

17 "Initiative Use," Initiative and Referendum Institute, last modified September 2010, www.iandrinstitute.org/IRI%20Initiative%20Use%20(2010-1).pdf.

18 There are multiple examples of this finding, including the work of scholars such as Stephen M. Nichols and Gregory A. Strizek, "Electronic Voting Machines and Ballot Roll-Off," *American Politics Quarterly*, 23(1995):300–318; Nichols, "State Referendum Voting"; Susan King Roth, "Disenfranchised by Design: Voting Systems and the Election Process," *Information Design Journal* 9(1998):29–38; David C. Kimball and Martha Kropf., "Voting Technology, Ballot Measures and Residual Votes," *American Politics Research*, 36(2008):479–509.

19 Paul S. Herrnson, et al., *Voting Technology: The Not-So-Simple Act of Casting a Ballot* (Washington, DC: Brookings Institution Press, 2008).

20 Ibid.

21 We have placed some examples of full-face ballot layouts on the Internet at www.umsl.edu/~kimballd/havalimits.html.

22 Kimball and Kropf, "Voting Technology, Ballot Measures and Residual Votes."

23 In elections with multiple ballot measures, we compute the average residual vote rate for all questions on the ballot. The patterns in Figure 3.5 are the same if we examine a single measure in each election.

24 Kimball and Kropf, "Voting Technology, Ballot Measures and Residual Votes," 497–499.

25 Very similar results hold when examining other ballot measures in the same election.

4 At What Cost? The Unintended Consequences of Reform

1 For an excellent discussion and assessment of arguments against electronic voting machines, see Alvarez and Hall, *Electronic Elections: The Perils and Promises of Digital Democracy*.

2 Electionline.org, "Back to Paper: A Case Study," February 21, 2008, www.pewcenteronthestates.org/report_detail.aspx?id=35628 (accessed March 15, 2008).

3 Richard Wolf, "Voting Equipment Changes Could Get Messy on Nov. 4," *USA Today*, October 29, 2008, www.usatoday.com/news/politics/election2008/2008-10-28-votingequipment_N.htm (accessed July 9, 2010).

4 For a more detailed summary of security issues, see Saltman, *The History and Politics of Voting Technology: In Quest of Integrity and Public Confidence*; Alvarez and Hall, *Electronic Elections*; and Saltman, *Accuracy, Integrity and Security*.

5 Saltman, *History and Politics of Voting Technology*, ch. 6.

6 Alvarez et al., "Are Americans Confident Their Ballots Are Counted?"; Charles Stewart, III, "Election Technology and the Voting Experience in 2008," Caltech/MIT Voting Technology Project. VTP Working Paper #71, March 2009; Thad E. Hall, "Electronic Elections in a Politicized Polity," Caltech/MIT Voting Technology Project, VTP Working Paper #76, June 2009.

7 Herrnson, et al., *Voting Technology*. For another comparison of voting system performance, see Alvarez and Hall, *Electronic Elections*, ch. 6.

8 Alvarez and Hall, *Electronic Elections*; Charles S. Bullock, III, M.V. Hood, III, and Richard Clark, "Punch Cards, Jim Crow and Al Gore: Explaining Voter Trust in the Electoral System in Georgia, 2000," *State Politics & Policy Quarterly* 5(2005): 284–294.

9   Alvarez and Hall, *Electronic Elections*, ch. 4.
10 For example, see Tadayoshi Kohno, Adam Stubblefield, Aviel D. Rubin, and Dan S. Wallach, *Analysis of an Electronic Voting System*, Technical Report TR-2003-19 (Baltimore: Johns Hopkins University Information Security Institute, 2003).
11 "Don't Rush," *Crain's Business Cleveland*, December 11, 2000 (accessed via Newsbank, August 2, 2010).
12 "Ohio Voters Whiplashed by Changes," *Dayton Daily News*, January 14, 2005, A8 (accessed via Newsbank, August 2, 2010).
13 See Election Law@Moritz for a summary of the major election court cases monitored by the Moritz College of Law at Ohio State University. http://moritzlaw.osu.edu/ electionlaw/ (accessed July 30, 2010).
14 "A Statewide Voting Standard," *Toledo Blade*, February 18, 2001, B4 (accessed via Newsbank, August 2, 2010).
15 Lee Leonard, "Legislature May Be Stuffing the Ballot Box on Voting Reforms," *Columbus Dispatch*, October 15, 2001, 7A (accessed via Newsbank, August 2, 2010).
16 Sabrina Eaton, "Elections Officials Eager to Repair Shortcomings," *Cleveland Plain Dealer*, December 18, 2000 (accessed via Newsbank, August 2, 2010).
17 Richard B. Saphire and Paul Moke, "Litigating *Bush v. Gore* in the States: Dual Voting Systems and the Fourteenth Amendment," *Villanova Law Review*, 51(2006):229–298. In the interest of full disclosure, we assisted in the ACLU lawsuit to replace punch card ballots in Ohio.
18 Mark Naymik and Julie Carr Smyth, "State to Buy Voting Machines," *Cleveland Plain Dealer*, February 26, 2003, B1 (accessed via Newsbank, August 2, 2010).
19 Fritz Wenzel, "State Halts Lucas Plans for New Voting Machines," *Toledo Blade*, February 26, 2003, A1 (accessed via Newsbank, August 2, 2010). Lucas County began to make plans to lease equipment. Allen County leased DREs for its May 2003 primary. At least two other small counties borrowed/leased touch screen machines as well.
20 Paul E. Kostyu, "Electronic Voting Expected by 2004 Election," *Times Reporter*, April 23, 2003 (accessed via Newsbank, August 2, 2010).
21 "New Voting Machines Flawed, Experts Claim," *Toledo Blade*, July 25, 2003, B1 (accessed via Newsbank, August 2, 2010).
22 Julie Carr Smyth, "State Postpones Vote Machine Deadlines," *Cleveland Plain Dealer*, August 20, 2003, B3 (accessed via Newsbank, August 2, 2010).
23 Kim Bates, "Wood County Asked to OK Funds to Buy Vote Machines," *Toledo Blade*, November 12, 2003, B1 (accessed via Newsbank, August 2, 2010).
24 Julie Carr Smyth, "Statewide Electronic Voting Delayed: Review Uncovers Security Problems," *Cleveland Plain Dealer*, December 3, 2003, A1 (accessed via Newsbank, August 2, 2010).
25 Michael Scott, "Lake County Scraps Old Electronic Voting Machines," *Cleveland Plain Dealer*, September 8, 2006, B1 (accessed via Newsbank, August 3, 2010).
26 Ann McFeatters, "Congress Certifies Bush Re-Election: Democrats Force Four-Hour Delay with Rarely Invoked Challenge," *Toledo Blade*, January 7, 2005, A3 (accessed via Newsbank, August 3, 2010).
27 Alvarez and Hall, *Electronic Elections*, 122.
28 Michael Powell and Peter Slevin, "Several Factors Contributed to 'Lost' Voters in Ohio," *Washington Post*, December 15, 2004, A1.
29 Benjamin Highton, "Long Lines, Voting Machine Availability, and Turnout: The Case of Franklin County, Ohio in the 2004 Presidential Election," *PS: Political Science and Politics*, January(2006):65–68.
30 Julie Carr Smyth, "Ohio Pulls Plug on Electronic Voting," *Cleveland Plain Dealer*, January 13, 2005, A1 (accessed via Newsbank, August 3, 2010).

31 "Dumping the Touch-Screens," *Toledo Blade*, January 16, 2005, B4 (accessed via Newsbank, August 3, 2010).

32 Robert Vitale, "Paper Ballots Could Cost County," *Columbus Dispatch*, January 29, 2005, 01C (accessed via Newsbank, August 3, 2010).

33 Robert Vitale and Mark Niquette, "5 Counties Defy Blackwell's Edict," *Columbus Dispatch*, February 10, 2005, 01A (accessed via Newsbank, August 3, 2010).

34 Jim Provance, "Blackwell Upbraided for Voting Decision—State Official Not Empowered to Certify Single Balloting System, Petro Says," *Toledo Blade*, February 9, 2005, A3 (accessed via Newsbank, August 3, 2010).

35 Erika D. Smith and Lisa A. Abraham, "Diebold's Touch-Screen System OK'ed—Blackwell Lets Ohio Counties Use E-Voting Rather Than Optical Scan," *Akron Beacon Journal*, April 15, 2005, A1 (accessed via Newsbank, August 3, 2010).

36 Mark Niquette, "Ohio Wrapping Up Mission to Upgrade Voting Machines," *Columbus Dispatch*, January 4, 2006, 01E (accessed via Newsbank, August 3, 2010).

37 Ibid.

38 Marc L. Songini, "Paper Trail Flawed in Ohio Election, Study Finds," *Computerworld*, August 21, 2006, www.computerworld.com/s/article/9002610/Paper_Trail_Flawed_in_Ohio_Election_Study_Finds (accessed July 29, 2010).

39 Joan Mazzolini, "Commissioners Want New Voting Machines: $17 Million Touch Screens Can't Handle Big Elections," *Cleveland Plain Dealer*, November 29, 2006, A1 (accessed via Newsbank, August 3, 2010).

40 Joan Mazzolini and Michael O'Malley, "Ohio is Keeping Its Touch Screens: Brunner Plans Review to Improve Voting," *Cleveland Plain Dealer*, February 3, 2007, A1 (accessed via Newsbank, August 4, 2010).

41 Everest Project and Ohio Secretary of State, "Everest Testing Reports, Project Executive Summary," www.sos.state.oh.us/Text.aspx?page=4519 (accessed May 16, 2011). It appears that the Ohio secretary of state's website was reorganized following Secretary of State Jon Husted taking office in January 2011. The report is still available as of May, 2011, but may be obtained from the authors if the reader is unable to access it at a later date.

42 A copy of the ACLU complaint is available at http://moritzlaw.osu.edu/electionlaw/litigation/documents/ACLU-Complaint1-17-08.pdf (accessed July 30, 2010). In the interest of full disclosure, we assisted the ACLU in this lawsuit too.

43 Lynn Hulsey and William Hershey, "Election Officials Have Mixed Reaction to Brunner Plan," *Dayton Daily News*, January 4, 2008, A7 (accessed via Newsbank, August 4, 2010).

44 William Hershey, "Counties Reject Brunner's Proposal," *Dayton Daily News*, January 23, 2008, A4 (accessed Newsbank, August 4, 2010).

45 Lawrence Norden with Jesse Allen, *Final Report: 2008–2009 Ohio Election Summit and Conference* (Brennan Center at the NYU School of Law, 2009) http://brennan.3cdn.net/9ccb57cb5de1711173_nkm6bqc3y.pdf,20 (accessed July 16, 2010).

46 Some election officials are confident that they can continue using the same voting technology for a long time—maybe up to a decade. Personal interview with Bryan A. Caskey, Assistant State Election Director, Kansas Secretary of State's Office, Topeka, Kansas, April 8, 2011.

47 Eliza Newlin Carney, "Rules of the Game: Voting Machine Monopoly Threatens Elections," *National Journal*, September 21, 2009, http://nationaljournal.com/columns/rules-of-the-game/voting-machine-monopoly-threatens-elections-20090921 (March 4, 2011).

48 State of Hawaii, Office of Elections, *Proposed Precinct Closings for the 2010 Elections: The Procurement of a Voting System for the State of Hawaii*, last modified June 15, 2009, http://hawaii.gov/elections/documents/precinct_closings_proposed_2010.pdf (accessed July 15, 2010).

49 Note that the jurisdictions included all the counties which reported having used optical scan ballots or hand-counted paper ballots. See Kimball and Kropf, "Ballot Design and Unrecorded Votes on Paper-Based Ballots."

50 Ewald, *The Way We Vote: The Local Dimension of American Suffrage.*

51 U.S. Election Assistance Commission, *2008 Election Administration and Voting Survey,* November 9–10, 2009 .

52 Robert M. Stein and Greg Vonnahme, "Engaging the Unengaged Voter: Vote Centers and Voter Turnout," *Journal of Politics,* 82(2008):487–497.

53 For 2000, we obtained 2,178 county data points, 2,402 for 2004, and 2,573 for 2008. For the most part, we gathered data on polling places, rather than precincts. Where only precinct data are available, we included data on the number of precincts for each of the elections.

54 A table comparing the polling place changes in each state is at www.umsl.edu/~kimballd/havalimits.htm.

55 Henry E. Brady and John E. McNulty, "Turning Out to Vote: The Costs of Finding and Getting to the Polling Place," *American Political Science Review* 105(2011):115–134.

56 Joshua J. Dyck and James G. Gimpel, "Distance, Turnout and the Convenience of Voting," *Social Science Quarterly,* 86(2005):531–548; J.G. Gimpel and J.E. Schuknecht, "Political Participation and the Accessibility of the Ballot Box," *Political Geography* 22(2003):471–488; Moshe Haspel and H. Gibbs Knotts, "Location, Location, Location: Precinct Placement and the Costs of Voting," *Journal of Politics* 67(2005):560–573; John E. McNulty, Conor M. Dowling, and Margaret H. Ariotti, "Driving Saints to Sin: How Increasing the Difficulty of Voting Dissuades Even the Most Motivated Voters," *Political Analysis* 17(2009):435–455.

57 Stein and Vonnahme, "Engaging the Unengaged Voter."

58 Monte Whaley and Joey Bunch, "Vote Centers 'a Total Fiasco,'" *Denver Post,* November 9, 2006, www.denverpost.com/election/ci_4627496 (accessed August 14, 2009).

59 See for example, Gary H. Roseman, Jr. and E. Frank Stephenson, "The Effects of Voting Technology on Voter Turnout: Do Computers Scare the Elderly?" *Public Choice* 123(2005):39–47.

60 Stephen M. Nichols, David C. Kimball, and Paul Allen Beck, "Voter Turnout in the 1996 Election: Resuming the Downward Spiral?" in Herbert F. Weisberg and Janet M. Box-Steffensmeier (eds.), *Reelection 1996: How Americans Voted* (New York: Chatham House, 1999), 32–33.

61 Michael McDonald, "United States Election Project," George Mason University (http://elections.gmu.edu/voter_turnout.htm), last accessed May 5, 2011.

62 Sam Tyson, "Poll: DeMint Heavily Favored in SC Senate Race," June 15, 2010, www.live5news.com/Global/story.asp?S=12652227 (accessed July 15, 2010).

63 Manuel Roig-Franzia, "Election Speculation Comes from All Corners After S.C. Primary," *Washington Post,* June 15, 2010, www.washingtonpost.com/wp-dyn/content/article/2010/06/14/AR2010061405215.html (accessed July 15, 2010).

64 David C. Kimball, "Voting and Ballots," in Paul S. Herrnson, Colton C. Campbell, Marni Ezra, and Stephen K. Medvic (eds.), *Guide to Political Campaigns in America* (Washington, DC: CQ Press, 2005), 52–69.

5 We Mostly Eliminated the Butterfly Ballot…Isn't That Enough?

1 ABC News, "Butterfly Ballot Designer Speaks Out: Election Official LePore Talks About the Controversial Butterfly Ballot," December 21, 2001, http://abcnews.go.com/Politics/story?id=122175&page=1 (accessed March 29, 2011).

2 Melissa Block, "New Ballot Design in Florida County," *All Things Considered,* August 26, 2004 (www.npr.org/templates/story/story.php?storyid=3873016).

3 We downloaded the Florida precinct data November 7, 2001, from www.usatoday. com/news/politics/nov01/ballots-usat.htm. The precinct figures compiled by the newspaper consortium did not include data for Glades County, a small county in southern Florida. There also was a disparity between official election results and the newspaper data for Martin County, another small county that used lever machines in the 2000 election. The newspaper data indicated no residual votes in the county. Thus, we exclude Martin County from our analysis.

4 For example, see Matthew J. Streb, *Rethinking American Electoral Democracy* (2nd ed., New York: Routledge, 2011), 83–84.

5 Wand, et al., "The Butterfly Did It"; Robert C. Sinclair, et al., "Psychology: An Electoral Butterfly Effect," *Nature* 408(2000):665–666.

6 This case is not ideal to compare voting equipment versus ballot design. None of the Florida counties using precinct-count optical scan systems produced ballots with the two-column presidential layout. Nevertheless, in a more rigorous analysis that controlled for several demographic and election administration factors, the two-column ballot design was the biggest source of overvotes and residual votes. Results are available from the authors. The general problem with the two-column ballot layout in Florida was first reported by Aubrey Jewett, "Explaining Variation in Ballot Invalidation Among Florida Counties in the 2000 Election" (paper presented at the annual meeting of the American Political Science Association San Francisco, August 2001). Also see Dennis Cauchon, "Errors Mostly Tied to Ballots, not Machines," *USA Today*, November 7, 2001, 6A.

7 Richard G. Niemi and Paul S. Herrnson, "Beyond the Butterfly: The Complexity of U.S. Ballots," *Perspectives on Politics* 1(2003):317–326; Kimball and Kropf, "Ballot Design and Unrecorded Votes on Paper-Based Ballots," ; Herrnson, et al., *Voting Technology*; and Susan King Roth, "The Unconsidered Ballot: How Design Affects Voting Behavior," *Visible Language* 28(1994):48–67.

8 See U.S. Election Assistance Commission, *Effective Designs for the Administration of Federal Elections*, June, 2007, www.eac.gov/assets/1/Page/EAC_Effective_Election_ Design.pdf (accessed March 30, 2011).

9 For more information on this design initiative, see AIGA's website www.aiga.org/ content.cfm/design-for-democracy (accessed May 7, 2011) and Marcia Lausen, *Design for Democracy: Ballot and Election Design* (Chicago: University of Chicago Press, 2007). According to its website, AIGA stands for American Institute of Graphic Arts, but the organization simply goes by AIGA, the professional association for design.

10 Lawrence Norden, et al., *Better Ballots* (Brennan Center for Justice, 2008), citing, *Voluntary Voting System Guidelines Recommendations to the Election Assistance Commission*, prepared at the direction of the Technical Guidelines Development Committee, August 31, 2007 (www.eac.gov).

11 John Pierson, "Preparing for the 2000 Census, Bureau Tests Carrots vs. Sticks," *Wall Street Journal*, May 2, 1996, B1.

12 See for example, Don A. Dillman, Michael D. Sinclair, and Jon R. Clark, "Effects of Questionnaire Length, Respondent-Friendly Design, and a Difficult Question on Response Rates for Occupant-Addressed Census Mail Surveys," *Public Opinion Quarterly* 57(1993):289–304.

13 Dillman suggested that his research might apply to ballots in a presidential address to the American Association of Public Opinion Research. See Don A. Dillman, "Navigating the Rapids of Change: Some Observations on Survey Methodology in the Early 21st Century," *Public Opinion Quarterly* 66(2002):473–494. For an extensive review of the survey design literature, see Don A. Dillman, Jolene D. Smyth, and Leah Melani Christian, *Internet, Mail, and Mixed-Mode Surveys: The Tailored Design Method* (3rd ed., New York: John Wiley, 2009). For more detailed discussion of the ballot features evaluated here, see Kimball and Kropf, "Ballot Design and Unrecorded Votes on Paper-Based Ballots," and Norden, et al., *Better Ballots*.

14 Interestingly, those who conduct research on public opinion surveys have been conducting considerable research on how to make web surveys more usable as well. While we argue that many of the principles laid out here apply to DREs as well, some of the web survey research may as well. See Mick Couper, *Designing Effective Web Surveys* (Cambridge: Cambridge University Press, 2008).

15 See Don A. Dillman, *Mail and Internet Surveys: The Tailored Design Method* (New York: John Wiley, 2000), 107; and Charles Wallschlaeger and Cynthia Busic-Snyder, *Basic Visual Concepts and Principles for Artists, Architects and Designers* (Dubuque, IA: William C. Brown, 1992).

16 Cleo R. Jenkins and Don A. Dillman, "Towards a Theory of Self-Administered Questionnaire Design," in Lars Lyberg, et al. (eds.), *Survey Measurement and Process Quality* (New York: Wiley Inter-Science, 1997), 165–196.

17 Dillman, *Mail and Internet Surveys*, 113; Roth, "Unconsidered Ballot," 59.

18 William F. Long, et al., "The Ergonomics of Reading," In *Vision and Reading*, ed., Ralph P. Garzia (St. Louis, MO: Mosby, 1996), 91; Colin Wheildon, *Type and Layout: How Typography and Design Can Get your Message Across – Or Get in the Way* (Berkeley, CA: Strathmoor Press, 1995),62.

19 HAVA 2002, Title III, Section 301.a.1.B.

20 Dillman, *Mail and Internet Surveys*,106.

21 Lausen, *Design for Democracy*.

22 Dillman, *Mail and Internet Surveys*,118.

23 Jenkins and Dillman, "Towards a Theory of Self-Administered Questionnaire Design."

24 Kimball and Kropf, "Ballot Design and Unrecorded Votes on Paper-Based Ballots," 522–526; Charles S. Bullock, III and M. V. Hood, III, "One Person—No Vote; One Vote; Two Votes: Voting Methods, Ballot Types, and Undervote Frequency in the 2000 Presidential Election," *Social Science Quarterly* 83(2002):981–993.

25 Chris Janiszewski, "The Influence of Display Characteristics on Visual Exploratory Search Behavior," *Journal of Consumer Research* 25(1998):290–301.

26 See for example Dillman, *Mail and Internet Surveys*; and Earl Babbie, *Survey Research Methods* (2nd ed., Belmont: Wadsworth, Cengage Learning, 1990).

27 Niemi and Herrnson, "Beyond the Butterfly."

28 Kimball and Kropf, "Ballot Design and Unrecorded Votes on Paper-Based Ballots" ; David C. Kimball, Chris T. Owens, and Katherine McAndrew Keeney, "Unrecorded Votes and Political Representation," in Robert P. Watson (ed.), *Counting Votes: Lessons from the 2000 Presidential Election in Florida* (Gainesville, FL: University of Florida Press, 2004).

29 See also Nichols, "State Referendum Voting, Ballot Roll-Off, and the Effect of New Electoral Technology"; Darcy and Schneider, "Confusing Ballots, Roll-Off, and the Black Vote," 360; Niemi and Herrnson, "Beyond the Butterfly."

30 In four states (Illinois, Missouri, Maryland, and Virginia), some cities have separate election administration authorities. These cities are treated as separate jurisdictions in this analysis. We treat Alaska as one observation since elections are administered by the Alaska state government.

31 For each state with more than one ballot proposition, we chose to examine the one with the closest outcome (see Table 5.4 for the list of ballot issues and states in our data).

32 Ballots we obtained from the 2004 election can be viewed online at http://vote.nist. gov. Many of the ballots we coded from the 2002 election are available at www.umsl. edu/~kimballd/ballots.htm.

33 Both readability scores are based on the length of words and sentences. Let the average number of words in a sentence be ASL, and the average number of syllables per word by ASW. The formula for the Flesch reading ease score is 206.835 − (1.015 x ASL) − (84.6 x ASW). The formula for computing the Flesch–Kincaid score is (.39 x ASL)

+ (11.8 x ASW) − 15.59. In Microsoft Word, the "Spelling and Grammar" feature reports readability scores for a document. The use and validity of these readability measures are supported by other studies. See Thomas Heilke, Mark R. Joslyn, and Alex Aguado, "The Changing Readability of Introductory Political Science Textbooks: A Case Study of Burns and Peltason, *Government by the People*," *PS: Political Science and Politics* 36(2003):229–232; Mark S. Sanders and Ernest J. McCormick, *Human Factors in Engineering and Design* (7th ed., New York: McGraw Hill, 1993); and Chafai Tefki, 1987, "Readability Formulas: An Overview," *Journal of Documentation* 43(1987): 261–273.

34 David Magleby, *Direct Legislation: Voting on Ballot Propositions in the United States* (Baltimore: Johns Hopkins University Press, 1984); and Shauna Reilly and Sean Richey, "Ballot Question Readability and Roll-Off: The Impact of Language Complexity," *Political Research Quarterly* 64(2011):59–67.

35 See Kimball et al., "Unrecorded Votes and Political Representation."

36 North Carolina and South Carolina have a straight-party option but it comes after the presidential contest and thus does not apply to the presidential contest. We code these two states as not having a straight-party option for our analysis of the presidential election, but we code both states as having a straight-party feature for the analysis of ballot measures.

37 The attentive reader may notice that this is somewhat different from the expected results of residual votes modeled in Chapter 3. The model in Chapter 3 is a fixed effects model, so the turnout variable is measuring whether an increase in turnout from one election to the next is associated with an increase in the residual vote rate. Stewart (2006) found a positive effect, although we find statistically insignificant effects (positive in 2004 but negative in 2008). The model in Chapter 5 is a cross-sectional model, so the turnout variable is measuring whether residual vote rates tend to be higher in smaller jurisdictions, which is what we tend to find (like other studies). It is consistent (although complicated) for both things to be happening: residual votes tend to be more frequent in small jurisdictions, but residual votes become more common when turnout increases. See Knack and Kropf, "Voided Ballots in the 1996 Presidential Election," 887; Ansolabehere and Stewart, III, "Residual Votes Attributable to Technology"; and Charles Stewart, III, "Residual Vote in the 2004 Election."

38 For these types of data, we estimate a negative binomial regression model to estimate the effects of the independent variables on the number of residual votes. A negative binomial model is superior to ordinary least squares regression because it is more appropriate for count data with heavily skewed distributions. In addition, the negative binomial model allows for extra variation, or overdispersion, in residual votes.

39 The idea of the concentration of residual votes in some areas is called "overdispersion." In the negative binomial model, larger values of the alpha parameter indicate higher levels of overdispersion. Since jurisdictions within the same state may not be independent (because they fall under the same state election laws and procedures), we estimate standard errors that are corrected for clustering within states. In this chapter, we use the same model procedures outlined in our article published in *Public Opinion Quarterly* in 2005 (Kimball and Kropf, "Ballot Design and Unrecorded Votes on Paper-Based Ballots"). For a more detailed justification of the use of a negative binomial model for residual vote data, see Bullock and Hood, "One Person—No Vote"; and Sinclair and Alvarez, "Who Overvotes, Who Undervotes, Using Punchcards?"

40 Complete model estimates for the effects estimated in this chapter are available in an online appendix at www.umsl.edu/~kimballd/havalimits.htm.

41 Residual vote rates are similar for ballot measures in the same state, in part because they tend to be grouped together in the same area of the ballot. For a comparison of

the within-state and between-state variance in residual votes for all ballot measures in 2004, see the online appendix at www.umsl.edu/~kimballd/havalimits.htm.

42 Jenkins and Dillman, "Towards a Theory of Self-Administered Questionnaire Design."

43 Many scholars have discussed this issue. For additional evidence, see Magleby, *Direct Legislation*; Shaun Bowler, Todd Donovan, and Trudi Happ, "Ballot Propositions and Information Costs: Direct Democracy and the Fatigued Voter," *Western Political Quarterly* 45(1992):559–568.

44 Reilly and Richey, "Ballot Question Readability and Roll-Off."

45 Cronback's alpha (a measure of scale reliability) for the issue salience scale is .89, indicating a reliable measure.

46 The full model estimates are at www.umsl.edu/~kimballd/havalimits.htm.

47 Herrnson, et al., *Voting Technology*, especially chs. 3 and 4.

48 Ibid. See also Herrnson et al., "Voters' Evaluations of Electronic Voting Systems: Results from a Usability Field Study," *American Politics Research* 36(2008): 580–611.

49 Our review of this election is based on Frisina, et al., "Ballot Formats, Touchscreens, and Undervotes: A Study of the 2006 Midterm Elections in Florida."

50 Florida Department of State, Analysis and Report of Overvotes and Undervotes for the 2004 General Election, January 2005; Florida Department of State, Analysis and Report of Overvotes and Undervotes for the 2008 Election, January 2009.

51 For a more complete review of these design issues on optical scanners in Florida, see Mary K. Garber, *Examining Florida's High Invalid Vote Rate in the 2008 General Election* (Florida Fair Elections Center, June 23, 2009).

52 Unfortunately, many counties do not count the number of undervotes and overvotes.

53 See Martha Kropf, "The Evolution (or not) of Ballot Design Ten Years after *Bush v. Gore*," (paper prepared for presentation at "*Bush v Gore*, 10 Years Later: Election Administration in the United States," April 16–17, 2011, Laguna Beach, CA).

6 Defining the Problem in Human Terms

1 The Colbert Report, aired June 3, 2010. Colbert is speaking about the magazine, *Consumer Reports*, but we think it fits here, too.

2 See for example, Daniel P. Tokaji, "The Birth and Rebirth of Election Administration," *Election Law Journal* 6(2007):118–131; Ewald, *The Way We Vote*; and Kenneth J. Mayer, "Comparative Election Administration: Can We Learn Anything from the Australian Election Commission?" (paper prepared for delivery at the 2007 Annual Meeting of the American Political Science Association, Chicago, IL, August 30–September 2, 2007).

3 "How America Doesn't Vote," *New York Times*, February 15, 2004, www.nytimes. com (accessed December 22, 2004).

4 Blackwell ruled that only provisional ballots cast in the correct precinct would be counted. He also decided that only voter registration applications on a certain weight of paper could be accepted (see House Judiciary Committee Democratic Staff, "Preserving Democracy: What Went Wrong in Ohio," January 5, 2005. This report is no longer available on the House.gov website where we originally found it. It is now available at www.verifiedvoting.org/article.php?id=5420 (accessed May 17, 2011) or one may purchase it on Amazon.com.

5 Lynn Hulsey, "Sen. Can Vote Here—Justices Say Secretary of State Improperly Applied Law; Jon Husted Accuses Brunner of Trying to Damage Him," *Dayton Daily News*, October 7, 2009, A1.

6 Nancy Vogel, "U.S. Orders State to Repay $536,000 in Election Funds," *Los Angeles Times*, May 13, 2006, B3.

7 Daniel P. Tokaji, "First Amendment Equal Protection: On Discretion, Inequality and Participation," *Michigan Law Review* 101(2003):2409–2524, 2411.

8 Wand, et al., "The Butterfly Did It."

9 Richard L. Hasen, "Introduction: Developments in Election Law," *Loyola of Los Angeles Law Review* 42(2009)565–574; Daniel P. Tokaji, "Early Returns on Election Reform: Discretion, Disenfranchisement, and the Help America Vote Act," *George Washington Law Review* 74(2005):1206–1253. People are even biased in favor of their own party when recounting votes in a close election. See Kyle C. Kopko et al., "In the Eye of the Beholder? Motivated Reasoning in Disputed Elections," *Political Behavior* 33(2011):271–290.

10 For an example of the Republican point of view on election reform, see John Fund, *Stealing Elections: How Voter Fraud Threatens Our Democracy* (New York: Encounter Books, 2004). For the Democratic perspective, see Piven and Cloward, *Why Americans Don't Vote*.

11 Ewald, *The Way We Vote*; Richard Franklin Bensel, *The American Ballot Box in the Mid-Nineteenth Century* (New York: Cambridge University Press, 2004).

12 See for example, "Election Integrity: Restoring Honor to a Disgraced Political Office," *San Diego Union Tribune*, March 17, 2005; Richard L. Hasen, "Beyond the Margin of Litigation: Reforming Election Administration to Avoid Electoral Meltdown," *Washington & Lee Law Review* 62(2005):937–999; Robert A. Pastor, "Improving the U.S. Electoral System: Lessons from Canada and Mexico," *Election Law Journal* 3(2004):584–593; Ann Shornstein, "Politicizing the Election Process: 'The Katherine Harris Effect'," *Florida Coastal Law Journal* 2(2001):373–380; Committee on Federal Election Reform, *Building Confidence in U.S. Elections*; Fair Election International, *2004 U.S. Election: An International Perspective*, November 2004, United States Observation Report, www.truthinvoting.org/fairelectionreport.pdf (or available from authors) (accessed September 4, 2004).

13 R. Michael Alvarez, Thad Hall, and Morgan Llewellyn, "Who Should Run Our Elections? Public Opinion About Election Governance in the United States," *Policy Studies Journal* 36(2008):325–346.

14 David C. Kimball and Martha Kropf, 2006. "The Street-Level Bureaucrats of Elections: Selection Methods for Local Election Officials," *Review of Policy Research* 23(2006):1257–1268. See the Appendix of that study for information on the selection methods used in each state.

15 Susan A. MacManus and Charles S. Bullock, III, "The Form, Structure and Composition of America's Municipalities in the New Millennium," *Municipal Yearbook* (International City Managers' Association, 2003). See also Charles Adrian, "A Typology for Nonpartisan Elections," *Western Political Quarterly* 12(1959):449–458.

16 David C. Kimball and Brady Baybeck, "Is There a Partisan Way to Administer Elections?" (paper presented at the annual meeting of the Midwest Political Science Association, Chicago, April 2010).

17 Donald P. Moynihan and Carol L. Silva, "The Administrators of Democracy: A Research Note on Local Election Officials," *Public Administration Review* September/October(2008):816–827.

18 Lydia Saad, "'Conservatives' Are Single-Largest Ideological Group" (June 15, 2009). www.gallup.com/poll/120857/conservatives-single-largest-ideological-group.aspx (accessed June 12, 2010).

19 James C. Garand, Catherine T. Parkhurst, and Rusanne Jourdan Seoud, "Testing the Bureau Voting Model: A Research Note on Federal and State-Local Employees," *Journal of Public Administration Research and Theory* 1(1991):229–233. Admittedly, the surveys cited here are somewhat old, but they give us a rough comparison.

According to Gallup.com, as many as 43 percent of Americans reported being conservative in 1992, a roughly similar time period.

20 Moynihan and Silva, "Administrators of Democracy."

21 Eric A. Fischer and Kevin J. Coleman, *Election Reform and Local Election Officials: Results of Two National Surveys* (Washington, DC: Congressional Research Service, 2008).

22 Timothy Vercellotti, "Embracing Change at the Polls: Election Administrators and the Provisional Ballot in 2004" (paper presented at the annual meeting of the Midwest Political Science Association, Chicago, April 15, 2007).

23 Martha Kropf, L. Timothy Vercellotti, and David C. Kimball, "Representative Bureaucracy and Partisanship: the Implementation of Election Law" (manuscript, University of North Carolina at Charlotte, 2009).

24 Kimball and Baybeck, "Is There a Partisan Way to Administer Elections?"

25 Hong-Hai Lim, "Representative Bureaucracy: Rethinking Substantive Effects and Active Representation," *Public Administration Review* 66(2006):193–204.

26 David C. Kimball, Martha Kropf, and Lindsay Battles, "Helping America Vote? Election Administration, Partisanship and Provisional Voting in the 2004 Presidential Election," *Election Law Journal* 5(2006):447–461. Also see David C. Kimball and Edward B. Foley, "Unsuccessful Provisional Voting in the 2008 General Election," Report for Pew Center on the States, August 26, 2009, www.pewcenteronthestates.org/report_detail.aspx?id=54831. For evidence of wide variation in provisional voting across precincts within the same local jurisdiction, see David Kimball and Brady Baybeck, "The Political Geography of Provisional Ballots" (paper presented at the annual meeting of the American Political Science Association, Boston, September 2008).

27 The states with lawsuits over whether to count provisional ballots cast outside a voter's precinct were Arizona, Colorado, Florida, Michigan, Missouri, North Carolina, and Ohio (see Tokaji, "Early Returns on Election Reform," fn. 195).

28 Tokaji, "Early Returns on Election Reform." See also "Toward a Greater State Role in Election Administration," *Harvard Law Review* 118(2005):2314–2335.

29 James W. Ceaser and Andrew Busch, *The Perfect Tie: The True Story of the 2000 Presidential Election* (Lanham, MD: Rowman & Littlefield, 2001).

30 Kosuke Imai and Gary King, "Did Illegal Overseas Absentee Ballots Decide the 2000 U.S. Presidential Election?" *Perspectives on Politics* 2(2004):537–549.

31 Anna Bassi, Rebecca Morton, and Jessica Troustine, "Local Implementation of State and Federal Election Law" (paper presented at the State Politics and Policy Conference, Raleigh NC, May 2009).

32 Stuart, "Databases, Felons, and Voting: Bias and Partisanship of the Florida Felons List in the 2000 Elections."

33 James T. Hamilton and Helen F. Ladd, "Biased Ballots? The Impact of Ballot Structure on North Carolina Elections in 1992," *Public Choice* 87(1996):259–280.

34 William A. Lund, "What's in a Name? The Battle Over Ballot Titles in Oregon," *Willamette Law Review,* 34(1998):143–167; Ronald Hayduk, *Gatekeepers to the Franchise: Shaping Election Administration in New York* (DeKalb, IL: Northern Illinois University Press, 2005).

35 Josh Dyck and Nicholas R. Seabrook, "The Problem with Vote-By-Mail" (paper presented at the 67th Annual Meeting of the Midwest Political Science Association, Chicago, IL, April 2009).

36 Dyck and Seabrook, "Problem with Vote-By-Mail," 18.

37 Jay Weiner, *This is Not Florida: How Al Franken Won the Minnesota Senate Recount* (Minneapolis: University of Minnesota Press, 2010).

38 Hasen, "Beyond the Margin of Litigation," fn 148, 973.

39 Draft Legislation for State Independent Election Commissions, Draft 11–22–2006, www1.american.edu/ia/cdem/pdfs/legislation_npml.pdf (accessed June 18, 2010).

40 Common Cause, "Ethics and Accountability in Election Administration" (2006).

41 Hasen, "Beyond the Margin of Litigation." In a more pertinent example, Randall D. Lloyd notes that federal judges are less likely to vote against redistricting plans passed by state legislatures from their own party (see "Separating Partisanship from Party in Judicial Research: Reapportionment in the U.S. District Courts," *American Political Science Review* 89(1995):413–420).

42 Mayer, "Comparative Election Administration."

43 Ibid., 26.

44 "NASS Resolution Affirming Conduct of Elections in a Non-Partisan Manner." Approved February 7, 2005 and Reaffirmed February 1, 2010, National Association of Secretaries of State. www.nass.org (accessed June 15, 2010).

45 For example, in one of the smaller New England states, Rhode Island, 37 of 39 towns and cities are governed by home rule charters.

46 "NASS Resolution Affirming Conduct of Elections in a Non-Partisan Manner."

47 Heather Gerken, *The Democracy Index: Why Our Election System is Failing and How to Fix It* (Princeton: Princeton University Press, 2009), 19.

48 Gerken, *Democracy Index.*

49 Vercellotti, "Embracing Change at the Polls."

50 Wendy Noren, Boone County Clerk and Legislative Co-Chair of the Missouri Association of County Clerks and Election Authorities, April 16, 2003, Columbia, MO quoted in Martha Kropf, "Dogs and Dead People: Incremental Election Reform in Missouri," in *Election Reform: Politics and Policy*, ed. Daniel J. Palazzollo and James W. Ceaser (Lanham: Lexington Books, 2005).

51 According to a report prepared about early voting by the Secretary of State's Office, election officials in Missouri estimate it will cost approximately $2.4 million dollars statewide (about one million would be one-time costs such as equipment purchase), or about $21,000 per election district. The majority of the counties reported they would hold early voting only at their central office.

52 Richard H. Pildes, "The Future of Voting Rights Policy from Anti-Discrimination to the Right to Vote." *Howard Law Journal* 49(2006):741–765.

53 Ewald, *The Way We Vote.*

7 Conclusion

1 Michael Traugott, quoted in: Associated Press, "No Clear Winner in Race to Decide Best Machines—Voting: Some Studies Show that Low-Tech Methods Work More Effectively than State-of-the-Art Systems," *Dubuque Telegraph Herald*, Monday, March 19, 2001, A2 (accessed via Newsbank, June 14, 2011).

2 For example, see Arend Lijphart, *Patterns of Democracy: Government Forms and Performance in Thirty-Six Countries* (New Haven, CT: Yale University Press, 1999).

3 Weiner, *This is Not Florida: How Al Franken Won the Minnesota Senate Recount.*

4 Becky Bohrer, "Alaska Judge Rejects Suit over Murkowski Write-in" *Associated Press*, December 11, 2010 http://articles.sfgate.com/2010–12–11/news/25186780_1_miller-last-month-ballots-write-in-votes (accessed December 12, 2010).

5 Edward B. Foley, "Ohio Provisional Ballot Case: What is Going On?" Free & Fair blog, January 14, 2011 http://moritzlaw.osu.edu/electionlaw/freefair/index.php?ID=8055.

6 Craig Gilbert, "Big Vote Adjustment Brings Waukesha Turnout More in Line With Nearby GOP Counties," The Wisconsin Voter blog, April 7, 2011, www.jsonline.com/blogs/news/119442229.html.

7 Edward B. Foley, "Uncounted Ballots: A Measure of Vulnerability?" Free & Fair blog, November 5, 2009 http://moritzlaw.osu.edu/electionlaw/freefair/index.php?ID=6943.

8 U.S. Election Assistance Commission, 2008 Election Administration and Voting Survey, 10.

9 Gerken, *Democracy Index*; Todd Donovan, "A Goal for Reform," in Bruce E. Cain, Todd Donovan, and Caroline J. Tolbert (eds.), *Democracy in the States: Experiments in Election Reform* (Washington, DC: Brookings Institution Press, 2008), 197.

10 Fred Bowen, "In Pursuit of Baseball Perfection," *Washington Post*, May 11, 2011, www. washingtonpost.com/lifestyle/style/in-pursuit-of-baseball-perfection/2011/05/09/AF7TFrsG_story.html (accessed May 12, 2011).

11 National Conference of State Legislatures, "Absentee and Early Voting," last updated October 10, 2010, www.ncsl.org/default.aspx?tabid=16604 (accessed May 9, 2011).

12 Patrick O'Donnell, "Voter Error on the Rise as Mail-In Voting Becomes More Popular in Cuyahoga County," *Cleveland Plain Dealer*, July 29, 2010, http://blog.cleveland.com/metro/2010/07/voter_error_on_the_rise_as_mai.html (accessed August 6, 2010).

13 For example, see Dennis Thompson, "Election Time: Normative Implications of Temporal Properties of the Electoral Process in the United States," *American Political Science Review* 98(2004):51–64. For examinations of the impact of early voting on turnout, see Paul Gronke, Eva Galanes-Rosenbaum, Peter A. Miller, and Daniel Toffey, "Convenience Voting," *Annual Review of Political Science* 11(2008):437–455; and Joseph D. Giammo and Brian J. Brox, "Reducing the Cost of Participation: Are States Getting a Return on Early Voting?" *Political Research Quarterly* 63(2010): 295–303. See also John Hansen, "Early Voting, Unrestricted Absentee Voting, and Voting by Mail," in "To Assure Pride and Confidence in the Electoral Process, Report of the Task Force to Accompany the National Commission on Election Reform, 2001," manuscript, Miller Center for Public Affairs, University of Virginia (available at www.millercenter.virginia.edu).

14 Thompson, "Election Time," 58.

15 Martha Kropf, David Swindell, and Elizabeth Wemlinger, "The Effects of Early Voting on Social Ties: Using Longitudinal Data" (paper presented at the 2009 North Carolina Political Science Association Meeting, Greensboro, NC, February 2009 and at Time Shifting the Vote: The Early Voting Revolution in Election Administration, October 9–10, 2009, Reed College, Portland, Oregon).

16 Ewald, *The Way We Vote*, see especially 9–10.

17 Gerken, *Democracy Index*.

18 Matthew J. Streb, *Rethinking American Electoral Democracy* (2nd ed., New York: Routledge, 2011), 100, 184.

19 Daniel Tokaji and Thad Hall, "Money for Data: Funding the Oldest Unfunded Mandate," Commentary, Election Law @Moritz blog, June 5, 2007 (http://moritzlaw.osu.edu/electionlaw). Also, see Chris Elmendorf, "Two Models for Building Public Confidence in the Electoral Process," Election Law Blog, November 9, 2008 (http://electionlawblog.org).

20 In the 111th Congress, Representative Steve Israel (NY) introduced similar legislation in the House—H.R. 4033. 111th Congress (2009–2010). Thomas On-Line. http://thomas.loc.gov (accessed June 21, 2010).

21 National Association of Secretaries of State, NASS Position on Funding and Authorization of the U.S. Election Assistance Commission, July 20, 2010, www.nass.org/index.php?option=com_content&view=article&id=75&Itemid=470   (accessed May 17, 2011).

22 The bill to eliminate the EAC is HR 672.

23 Frank R. Baumgartner, Jeffrey M. Berry, Marie Hojnacki, David C. Kimball, and Beth L. Leech, *Lobbying and Policy Change: Who Wins, Who Loses, and Why* (Chicago: University of Chicago Press, 2009), 18.

24 See for example, Social Science Research Commission, 2004. *Interim Report on Alleged Irregularities in the United States Presidential Election of 2 November 2004*, http://elections.ssrc.org/research/InterimReport122204.pdf (accessed September 7, 2004).

25 Doug Chapin, "Baby, Not Bathwater—Don't Toss the EAC's Election Day Survey"; electionline.org, March 3, 2011, http://www.pewcenteronthestates.org/uploadedFiles/wwwpewcenteronthestatesorg/Reports/Electionline_Reports/electionlineWeekly03.31.11.pdf. Also, David C. Kimball, "Evidence-Based Democracy," *Election Law Journal* 9(2010):161–164. We are not unbiased observers, as we have used data from the Election Day Surveys for this book.

REFERENCES

ABC News. 2001. "Butterfly Ballot Designer Speaks Out: Election Official LePore Talks About the Controversial Butterfly Ballot." December 21, http://abcnews.go.com/Politics/story?id=122175&page=1 (accessed 29 March 2011).

Alvarez, R. Michael, Stephen Ansolabehere, and Charles Stewart, III. 2005. "Studying Elections: Data Quality and Pitfalls in Measuring of Effects of Voting Technologies." *Policy Studies Journal* 33:15–24.

Alvarez, R. Michael and Thad E. Hall. 2008. *Electronic Elections: The Perils and Promises of Digital Democracy*. Princeton, NJ: Princeton University Press.

Alvarez, R. Michael, Thad Hall and Susan Hyde. eds. 2008. *Election Fraud: Detecting and Deterring Electoral Manipulation*. Washington, DC: Brookings Institution Press.

Alvarez, R. Michael, Thad E. Hall and Morgan H. Llewellyn. 2008. "Are Americans Confident Their Ballots Are Counted?" *Journal of Politics* 70:754–766.

Alvarez, R. Michael, Stephen Ansolabehere, Adam Berinsky, Gabriel Lenz, Charles Stewart, III, and Thad Hall. 2009. "2008 Survey of the Performance of American Elections: Final Report." www.pewcenteronthestates.org/uploadedFiles/Final%20report20090218.pdf (accessed February 5, 2011).

Ansolabehere, Stephen, and Charles Stewart, III. 2005. "Residual Votes Attributable to Technology." *Journal of Politics* 67: 365–389.

Associated Press. 2001. "California Sued Over Ballots." *Miami Herald*, April 18, A16.

Associated Press. 2001. "Task Force Decides Against Unified Voting System." *Dubuque Telegraph Herald*, May 15, A5.

Associated Press. 2011. "No Clear Winner in Race to Decide Best Machines—Voting: Some Studies Show that Low-Tech Methods Work More Effectively than State-of-the-Art Systems." *The Dubuque Telegraph Herald*, Monday, March 19, 2001, A2.

Atlanta Journal-Constitution. 2000. "Antiquated Voting System Needs Permanent Upgrade." November 13, A12.

Babbie, Earl. 2010. *The Practice of Social Research, 12th edition*. Belmont: Wadsworth, Cengage Learning, 2010.

Bassi, Anna, Rebecca Morton, and Jessica Troustine, 2009. "Local Implementation of State and Federal Election Law." Paper presented at the State Politics and Policy Conference, Raleigh, NC, May 2009.

Bates, Kim. 2003. "Wood County Asked to OK Funds to Buy Vote Machines." *Toledo Blade*, November 12, B1 (accessed via Newsbank, August 2, 2010).

Baumgartner, Frank R., Jeffrey M. Berry, Marie Hojnacki, David C. Kimball, and Beth L. Leech. 2009. *Lobbying and Policy Change: Who Wins, Who Loses, and Why*. Chicago: University of Chicago Press.

Berinsky, Adam. 2004. "The Perverse Consequences of Electoral Reform in the United States." *American Politics Research* 31:1–21.

Blunt, Matt. 2001. "Mandate for Reform: Election Turmoil in St. Louis," November 7, 2000. Missouri Secretary of State's Office, July 24.

Block, Melissa. 2004. "New Ballot Design in Florida County," *All Things Considered*, August 26, www.npr.org/templates/story/story.php?storyid=3873016.

Bohrer, Becky. 2010. "Alaska Judge Rejects Suit over Murkowski Write-in." *Associated Press*, December 11, http://articles.sfgate.com/2010–12–11/news/25186780_1_miller-last-month-ballots-write-in-votes (accessed December 12, 2010).

Bond, Christopher S. 2001. "'Motor Voter', Out of Control." *Washington Post*, June 27 (accessed via Lexis/Nexis, July 2, 2007).

Bousquet, Steve. 2001. "Florida's Best Buy for Better Elections Not Clear." *Miami Herald*, January 20, A1.

Bowen, Fred. 2011. "In Pursuit of Baseball Perfection." *Washington Post*, May 11, www.washingtonpost.com/lifestyle/style/in-pursuit-of-baseball-perfection/2011/05/09/AF7TFrsG_story.html (accessed May 12, 2011).

Bowler, Shaun, Todd Donovan, and Trudi Happ, 1992. "Ballot Propositions and Information Costs: Direct Democracy and the Fatigued Voter." *Western Political Quarterly* 45:559–568.

Brady, Henry E. and John E. McNulty. 2011. "Turning Out to Vote: The Costs of Finding and Getting to the Polling Place." *American Political Science Review* 105: 115–134.

Broder, David. 2001. "Election Report Delivered to Bush." *Washington Post*, August 1.

Buchler, Justin, Matthew Jarvis, and John E. McNulty. 2004. "Punch Card Technology and the Racial Gap in Residual Votes." *Perspectives on Politics* 2:517–524

Bullock, Charles and Richard E. Dunn. 1996. "Election Roll-Off: A Test of Three Explanations." *Urban Affairs Review* 32:71–86

Bullock, Charles S. III, M.V. Hood III, and Richard Clark. 2000. "Punch Cards, Jim Crow and Al Gore: Explaining Voter Trust in the Electoral System in Georgia, 2000." *State Politics & Policy Quarterly* 5:283–294.

Bush v. Gore, 531 U.S. 98 (2000).

Ceaser, James W. and Andrew Busch. 2001. *The Perfect Tie: The True Story of the 2000 Presidential Election*. Lanham, MD: Rowman & Littlefield.

Caltech/MIT Voting Technology Project. 2001. *Voting: What Is, What Could Be*. July. www.vote.caltech.edu (accessed December 15, 2001).

Carney, Eliza Newlin. 2009. "Rules of the Game: Voting Machine Monopoly Threatens Elections." *National Journal*, September 21, http://nationaljournal.com/columns/rules-of-the-game/voting-machine-monopoly-threatens-elections-20090921 (March 4, 2011).

Cauchon, Dennis. 2001. "Errors Mostly Tied to Ballots, not Machines." *USA Today*, November 7, 6A.

Century Foundation Working Group on State Implementation of Election Reform. 2005. *Balancing Access and Integrity*. New York: Century Foundation Press.

Christopher, Warren. 2002. "The Stalling of Election Reform." *New York Times*, September 15 (accessed via Lexis/Nexis).

Cobb, Roger W. and Charles D. Elder. 1972. *Participation in American Politics: The Dynamics of Agenda Building*. Boston: Allyn and Bacon.

Conyers, John. 2002. "Voting Rights in Peril." *New York Times*, January 30.

Darcy, Robert and Anne Schneider. 1989. "Confusing Ballots, Roll-Off, and the Black Vote." *Western Political Quarterly* 42:347–364.

Dillman, Don A. 2000. *Mail and Internet Surveys: The Tailored Design Method*. New York: John Wiley.

Dillman, Don A. 2002. "Navigating the Rapids of Change: Some Observations on Survey Methodology in the Early 21st Century." *Public Opinion Quarterly* 66:473–494.

Dillman, Don A., Michael D. Sinclair, and Jon R. Clark. 1993. "Effects of Questionnaire Length, Respondent-Friendly Design, and a Difficult Question on Response Rates for Occupant-Addressed Census Mail Surveys." *Public Opinion Quarterly* 57:289–304.

Dillman, Don A., Jolene D. Smyth, and Leah Melani Christian. 2009. *Internet, Mail, and Mixed-Mode Surveys: The Tailored Design Method*, 3rd ed., New York: John Wiley and Sons.

Donovan, Todd. 2008. "A Goal for Reform." In Bruce E. Cain, Todd Donovan, and Caroline J. Tolbert (eds.), *Democracy in the States: Experiments in Election Reform*. Washington, DC: Brookings Institution Press, 186–198.

"Don't Rush." 2000. *Crain's Business Cleveland*, December 11 (Accessed via Newsbank, August 2, 2010).

"Dumping the Touch-Screens." 2005. *The Toledo Blade*. January 16, B4 (accessed via Newsbank, August 3, 2010).

Dyck, Joshua J. and James Gimpel. 2005. "Distance, Turnout and the Convenience of Voting." *Social Science Quarterly* 86:531–548.

Dyck, Josh and Nicholas R. Seabrook. 2009. "The Problem of Vote-By-Mail." Paper presented at the 67th Annual Meeting of the Midwest Political Science Association, Chicago, IL.

Eagleton Institute of Politics. 2006. Report to the U.S. Election Assistance Commission On Best Practices to Improve Provisional Voting: Pursuant to the HELP AMERICA VOTE ACT OF 2002, Public Law 107-252. Rutgers, State University of New Jersey and the Moritz College of Law, Ohio State University, June 28.

Eaton, Sabrina. 2000. "Elections Officials Eager to Repair Shortcomings." *Cleveland Plain Dealer*, December 18 (accessed via Newsbank, August 2, 2010).

Electionline.org. 2005. "Assorted Rolls: Statewide Voter Registration Databases Under HAVA." June 1, www.pewcenteronthestates.org/report_detail.aspx?id=35430 (accessed May 17, 2011).

Electionline.org. 2008. "Back to Paper: A Case Study." February 21, www.pewcenteronthestates.org/report_detail.aspx?id=35628 (accessed March 15, 2008).

Everest Project and Ohio Secretary of State. [no date given]. "Everest Testing Reports, Project Executive Summary." www.sos.state.oh.us/Text.aspx?page=4519 (accessed May 16, 2011).

Ewald, Alec C. 2009. *The Way We Vote: The Local Dimension of American Suffrage*. Nashville: Vanderbilt University Press.

Federal Election Commission. 1982. *Voting System Standards: A Report to the Congress on the Development of Voluntary Engineering and Procedural Performance Standards for*

Voting Systems. Washington, DC: National Clearinghouse on Election Administration of the Federal Election Commission.

Fineout, Gary. 2007. "Voting Change Irks Supervisors." *Miami Herald*, May 24. www.miamiherald.com/515/v-print/story/116688.html (accessed June 6, 2007).

Florida Department of State. 2005. Analysis and Report of Overvotes and Undervotes for the 2004 General Election, January.

Florida Department of State. 2009. Analysis and Report of Overvotes and Undervotes for the 2008 Election, January.

Frisina, Laurin, Michael C. Herron, James Honaker, and Jeffrey B. Lewis. 2008. "Ballot Formats, Touchscreens, and Undervotes: A Study of the 2006 Midterm Elections in Florida." *Election Law Journal* 7:25–47.

Fund, John. 2004. *Stealing Elections: How Voter Fraud Threatens our Democracy.* New York: Encounter Books.

Garber, Mary K. 2009. *Examining Florida's High Invalid Vote Rate in the 2008 General Election.* Florida Fair Elections Center, June 23.

General Accounting Office. 2001. *The Scope of Congressional Authority in Election Administration.* March. www.gao.gov/new.items/d01470.pdf (accessed July 27, 2007).

Giammo, Joseph D. and Brian J. Brox. 2010. "Reducing the Cost of Participation: Are States Getting a Return on Early Voting?" *Political Research Quarterly* 63: 295–303.

Gillon, Steven M. 2000. *"That's Not What We Meant to Do": Reform and Its Unintended Consequences in 20th Century America.* New York: Norton.

Gimpel, James and Joshua J. Dyck. 2005. "Maryland: Policy Entrepreneurship in a One-Party State." In Daniel J. Palazzolo and James W. Ceaser (eds.), *Election Reform: Politics and Policy.* Lanham, MD: Lexington Books, 74–89.

Gimpel, J.G. and J.E. Schuknecht. 2003. "Political Participation and the Accessibility of the Ballot Box." *Political Geography* 22:471–488.

Goodman, Peter S. 2000. "An Outcome Driven by Technology, High and Low." *Washington Post*, November 10, E1.

Gore, Al. 2000. "Vice President Al Gore Delivers Remarks." December 13. http://archives.cnn.com/2000/ALLPOLITICS/stories/12/13/gore.ends.campaign/index.html (accessed June 26, 2007).

Hall, Thad E. 2009. "Electronic Elections in a Politicized Polity." Caltech/MIT Voting Technology Project, VTP Working Paper #76, June.

Hamilton, James T. and Helen F. Ladd. 1996. "Biased Ballots? The Impact of Ballot Structure on North Carolina Elections in 1992." *Public Choice* 87:259–280.

Hanmer, Michael J., Won-Ho Park, Michael W. Traugott, Richard G. Niemi, Paul S. Herrnson, Benjamin Bederson, and Frederick C. Conrad. 2010. "Losing Fewer Votes: The Impact of Changing Voting Systems on Residual Votes." *Political Research Quarterly* 63:129–142.

Hanmer, Michael J. and Michael W. Traugott. 2004. "The Impact of Vote-By-Mail on Voter Behavior." *American Politics Research* 32:375–405.

Hasen, Richard L. 2004. "After the Storm: The Uses, Normative Implications, and Unintended Consequences of Voting Reform Research in Post-*Bush v. Gore* Equal Protection Challenges." In Ann N. Crigler, Marion R. Just, and Edward J. McCaffery (eds.), *Rethinking the Vote: The Politics and Prospects of American Election Reform.* New York: Oxford University Press, 185–199.

Haspel, Moshe and H. Gibbs Knotts. 2005. "Location, Location, Location: Precinct Placement and the Costs of Voting." *Journal of Politics* 67:560–573.

Hayduk, Ronald. 2005. *Gatekeepers to the Franchise: Shaping Election Administration in New York*. DeKalb, IL: Northern Illinois University Press.

Heilke, Thomas, Mark R. Joslyn, and Alex Aguado. 2003. "The Changing Readability of Introductory Political Science Textbooks: A Case Study of Burns and Peltason, *Government by the People*." *PS: Political Science and Politics* 36:229–232.

Help America Vote Act of 2002. U.S. Public Law 252. 107th Congress, 2nd session, 29 October 2002.

Hernson, Paul S., Richard G. Niemi, Michael J. Hanmer, Benjamin B. Bederson, Frederick C. Conrad, and Michael Traugott. 2008. *Voting Technology: The Not-So-Simple Act of Casting a Ballot*. Washington, DC: Brookings Institution Press.

Herron, Michael C. and Jasjeet S. Sekhon. 2003. "Overvoting and Representation: An Examination of Overvoted Presidential Ballots in Broward and Miami-Dade Counties." *Electoral Studies* 22:21–47

Herron, Michael C. and Jasjeet S. Sekhon. 2005. "Black Candidates and Black Voters: Assessing the Impact of Candidate Race on Uncounted Vote Rates." *Journal of Politics* 67:154–177.

Hershey, William. 2008. "Counties Reject Brunner's Proposal." *Dayton Daily News*, January 23, A4 (accessed Newsbank, August 4, 2010).

Highton, Benjamin. 2006. "Long Lines, Voting Machine Availability, and Turnout: The Case of Franklin County, Ohio in the 2004 Presidential Election." *PS: Political Science and Politics* January:65–68.

House Judiciary Committee Democratic Staff, "Preserving Democracy: What Went Wrong in Ohio," January 5, 2005.

"How America Doesn't Vote." 2004. *New York Times*, February 15, www.nytimes.com (accessed December 22, 2004).

Hulsey, Lynn. 2009. "Sen. Can Vote Here; Justices Say Secretary of State Improperly Applied Law; Jon Husted Accuses Brunner of Trying to Damage Him." *Dayton Daily News*, October 7, A1.

Hulsey, Lynn and William Hershey. 2008. "Election Officials Have Mixed Reaction to Brunner Plan." *Dayton Daily News*, January 4, A7 (accessed via Newsbank, August 4, 2010).

Imai, Kosuke and Gary King. 2004. "Did Illegal Overseas Absentee Ballots Decide the 2000 U.S. Presidential Election?" *Perspectives on Politics* 2:537–549.

"Initiative Use," Initiative and Referendum Institute, last modified September 2010, www.iandrinstitute.org/IRI%20Initiative%20Use%20(2010-1).pdf

Janiszewski, Chris. 1998. "The Influence of Display Characteristics on Visual Exploratory Search Behavior." *Journal of Consumer Research* 25:290–301.

Jenkins, Cleo R. and Don A. Dillman. 1997. "Towards a Theory of Self-Administered Questionnaire Design." In Lars Lyberg, Paul Biemer, Martin Collins, Edith deLeeuw, Cathryn Dippo, Norbert Schwarz, and Dennis Trewin (eds.), *Survey Measurement and Process Quality*. New York: Wiley Inter-Science, 165–196.

Jewett, Aubrey. 2001. "Explaining Variation in Ballot Invalidation Among Florida Counties in the 2000 Election." Paper presented at the annual meeting of the American Political Science Association, San Francisco, CA.

Johnson, Kevin. 2008. "States Grapple with Voting Status of Felons." *USA Today*, November 3. www.usatoday.com/news/politics/election2008/2008-11-02-prison-vote_N.htm (accessed December 2, 2008).

Jones, Bryan D. and Frank R. Baumgartner. 2005. *The Politics of Attention: How Government Prioritizes Problems*. Chicago: University of Chicago Press.

Jones, Douglas W. 2004. "Confusion of Myth and Fact in Maryland." University of Iowa, Department of Computer Science. www.divms.uiowa.edu/~jones/voting/myth-fact-md.html (accessed August 18, 2009).

Keyssar, Alexander. 2000. *The Right to Vote: The Contested History of Democracy in the United States.* New York: Basic Books.

Kimball, David C. 2005. "Voting and Ballots." In Paul S. Herrnson, Colton C. Campbell, Marni Ezra, and Stephen Medvic (eds.), *Guide to Political Campaigns in America.* Washington, DC: CQ Press, 52–69.

Kimball, David C. 2010. "Evidence-Based Democracy." *Election Law Journal* 9:161–164.

Kimball, David C. and Martha Kropf. 2005. "Ballot Design and Unrecorded Votes on Paper-Based Ballots." *Public Opinion Quarterly* 69:508–529.

Kimball, David C. and Martha Kropf. 2008. "Voting Technology, Ballot Measures and Residual Votes." *American Politics Research* 36:479–509.

Kimball, David C., Chris T. Owens, and Katherine M. Keeney. 2003. "Unrecorded Votes and Election Reform." *Spectrum: The Journal of State Government* 76:34–37

Kimball, David C., Chris T. Owens, and Katherine M. Keeney. 2004. "Unrecorded Votes and Political Representation." In Robert P. Watson (ed.), *Counting Votes: Lessons from the 2000 Presidential Election in Florida.* Gainesville, FL: University Press of Florida, 135–150.

Kingdon, John W. 1995. *Agendas, Alternatives and Public Policies,* 2nd ed., New York: Harper Collins.

Knack, Stephen and Martha Kropf. 2002. "Who Uses Inferior Voting Technology?" *PS: Political Science and Politics* 35:541–548.

Knack, Stephen and Martha Kropf. 2003. "Voided Ballots in the 1996 Presidential Election: A County-Level Analysis." *Journal of Politics* 65:881–897.

Knack, Stephen and Martha Kropf. 2003. "Roll-Off at the Top of the Ballot: Intentional Undervoting in American Presidential Elections." *Politics & Policy* 31(4):575–594.

Kohno, Tadayoshi, Adam Stubblefield, Aviel D. Rubin, and Dan S. Wallach. 2003. *Analysis of an Electronic Voting System.* Technical Report TR-2003–19. Baltimore: Johns Hopkins University Information Security Institute.

Kopko, Kyle C., Sarah McKinnon Bryner, Jeffrey Budziak, Christopher J. Devine and Steven P. Nawara. 2011. "In the Eye of the Beholder? Motivated Reasoning in Disputed Elections." *Political Behavior* 33(2):271–290.

Kostyu, Paul E. 2003. "Electronic Voting Expected by 2004 Election." *Times Reporter,* April 23 (accessed via Newsbank, August 2, 2010).

Kropf, Martha. 2005. "Dogs and Dead People: Incremental Election Reform in Missouri." In Daniel J. Palazzollo and James W. Ceaser (eds.), *Election Reform: Politics and Policy.* Lanham, MD: Lexington Books, 157–174.

Kropf, Martha. 2011. "The Evolution (or not) of Ballot Design Ten Years After *Bush v. Gore.*" Paper prepared for presentation at "*Bush v Gore,* 10 Years Later: Election Administration in the United States," Laguna Beach, CA.

Kropf, Martha, Janine Parry, Jay Barth, and E. Terrence Jones. 2008. "Pursuing the Early Voter: Does the Early Bird Get the Worm?" *Journal of Political Marketing* 7:131–150.

Kropf, Martha, David Swindell, and Elizabeth Wemlinger. 2009. "The Effects of Early Voting on Social Ties: Using Longitudinal Data." Paper presented at the 2009 North Carolina Political Science Association Meeting, Greensboro, NC, February 2009 and at Time Shifting the Vote: The Early Voting Revolution in Election Administration, October 9–10, 2009, Reed College, Portland, Oregon.

Lausen, Marcia. 2007. *Design for Democracy: Ballot and Election Design.* Chicago: University of Chicago Press.

Leonard, Lee. 2001. "Legislature May be Stuffing the Ballot Box on Voting Reforms." *Columbus Dispatch*, October 15, 7A (accessed via Newsbank, August 2, 2010).

Liebschutz, Sarah F. and Daniel J. Palazzolo. 2005. "HAVA and the States." *Publius* 35:497–515.

Lijphart, Arend. 1999. *Patterns of Democracy: Government Forms and Performance in Thirty-Six Countries.* New Haven, CT: Yale University Press.

Lipton, Eric. 2003. "Vote Machine Replacement Lags, Despite Age." *New York Times*, October 20, A1.

Lloyd, Richard D. 1995. "Separating Partisanship from Party in Judicial Research: Reapportionment in the U.S. District Courts." *American Political Science Review* 89:413–420.

Long, William F., Ralph P. Garzia, Timothy Wingert, and Sylvia R. Garzia. 1996. "The Ergonomics of Reading." In Ralph P. Garzia (ed.), *Vision and Reading.* St. Louis, MO: Mosby, 71–110.

Lund, William A. 1998. "What's in a Name? The Battle Over Ballot Titles in Oregon." *Willamette Law Review* 34:143–167.

Lynch, James Q. 2002. "Old Voting Machines on Way Out." *Gazette*, October 15 (accessed via Newsbank, Record #1198723).

Magleby, David. 1984. *Direct Legislation: Voting on Ballot Propositions in the United States.* Baltimore: Johns Hopkins University Press.

Martinez, Michael D., and Jeff Gill. 2005. "The Effects of Turnout on Partisan Outcomes in U.S. Presidential Elections 1960–2000." *Journal of Politics* 67:1248–1274.

Mazzolini, Joan. 2006. "Commissioners Want New Voting Machines: $17 Million Touch Screens Can't Handle Big Elections." *Cleveland Plain Dealer*, November 29, A1 (accessed via Newsbank, August 3, 2010).

Mazzolini, Joan and Michael O'Malley. 2007. "Ohio is Keeping Its Touch Screens: Brunner Plans Review to Improve Voting." *Cleveland Plain Dealer*, February 3, A1 (accessed via Newsbank, August 4, 2010).

Merzer, Martin. 2001. "Review Shows Ballots Say Bush Floridians Zany, Creative in Spoiling Their Ballots." *Miami Herald*, April 4, A1 (accessed via Newsbank, February 5, 2011).

Mayer, Kenneth J. 2007. "Comparative Election Administration: Can We Learn Anything from the Australian Election Commission?" Paper prepared for delivery at the 2007 Annual Meeting of the American Political Science Association, Chicago, IL.

McDonald, Michael. 2010. "United States Election Project," George Mason University (http://elections.gmu.edu/voter_turnout.htm), last accessed on May 5, 2011.

McFeatters, Ann. 2005. "Congress Certifies Bush Re-Election: Democrats Force Four-Hour Delay with Rarely Invoked Challenge." *Toledo Blade*, January 7, A3 (accessed via Newsbank, August 3, 2010).

McNulty, John E., Conor M. Dowling, and Margaret H. Ariotti. 2009. "Driving Saints to Sin: How Increasing the Difficulty of Voting Dissuades Even the Most Motivated Voters." *Political Analysis* 17:435–455.

Moke, Paul and Richard B. Saphire. 2006. "The Voting Rights Act and the Racial Gap in Lost Votes." *Hastings Law Journal* 58:1–59.

Montjoy, Robert. 2005. "HAVA and the States." In Daniel J. Palazzollo and James W. Ceaser (eds.), *Election Reform: Politics and Policy.* Lanham, MD: Lexington Books, 16–34.

National Conference of State Legislatures. 2010. "Absentee and Early Voting," www.ncsl. org/default.aspx?tabid=16604 (accessed May 9, 2011).

Naymik, Mark and Julie Carr Smyth. 2003. "State to Buy Voting Machines." *Cleveland Plain Dealer*, February 26, B1 (accessed via Newsbank, August 2, 2010).

"New Voting Machines Flawed, Experts Claim" 2003. *Toledo Blade*, July 25, B1 (accessed via Newsbank, August 2, 2010).

Nichols, Stephen M. 1998. "State Referendum Voting, Ballot Roll-off, and the Effect of New Electoral Technology." *State and Local Government Review* 30:106–117.

Nichols, Stephen M., David C. Kimball, and Paul Allen Beck. 1999. "Voter Turnout in the 1996 Election: Resuming the Downward Spiral?" In Herbert F. Weisberg and Janet M. Box-Steffensmeier (eds.), *Reelection 1996: How Americans Voted*. New York: Chatham House.

Nichols, Stephen M. and Gregory A. Strizek. 1995. "Electronic Voting Machines and Ballot Roll-Off." *American Politics Quarterly* 23:300–318.

Niemi, Richard G. and Paul S. Herrnson. 2003. "Beyond the Butterfly: The Complexity of U.S. Ballots." *Perspectives on Politics* 1:317–326

Niquette, Mark. 2006. "Ohio Wrapping Up Mission to Upgrade Voting Machines." *Columbus Dispatch*, January 4, 01E (accessed via Newsbank, August 3, 2010).

Norden, Lawrence with Jesse Allen. 2009. *Final Report: 2008–2009 Ohio Election Summit and Conference*. New York: Brennan Center for Justice, http://brennan.3cdn. net/9ccb57cb5de1711173_nkm6bqc3y.pdf (accessed July 16, 2010).

Norden, Lawrence, David Kimball, Whitney Quesenbery, and Margaret Chen. 2008. *Better Ballots*. New York: Brennan Center for Justice.

"Ohio Voters Whiplashed by Changes." 2005. *Dayton Daily News*, January 14, A8 (accessed via Newsbank, August 2, 2010).

Palazzolo, Daniel J. 2005. "Election Reform After the 2000 Election." In Daniel J. Palazzollo and James W. Ceaser (eds.), *Election Reform: Politics and Policy*. Lanham, MD: Lexington Books, 3–15.

Pew Research Center for People and the Press. 2000. "Many Question Bush or Gore as Legitimate Winner." December 1. http://people-press.org/reports/display.php3? ReportID=22 (accessed July 29, 2007).

Pierson, John. 1996. "Preparing for the 2000 Census: Bureau Tests Carrots v. Sticks." *Wall Street Journal*, May 2, http://online.wsj.com/article/SB830988694388099000. html (accessed May 5, 2011).

Pildes, Richard H. 2006. "The Future of Voting Rights Policy from Anti-Discrimination to the Right to Vote." *Howard Law Journal* 49:741–765.

Piven, Frances Fox and Richard A. Cloward. 1988. *Why Americans Don't Vote*. New York: Pantheon Books.

Potter, Trevor and Marianne Holt Viray. 2004. "Federal Election Authority: Jurisdiction and Mandates." In Ann N. Crigler, Marion R. Just, and Edward J. McCaffery (eds.), *Rethinking the Vote: The Politics and Prospects of American Election Reform*. New York: Oxford University Press, 102–116.

Powell, Michael and Peter Slevin. 2004. "Several Factors Contributed to 'Lost' Voters in Ohio." *Washington Post*, December 15, A1.

Provance, Jim. 2005. "Blackwell Upbraided for Voting Decision—State Official Not Empowered to Certify Single Balloting System, Petro Says." *Toledo Blade*, February 9, A3 (accessed via Newsbank, August 3, 2010).

Rankin, Bill. 2001. "Uniform Voting System May Meet Opposition—2001 Georgia Legislature." *Atlanta Journal Constitution*, January 3, B6.

Rankin, Bill. 2000. "Cox: State's Vote Gap Nearly Twice U.S. Norm." *Atlanta Journal-Constitution*, December 29, D1.

Raspberry, William. 2001. "Post-Traumatic Suggestions." *Washington Post*, January 1 (accessed via Lexis/Nexis).

Reilly, Shauna and Sean Richey. 2011. "Ballot Question Readability and Roll-Off: The Impact of Language Complexity." *Political Research Quarterly* 64:59–67.

Roig-Franzia, Manuel. 2010. "Election Speculation Comes from All Corners After S.C. Primary." *Washington Post*, June 15, www.washingtonpost.com/wp-dyn/content/article/2010/06/14/AR2010061405215.html (accessed July 15, 2010).

Roseman, Gary H., Jr. and E. Frank Stephenson. 2005. "The Effects of Voting Technology on Voter Turnout: Do Computers Scare the Elderly?" *Public Choice* 123:39–47.

Roth, Susan King. 1994. "The Unconsidered Ballot: How Design Affects Voting Behavior." *Visible Language* 28:48–67.

Roth, Susan King. 1998. "Disenfranchised by Design." *Information Design Journal* 9:29–38.

Rubin, Aviel D. 2006. *Brave New Ballot: The Battle to Safeguard Democracy in the Age of Electronic Voting*. New York: Morgan Road Books.

Saltman, Roy G. 1988. "Accuracy, Integrity and Security in Computerized Vote-Tallying." *Communications of the Association for Computing Machinery* 31(10): 1184–1218.

Saltman, Roy G. 1988. *Accuracy, Integrity and Security in Computerized Vote-Tallying*. NBS Special Publication 500–158. www.itl.nist.gov/lab/specpubs/500-158.htm (accessed July 23, 2007).

Saltman, Roy. 2006. *The History and Politics of Voting Technology in the United States*. New York: Palgrave Macmillan.

Sanders, Mark S. and Ernest J. McCormick. 1993. *Human Factors in Engineering and Design*. 7th ed., New York: McGraw Hill.

Saphire, Richard B. and Paul Moke. 2006. "Litigating Bush v. Gore in the States: Dual Voting Systems and the Fourteenth Amendment." *Villanova Law Review* 51:229–298.

Schulte, Brigid. 2003. "Jolted Over Electronic Voting," *Washington Post*, August 11, sec. A1.

Scott, Michael. 2006. "Lake County Scraps Old Electronic Voting Machines." *Cleveland Plain Dealer*, September 8, B1 (accessed via Newsbank, August 3, 2010).

Silva, Mark. 2001. "Lawmakers Negotiating Election-Reform Bill." *Miami Herald*, May 1, B6.

Silva, Mark and Steve Bousquet. 2001. "Punch-Card Ballots Banished as of 2002." *Miami Herald*, May 5, A19.

Sinclair, D. E. "Betsy" and R. Michael Alvarez. 2004. "Who Overvotes, Who Undervotes, Using Punchcards? Evidence from Los Angeles County." *Political Research Quarterly* 57:15–25.

Sinclair, Robert C., Melvin M. Mark, Sean E. Moore, Carrie A. Lavis, and Alexander S. Soldat. 2000. "Psychology: An Electoral Butterfly Effect." *Nature* 408:665–666.

Sioux City Journal. 2001. "Testing the System." November 4 (accessed via Newsbank, Record Number: 4d2a68296c8dfd9b5992899a549c8faf97922048).

Smith, Erika D. and Lisa A. Abraham. 2005. "Diebold's Touch-Screen System OK'ed—Blackwell Lets Ohio Counties Use E-Voting Rather Than Optical Scan." *Akron Beacon Journal*, April 15, A1 (accessed via Newsbank, August 3, 2010).

Smyth, Julie Carr. 2003. "State Postpones Vote Machine Deadlines." *Cleveland Plain Dealer*, August 20, B3 (accessed via Newsbank, August 2, 2010).

Smyth, Julie Carr. 2003. "Statewide Electronic Voting Delayed: Review Uncovers Security Problems." *Cleveland Plain Dealer*, December 3, A1 (accessed via Newsbank, August 2, 2010).

Smyth, Julie Carr. 2005. "Ohio Pulls Plug on Electronic Voting." *Cleveland Plain Dealer*, January 13, A1 (accessed via Newsbank, August 3, 2010).

Songini, Marc L. 2006. "Paper Trail Flawed in Ohio Election, Study Finds." *Computerworld*, August 21, www.computerworld.com/s/article/9002610/Paper_Trail_Flawed_in_Ohio_Election_Study_Finds (accessed July 29, 2010).

Songini, Marc L. 2007. "Florida Bans Touch-Screen Voting Machines." *PC World*, May 22. http://www.pcworld.com/article/132138/florida_bans_touchscreen_voting_machines.html (accessed June 19, 2007).

State of Hawaii, Office of Elections, *Proposed Precinct Closings for the 2010 Elections: The Procurement of a Voting System for the State of Hawaii*, last modified June 15, 2009, http://hawaii.gov/elections/documents/precinct_closings_proposed_2010.pdf (accessed July 15, 2010).

"A Statewide Voting Standard." 2001. *Toledo Blade*, February 18, B4.

Stein, Robert M. and Greg Vonnahme. 2008. "Engaging the Unengaged Voter: Vote Centers and Voter Turnout." *Journal of Politics* 82:487–497.

Stewart, Charles III. 2006. "Residual Vote in the 2004 Election." *Election Law Journal* 5:158–169.

Stewart, Charles. 2009. "Election Technology and the Voting Experience in 2008." Caltech/MIT Voting Technology Project. VTP Working Paper #71, March 2009.

Stone, Deborah. 2002. *Policy Paradox: The Art of Political Decision Making*, Revised Edition. New York: Norton.

Strahan, Randall and Mathew Gunning. 2005. "Entrepreneurial Leadership and Election Reform in Georgia: 2001 to 2003." In Daniel J. Palazzollo and James W. Ceaser (eds.), *Election Reform: Politics and Policy*. Lanham, MD: Lexington Books, 74–90.

Streb, Matthew J. 2011. *Rethinking American Electoral Democracy*, 2nd ed., New York: Routledge.

Stuart, Guy. 2004. "Databases, Felons, and Voting: Bias and Partisanship of the Florida Felons List in the 2000 Elections." *Political Science Quarterly* 119:453–475.

Tefki, Chafai. 1987. "Readability Formulas: An Overview." *Journal of Documentation* 43:261–273.

Thomas, Norman C. 1968. "Voting Machines and Voter Participation in Four Michigan Constitutional Revision Referenda." *Western Political Quarterly* 21:409–419.

Thompson, Dennis. 2004. "Election Time: Normative Implications of Temporal Properties of the Electoral Process in the United States" *American Political Science Review* 98:51–64

Tokaji, Daniel P. 2003. "First Amendment Equal Protection: On Discretion, Inequality and Participation." *Michigan Law Review* 101:2409–2524.

Tokaji, Daniel P. 2005. "Early Returns on Election Reform: Discretion, Disenfranchisement, and the Help America Vote Act." *George Washington Law Review* 74:1206–1253.

Tokaji, Daniel P. 2007. "The Birth and Rebirth of Election Administration." *Election Law Journal* 6:118–131.

Traugott, Michael. W. 2004. "Why Electoral Reform Has Failed: If You Build It, Will They Come?" In Ann N. Crigler, Marion R. Just, and Edward J. McCaffery (eds.), *Rethinking the Vote: The Politics and Prospects of American Election Reform*. New York: Oxford University Press, 167–184.

Tomz, Michael and Robert P. Van Houweling. 2003. "How Does Voting Equipment Affect the Racial Gap in Voided Ballots?" *American Journal of Political Science* 47:46–60.

"Toward a Greater State Role in Election Administration." 2005. *Harvard Law Review* 118:2314–2335.

Tuft, Carolyn. 2000. "Bond Wants Federal Investigation of Problems at City Polls." *St. Louis Post-Dispatch*, November 10, 2000 (accessed via Newsbank, August 7, 2007).

Tyson, Sam. 2010. "Poll: DeMint Heavily Favored in SC Senate Race." June 15, www.live5news.com/Global/story.asp?S=12652227 (accessed July 15, 2010).

U.S. Commission on Civil Rights. 2001. "Voting Irregularities in Florida During the 2000 Presidential Election." June. www.usccr.gov/pubs/vote2000/report/main.htm (accessed July 29, 2007).

U.S. Commission on Civil Rights, Office of Civil Rights Evaluation. 2004. "Is America Ready to Vote? Election Readiness Briefing Paper." www.law.umaryland.edu/Marshall/usccr/documents/isamerreadyvote.pdf (accessed July 29, 2007).

U.S. Election Assistance Commission. 2007. "Effective Designs for the Administration of Federal Elections," June, www.eac.gov/assets/1/Page/EAC_Effective_Election_Design. pdf (accessed March 30, 2011).

U.S. Election Assistance Commission. 2009. 2008 Election Administration and Voting Survey.

Vanderleeuw, James M. and Glenn H. Utter. 1993. "Voter Roll-Off and the Electoral Context: A Test of Two Theses." *Social Science Quarterly* 74:664–673.

Vercellotti, Timothy. 2007. "Embracing Change at the Polls: Election Administrators and the Provisional Ballot in 2004." Paper presented at the 2007 Midwest Political Science Association Meeting, Chicago, IL.

Vitale Robert. 2005. "Paper Ballots Could Cost County." *Columbus Dispatch*, January 29, 01C (accessed via Newsbank, August 3, 2010).

Vitale, Robert and Mark Niquette. 2005. "5 Counties Defy Blackwell's Edict." *Columbus Dispatch*, February 10, 01A (accessed via Newsbank, August 3, 2010).

Vogel, Nancy. 2006. "U.S. Orders State to Repay $536,000 in Election Funds." *Los Angeles Times*, May 13, 2006, B3.

Wallschlaeger, Charles and Cynthia Busic-Snyder. 1992. *Basic Visual Concepts and Principles for Artists, Architects and Designers*. Dubuque, IA: William C. Brown.

Wand, Jonathan N., Kenneth W. Shotts, Jasjeet S. Sekhon, Walter R. Mebane, Jr., Michael C. Herron, and Henry E. Brady. 2001. "The Butterfly Did It: The Aberrant Vote for Buchanan in Palm Beach County, Florida." *American Political Science Review* 95:793–810.

Walsh, Edward. 2002. "Election Reform Bill Is Passed by Senate; $3.86 Billion Allotted for Improvements." *Washington Post*, October 17 (accessed via Lexis/Nexis, July 2, 2007).

Wang, Tova Andrea. 2004. "Missouri Miseries." *Century Foundation*. www.tcf.org (accessed July 24, 2007).

Wattenberg, Martin P., Ian McAllister and Anthony Salvanto. 2000. "How Voting is Like Taking an SAT Test: An Analysis of American Voter Roll-off." *American Politics Quarterly* 28:234–250.

Weiner, Jay. 2010. *This is Not Florida: How Al Franken Won the Minnesota Senate Recount*. Minneapolis: University of Minnesota Press.

Wenzel, Fritz. 2003. "State Halts Lucas Plans for New Voting Machines." *Toledo Blade*, February 26, A1 (accessed via Newsbank, August 2, 2010).

Whaley, Monte and Joey Bunch. 2006. "Vote Centers 'a Total Fiasco.'" *Denver Post*, November 9, www.denverpost.com/election/ci_4627496 (accessed 14 August 2009).

Wheildon, Colin. 1995. *Type and Layout: How Typography and Design Can Get your Message Across—Or Get in the Way*. Berkeley, CA: Strathmoor Press.

Whoriskey, Peter. 2000. "Protests Put West Palm 'On the Map' For Once…Focus Is not on Glitter across the Bay." *Miami Herald*, November 10 (accessed via Newsbank, July 23, 2007).

Wolf, Richard. 2008. "Voting Equipment Changes Could Get Messy on Nov. 4." *USA Today*, October 29, www.usatoday.com/news/politics/election2008/2008-10-28-votingequipment_N.htm (accessed July 9, 2010).

Wolter, Kirk, Diana Jergovic, Whitney Moore, Joe Murphy, and Colm O'Muircheartaigh. 2003. "Reliability of the Uncertified Ballots in the 2000 Presidential Election in Florida." *American Statistician* 57(1):1–14.

Zabarenko, Deborah. 2000. "A Chad is Born: Debuting in 1890, It Stuck Around." *Washington Post*, November 24, A41.

Zetter, Kim. 2003. "Maryland E-Voting Passes Muster." *Wired News*, September 25. www.wired.com/news/business/0,1367,60583,00.html

INDEX

Page numbers in bold refer to figures and tables.

absentee voting 56, 65, 69, 105, 107,
    113–14, 116–17
access versus integrity debates 4–5, 11,
    16–17, 97–8, 100–101, 102, 114
affidavit ballot *see* provisional voting
Alvarez, R.M. 69, 110
American Civil Liberties Association
    (ACLU) 21, 58, 62
Atlanta Journal and Constitution 15

ballot design 10; in 2002 and 2004
    elections 80–2; in 2000 Florida
    election 71–4; like a survey 74–9;
    and overvotes 86–8; and residual votes
    84–6, 91–3; and undervotes 86–8
ballot fatigue 91–2
ballot measures: in 2004 election 90;
    and ballot design 78–9; residual votes
    49–53, 88–93; salience of 91–2
barriers to voting *see* access versus
    integrity debates
Bassi, A. 105–6
Baumgartner, F. 11
Blackwell, K. 58–9, 61, 97
Blunt, M. 9
Bond, C. 9, 20, 24
Bowen, D. 115
Brady, H. 66–7
Brennan Center for Justice 75, 95

Brunner, J. 62–3, 97, 115
Buchanan, P. 7
Bush, G.W.: 2000 election 3, 5, 72, 96,
    105; 2004 election 60; Help America
    Vote Act (HAVA) 55
Bush, J. 21
Bush v. Gore 6, 18, 45–6, 59
butterfly ballot 6, 71, **73**, 97

Caltech/MIT Voting Technology
    Project 117–18
Carnahan, R. 115
Carney, E.N. 64
Carter Baker Commission 14
Center for Democracy and Election
    Management 108
Century Foundation 9, 24
central-count optical scan 34–5, 40, 62–3,
    83; decline in use 29–31; defined **29**;
    in Florida 2000 election 72; and
    residual votes 37, 41–4, 72
Christopher, W. 24
Cleveland Plain Dealer 60, 61, 116
Clinton, H.R. 10, 118
Colbert, S. 96
Coleman, N. 1, 107, 113
connect-the-arrow ballot style 77–8;
    and overvotes 87; and residual
    votes 83–5

Conyers, J. 18–19
Cox, C. 22
Cross, N. 51
Culver, C. 23

Damschroder, M. 61
Datavote punch cards 28; defined **29**;
    and residual votes 37
DeMint, J. 69
Democracy Index 110, 118
Design for Democracy 75
Dickerson, M. 111
Diebold 23, 59, 61
Dillman, D. 75, 130n13
direct recording electronic (DRE)
    voting machines 10, 21–2; costs 56,
    62, 114; defined 28–30; design 75,
    93; in Ohio 58–64; use 29, 31–2; and
    residual votes 37, 41–4, 46–7; security
    concerns 23, 55–7, 60–3, 69; *see also*
    full-face DRE, scrolling DRE,
    voter-verified paper trail
Dodd, C. 19
Dominion Voting Systems 64
DS 200 ballot scanner; and overvotes 94
Dyck, J. 107

early voting 51, 65–6, 111, 116–17,
    136n7
Ehrlich, R.L. 23
election adminstration: costs 63–5;
    jurisdiction size 103; local discretion
    96, 98, 103–5, 109–10, 114;
    nonpartisan 108–9; partisan conflict
    97, 104–6; *see also* polling place
    consolidation
Election Assistance Commission (EAC)
    13, 55, 75, 95, 118; creation 27–28;
    Election Day Survey 65, 118;
    proposals to dissolve 118
election day registration 26, 101
electronic voting machines 10; *see also*
    direct recording electronic (DRE)
    voting machines
ES&S 64
evidence-based democracy 117–18
Ewald, A. 111, 117

Federal Election Commission 26, 109, 118
Foley, E. 113
Franken, A. 1, 107, 113
full-face DRE 28, 79; decline in use 29,
    31–2; defined **29**; and residual votes
    49–53

Galarraga, A. 115
Garand, J. 101
Gerken, H. 110–11, 117
Goodman, P.S. 15
Gore, A. 3, 5, 72, 105
Greene, A. 69

Hall, T. 69, 110
Hamilton, J.T. 107
Harper, G. 118
Harris, K. 96
Hart InterCivic 61
Hasen, R. 108–9
Help America Vote Act (HAVA) 2–3, 49,
    111, 115–16; and ballot design 75, 77;
    election costs 63–4, 69; impact on local
    jurisdictions 64–5, 101, 114; preventing
    voting errors 34; provisional voting
    25, 26–7, 98, 102–4; replacing voting
    equipment 10–14, 23–6, 34–5, 55–8,
    59, 95, 112–13; voter identification 20;
    voter registration database 24–5; 27
Herrnson, P. 50, 53, 78, 93
Husted, J. 63

inactive voters 107
initiatives *see* ballot measures
issue definition *see* problem definition

Jones, B. 11
Joyce, J. 115

Kerry, J. 60
Kingdon, J.S. 112

Ladd, H.F. 107
Lausen, M. 75
LePore, T. 22, 71, 77, 95
lever voting machines 10, 15, 23, 28;
    decline in use 21, 25, 29–30, 52–3,
    59, 113; defined **29**; full-face layout 36,
    49, 50, 79, 124n51; and residual votes
    37, 40, 45, 47; use 29–30
Liebschutz, S. 27
local election officials: code of ethics
    108–9; methods of selection 99;
    oversight 106, 110; party affiliation
    99–101, 102–3, 105–7; policy attitudes
    100–3; provisional voting 104–6;
    voter turnout 106–7
LoParo, C. 59

McNulty, J. 66–7
Mayer, K.R. 109

Merzer, M. 34
Miami Herald 7, 21, 34
Military and Overseas Voter
   Empowerment (MOVE) Act 116
motor voter law *see* National Voter
   Registration Act
Morton, R. 105–6
Moynihan, D. 101
Murkowski, L. 113

National Association of Secretaries of
   State 109, 110, 118
National Commission on Federal
   Election Reform 19
National Conference of State
   Legislatures 116
National Institute of Standards and
   Technology (NIST) 7, 13, 27, 118
National Voter Registration Act
   (NVRA) 19, 20, 123n38
New York Times 18, 24
Niemi, R. 78
Norden, L. 130n10
Noren, W. 111

Obama, B. 118
office block ballot layout 89–91; and
   residual votes 92
Ohio State University Moritz College
   of Law 117–18
optical scan balloting 10, 28; use 29, 31;
   see also central-count optical scan,
   precinct-count optical scan
overvotes 8, 34, 40, 84; defined 36, 72;
   in Florida 2000 election 72–4; in 2002
   and 2004 elections 86–8; in 2008
   election 94

Palazzolo, D. 27
paper ballots 23, 28, 64, 79, 83; decline
   in use 29–30; defined 16, **29**; and
   residual votes 37, 40–4, 92
Parkhurst, C. 101
party column ballot layout 79, 89–92;
   and residual votes 92
Pew Center on the States 118
Pew Research Center 3
Pildes, R. 111
polling place consolidation 64–6; and
   voter turnout 66–8, 114
precinct-count optical scan 34, 40, 62,
   83–4; defined **29**; in Florida 2000
   election 72; increase in use 29–31;
   and overvotes 87–8; and residual

votes 37, 41–44, 47, 72, 85–6; and
   undervotes 87–8
Premier Election Solutions 64
problem definition 11
provisional voting 13, 20, 103, 113–14;
   local implementation 103–6; state
   laws 104
punch card ballots 6–7, 10, 15, 113;
   decline in use 29–30; in Florida 2000
   election 72; and residual votes 41–44,
   72, 113; *see also* Datavote punch
   cards, Votomatic punch cards

readability: ballot instructions 80–2,
   132n33; ballot measures 91–2
recount of ballots 1, 4, 6–7, 18, 34–5,
   45–6, 72, 105, 107, 113–14
Reilly, S. 91
residual votes 8, 22; and ballot design
   82–86; on ballot measures 88–93;
   and change in voting equipment 38–44,
   113; defined 8, 35, 82; economic
   disparity 46–49; in Florida 2000
   election 72–4; in presidential elections
   37; racial disparity 17–18, 46–49;
   rate 36; by voting equipment 37;
   within-state variation 45–6
Richey, S. 91
Rodriguez, R. 55
Rokita, T. 115

Saltman, R. 7, 13, 57
Saturday Night Live 1
Schumer, C. 10
scrolling DRE 30; defined **29**; increase
   in use 29, 31–32 ; and residual
   votes 49–53, 93
Seabrook, N.R. 107
Seoud, R.J. 101
Sequoia Voting Systems 60, 64
Shelley, K. 97
Silva, C. 101
Sioux City Journal 23
state election officials: code of ethics
   108–9, 115; methods of selection
   98; party affiliation 98; provisional
   voting 104
Stein, R. 67
Stevens, T. 1
Stewart, C. 41
straight-party device 18; and overvotes
   87–8; and residual votes 83–5,
   91–3
Stuart, G. 106–7

Tennant, N. 115
Thompson, D. 117
Tokaji, D.P. 97
Toledo Blade 59, 61
touch-screen voting *see* direct recording
electronic (DRE)
Traugott, M. 112
Trounstine, J. 105–6

undervotes 8, 34, 84; in 2002 and 2004
elections 86–8; on ballot measures
79; defined 22, 36; in Florida's 13th
congressional district 93
USA Today 55, 56, 72
usability of election materials 12, 53,
71, 75, 93, 95, 114; *see also* ballot
design
U.S. Commission on Civil Rights 8–9

Vonnahme, G. 67
voter confidence 4, 114

voter fraud *see* access versus integrity
voter identification 10, 101, 102
voter registration 101, 102; database 5, 8,
16, 20; purging lists 5, 20, 106–7
voter-verified paper trail 57, 60, 61, 70
voting centers 65; and voter turnout 67
voting equipment 10, 12; civil rights and
17–18; defined as problem in 2000
election 15–19; defined as problem in
HAVA 23–26, 53–54; error prevention
40, 62, 84–5, 113; state replacement
20–23; types 28–29
voting errors *see* overvotes, undervotes
Voting Rights Act 4, 19; renewal in
2006 111
Votomatic punch cards 28, 47; defined **29**;
and residual votes 37

Wang, T. 9
Washington Post 9, 15, 20, 60
Whoriskey, P. 7